Social Policies
for Children

Social Policies for Children

IRWIN GARFINKEL
JENNIFER L. HOCHSCHILD
SARA S. McLANAHAN
Editors

The Brookings Institution
Washington, D.C.

Copyright © 1996

THE BROOKINGS INSTITUTION

1775 Massachusetts Avenue, N.W., Washington, D.C. 20036

Library of Congress Cataloging-in-Publication Data
Social policies for children / [edited by] Irwin Garfinkel,
Jennifer L. Hochschild, Sara S. McLanahan.
    p.   cm.
    Includes bibliographical references and index.
    ISBN 0-8157-3666-5 (alk. paper). — ISBN 0-8157-3665-7
(pbk. : alk. paper)
    1. Child welfare—United States. 2. Children—Government
policy—United States. I. Garfinkel, Irwin. II. Hochschild,
Jennifer L., 1950—   . III. McLanahan, Sara S.
HV741.S62 1996
362.7'0973—dc20
                                                    95-25287
                                                      CIP

9 8 7 6 5 4 3 2 1

The paper used in this publication meets the minimum
requirements of the American National Standard for
Information Sciences—Permanence of Paper for Printed Library
Materials, ANSI Z39.48-1984.

Set in Palatino

Composition by Linda C. Humphrey
Arlington, Virginia

Printed by R. R. Donnelley and Sons Co.
Harrisonburg, Virginia

Foreword

SOCIAL POLICIES that succeed in helping children to achieve their potential are critical to our nation's future, both because a humane society owes this consideration to its most vulnerable members and as a means of developing human capital to ensure that American industries can compete around the world. Yet the status of children in the United States suggests that the nation's policies may not be serving them well. Infant and child mortality rates remain high; the proportion of children in poverty is high and increasing; the number of children who cannot read or calculate or think abstractly is unacceptable for the Information Age.

Social Policies for Children puts forth concrete, original proposals to address seven problems: poverty or income insecurity, poor schooling, inadequate child care, difficulties in moving from school to work, insufficient health care, lack of physical security, and child abuse. The proposals, each written by an expert in the field, would, if effected, make a significant difference in the lives of children.

These proposals grew out of a conference entitled Social Policies for Children that was held at the Woodrow Wilson School of Public and International Affairs at Princeton University on May 25–27, 1994. The conference was sponsored by James D. Wolfensohn, Inc.; the Foundation for Child Development; the Annie E. Casey Foundation; the Brookings Institution; and through an anonymous foundation grant.

The authors are grateful to Glenn Loury, William Galston, and Patrick Fagan for participating in the conference and for providing insight into the ethical conflicts that underlie the continuing debate over social policies for children. They also thank colleagues on the Princeton faculty—Timothy Besley, Jameson Doig, Amy Gutmann, Maria Hanratty, Alan Krueger, Kristin Luker, and Deanna Pagnini—who chaired the sessions and summarized the papers with skill and grace.

Henry Bienen, then dean of the Woodrow Wilson School of Public and International Affairs of Princeton University, and Michael Danielson, director of the Center for Domestic and Comparative Policy Studies at the Woodrow Wilson School, provided the institutional context within which vague ideas could be coaxed into completed projects. Vivian Shapiro contributed introductory comments, encouragement, and support.

Pulling the conference together and producing the book was a joint effort to which many people contributed. Cynthia Harper, Hongxin Zhao, and Amy Richardson provided essential research assistance, and Patricia Trinity and Caryn Siegel provided administrative support. Tom Mann, director of the Governmental Studies program at Brookings, made sure that the project stayed on track. Trish Weisman, Jim Schneider, and Steph Selice edited the manuscript; Laurel Imig verified its content; Inge Lockwood and Carlotta Ribar proofread it; and Julia Petrakis prepared the index.

The views expressed here are those of the authors and should not be ascribed to the institutions that supported this work or to the trustees, officers, or staff members of the Brookings Institution.

MICHAEL H. ARMACOST
President

February 1996
Washington, D.C.

Contents

Chapter 1

Introduction

Irwin Garfinkel, Jennifer L. Hochschild, and
Sara S. McLanahan

S UCCESSFUL SOCIAL POLICIES for children are critical to our
nation's future. Whether one thinks of developing human
capital so that American industries can compete around the world or of
what a humane society owes to its most vulnerable members, policies
for children are central. Yet the status of children in America suggests
that the nation's policies may not be serving them well. While infant
and child mortality rates in the United States have declined since 1960,
they remain high in comparison to other western industrialized countries. Child poverty rates, which had been falling since 1960, have
worsened in the past decade and a half; poor health care, child abuse,
and inadequate schooling and child care persist. This book presents an
array of social policies designed to alleviate these problems and, more
generally, to help satisfy the needs of all of the youngest Americans.

This call for new social policies for children comes at a moment of
extraordinary political complexity. In many ways, it is opportune.
President Bill Clinton campaigned on a slogan of "time for a change,"
and his administration has steadily signaled its concern for children;
thus one could plausibly expect greater attention to social policies for
children than in the administrations of his recent predecessors. After
all, President Clinton proclaimed 1993's National Children's Day by
affirming that "America's children are at once our most precious national resource and our most weighty responsibility. . . . Millions of
America's children grow up in stable and loving families. At the same
time, an alarmingly high number of our youth do not have the benefit
of such security; many grow up hungry, neglected, or abused. . . . We
all must take it upon ourselves to address these problems. . . ."[1]

Until November 1994, the president's concerns were echoed by political activists from both the left and right. Jesse Jackson proclaimed,

"When the nation's children are in trouble, our nation is in trouble."[2] William Bennett, secretary of education under President Ronald Reagan and director of the Office of National Drug Control Policy under President George Bush, noted in 1991, "If I learned one thing in those two jobs it's that this country has a challenge on its hands at home. And that challenge has to do with the well-being of our children."[3] In the late 1980s Senator Orrin Hatch (R.-Utah) told journalists that his cosponsored child care bill had become "my number one legislative agenda."[4]

The public has echoed—even amplified—politicians' call for action. In 1985, 62 percent of Americans thought children were better off than they themselves had been when they were growing up, and only 29 percent thought children were worse off. Almost a decade later, the reverse obtained: only 29 percent of adults believed children to be better off now, and 60 percent saw them as worse off.[5]

Even in the increasingly conservative political atmosphere of the mid-1990s, most Americans are willing to underwrite social policies for children. In December 1994, 47 percent of respondents to a *New York Times* poll thought that "government spending on programs for poor children" should be increased, compared with 9 percent who thought it should be decreased.[6] At the same time, fully 90 percent of Americans agreed that "the welfare system" should "help provide child care so a parent on welfare can work or look for work." More Americans (between 50 and 70 percent) would increase federal spending on combating crime, on the public school system, and on health care—all issues discussed in the chapters below—than would spend on public policies not closely related to children's needs, such as environmental protection or military defense.[7]

In other ways, this call for new social policies for children is not at all opportune. Since the midterm election of November 1994 brought Republican party majorities to both houses of Congress, few politicians or policy advocates have called for new federal programs for any group of Americans, never mind nonvoting children. As we write, concern about the federal budget deficit, the conviction that states can address social problems better than the federal government can, and the belief that welfare must be reformed almost to elimination all militate against new policy initiatives.

This book responds to both the new and the former political scenes. Some proposals are more in tune with liberals' inclinations for new programs or greater downward redistribution of wealth, whereas others are more compatible with conservatives' concerns about needless or harmful expenditures. More important, many of the authors seek to overcome partisan or substantive disagreements by proposing social policies that cut across ideological divides and that respond to the concerns of both liberals and conservatives. Many of these proposed policies, for example, could be implemented by states experimenting with block grant money, if such a shift occurs in the federal budget. All of the proposals will generate controversy (as would any proposal in the current political climate); all, if enacted, would help American children.

The Conference

This book grew out of a conference that, recognizing the context of shared apprehension but disparate solutions, was devoted to identifying a new set of social policies for children. (See list of conference participants.) Since no book or conference can address policies for all aspects of children's lives, our choices were guided by several considerations. First, we wanted to deal with the most important domains affecting children from birth through the passage to adulthood. Thus we chose proposals in seven major arenas: child care, schooling, transition to work, health care, income security, physical security, and child abuse.[8]

Second, we sought proposals that entailed serious departures from the status quo but were being advanced by important political groups. On this point we were initially successful beyond our expectations: shortly after we commissioned the chapter on transition to work, Congress adopted legislation to fund small-scale demonstrations similar to Robert Lerman's proposal for a youth apprenticeship system. (There was no causal connection.) The crime bill passed in August 1994 contained provisions for community policing and tougher criminal sanctions akin to those proposed by John DiIulio; whether it will stand in the new political climate of Capitol Hill remains to be seen.

Many of the other proposals are serious contenders, although by no means sure winners, in the policy competition. Most of the income security policies proposed here by Irwin Garfinkel were recommended by the National Commission on Children, a bipartisan commission appointed jointly by President Reagan and Congress and chaired by

Senator Jay Rockefeller, and many have been proposed by President Clinton. Barbara Bergmann's child care proposal is consistent with the commission's call for further expansion of public financing of child care. Julia Lear's school-based health clinics are up and running in some communities, and they are among the proposals that would-be reformers are now considering as an alternative to national health insurance.

Third, we sought to avoid merely "preaching to the choir" by encouraging participants to air disagreements as well as points of consensus. In particular, while the public and politicians agree that children are the nation's most essential resource and need help, they disagree on two crucial questions: What is the most important cause of the problems that children face in the 1990s? What is the role of government in trying to solve these problems?

With respect to causation, most liberals believe that lack of income is the major factor underlying children's problems and that government should do more to raise the incomes of poor families and to promote their economic security. Some conservatives agree that lack of economic resources is a serious problem for children, but they doubt that government can help. Indeed, many claim that government programs have made children worse off by creating incentives for families to break up and for parents to stop supporting their children.[9]

Others argue that values, rather than low income, are the root cause of children's most serious problems. But serious disagreements persist even among those who agree that children are not being taught enough about family commitments, duties, collective responsibility, or even sin and salvation. Rather than seeking to eliminate government, as do other conservatives, social conservatives want to redefine the relationship between citizens and government—from one based on the principle of individual entitlement and self-interest to one based on mutual responsibility and respect for authority.[10] Advocates of this position also believe that government policies should reinforce local and familial norms and values, including religious and moral beliefs. "New Democrats" express a similar concern with values, although their proposed solutions are often quite different from those of the social conservatives.[11] In particular, New Democrats usually envision a more active role for government in strengthening social values, mainly by providing new services and institutions that will help people live up to the values they espouse.

Americans are split exactly down the middle on the question of whether children's problems are more economic or moral in origin. Both in 1993 and 1994, respondents were evenly divided between agreement that "the social and economic problems that face America are mainly the result of," on the one hand, "a decline in moral values" or, on the other hand, "financial pressures and strains on the family."[12]

Given the equally deep philosophical and political splits in frameworks for thinking about social policies for children, we strove for ideological diversity in choosing both authors and discussants. Thus we sought proposals that would call for more, less, or different government. We also sought proposals that would variously call for governmental provision of money or of services, governmental reinforcement of cherished values, or abdication of involvement in private matters. At the same time, we strove to bring to light ideological convergence, even (or especially) among people who see themselves as being on opposite sides of the political spectrum. Thus we sought authors and discussants who were willing to look at old problems in new ways and to envision alliances among traditional competitors for the sake of children.

Finally, to ensure that the conference would focus on policy, we chose an unusual format. Even academics who intend to develop the policy implications of their analyses often do not get around to devoting the attention to the "so what?" that they lavish on the "what?" and "why?" Thus we began at the end, with detailed policy proposals as the centerpiece of each session. Each proposal included one or more specific policy option(s) designed to focus political debate and eventually to be implemented. Proposal writers were asked to (briefly) identify a problem that needed to be addressed, offer a fairly specific proposal for its solution, discuss the costs and benefits of the proposal, compare its advantages (and possible disadvantages) with alternatives, and assess its political prospects.

To keep the focus on workable policy solutions to identified problems, each proposal was evaluated by three types of respondents: (1) an academic expert to assess the intellectual grounding for the proposal, (2) a political analyst to consider the likely trajectory of the proposal during the process of enactment, and (3) an activist or administrator to discuss how the proposal would play out during the implementation process and how it would affect its ultimate recipients—American children. Before examining the specific proposals, however, let us first consider recent trends in the status of children.

The Status of Children

Determining just what is problematic about the status of children is not simple. After all, by some measures American children are better off today than they have ever been. The infant mortality rate is now two-thirds lower than it was in 1960, and educational attainment, by most indicators, is higher.[13] The National Assessment of Educational Progress shows that children have gained in basic reading and mathematical skills since testing began in the early 1970s.[14] Even childhood poverty and teenage motherhood, while more common in the United States than in comparable countries, are less frequent today than in the early 1960s.[15] (See table 1-1.)

The Decline in Children's Well-Being

Before concluding that this book is unnecessary, however, consider the recent past. As table 1-1 shows, nearly all of the improvements mentioned above occurred during the 1960s and early 1970s; many gains in children's well-being have stagnated or even receded since then. Rates of poverty among children, for example, were about 34 percent higher in 1990 than in 1970. Moreover, while both high school graduation rates and achievement test scores have remained stable or inched upward, young adults with only a high school degree have actually lost ground in terms of their future employment opportunities and earning trajectories. Changes in the labor market, due in part to new technologies and increases in international competition, have altered the demand for skilled workers, so that a high school degree is worth less today than it was thirty years ago.[16]

Other indicators of children's well-being paint an even bleaker picture. Both suicide and homicide rates among young men have tripled since 1960. The unemployment rate for young men is substantially higher today than it was in 1960, and the percentage of young men who are "idle"—neither at work nor in school—has risen precipitously. (See table 1-1.) While teenage motherhood has declined substantially since 1960, the proportion of teen mothers who are unmarried at the time of birth has risen dramatically. In 1960, 85 percent of all teen births were to married women; by 1990 the figure was only 35 percent.[17]

Children also have less access to their parents' time and money than their counterparts did in the past. Forty years ago, nine out of ten children lived with two parents, mostly two biological parents. By 1990 only 75 percent of children lived in two-parent families, and many of these lived with a stepfather rather than a biological father. More than half of all children born in the 1980s are expected to spend some time in a single-parent family before reaching age eighteen; many will spend their entire childhood in such a family.[18] Since single-parent families are primarily headed by women, the changes in family structure imply a major loss of fathers' time for children.

Single-parent families also mean a loss of parents' economic resources, since the average single-mother family is five times as likely to be poor as the average two-parent family. Most important, children who grow up with only one parent are less successful in adulthood than children who grow up with both parents. They are less likely to graduate from high school, more likely to become teen mothers, and more likely to have trouble finding and keeping a steady job.[19] Indeed, children in single-mother families score lower on nearly all of the indicators shown in table 1-1.[20]

Changes in gender roles have further undermined children's claim on mothers' time.[21] Women have been entering the paid labor force in greater numbers throughout the twentieth century. Since 1960, the increase has been especially pronounced among mothers with children at home, particularly preschool children. Today more than half of all mothers return to work outside the home before their infants are a year old.[22] Close to two-thirds of mothers with preschool children now work outside the home.[23] Employed mothers spend six hours a week, on average, in primary child care activities (dressing, feeding, playing with, and talking to children), just under half of the time devoted by mothers not working outside the home.[24]

Mothers' employment need not harm children so long as child care is adequate. But the current child care system is so uneven in quality that the United States has cause for concern about the effects on children of the increasing use of nonparental child care.[25] There are no national standards for day care centers, and many states lack guidelines on factors such as teacher qualifications and group size. Consequently, many children are cared for in settings that do not conform to professional standards, such as those set forth by the National Academy of Sciences Panel on Child Care Policy. While most center-based programs meet professional standards for group sizes and child-staff ratios, only about half of home-based programs

TABLE 1-1. *Selected Indicators of Trends in Child Well-Being, 1960–90*

Indicator	1960	1970	1980	1990
Infant mortality[a]				
All infants	26.0	20.0	12.6	9.2
Whites	22.9	17.8	11.0	7.7
Blacks	44.3	32.6	21.4	17.0
Low birth weight[b]				
All births	8.0	7.9	6.8	7.0
Whites	6.8	6.8	5.7	5.7
Blacks	12.8	13.9	12.5	12.9
High school dropout[c]				
All youth age 18 to 24	26.9	17.3	15.6	13.6
Whites	25.5	15.2	14.4	13.5
Blacks	36.7	33.3	23.5	15.1
Poverty (child < age 18)[d]				
All children	26.5	14.9	17.9	19.9
Whites	20.0	10.5	13.4	13.7
Blacks	65.5	41.5	42.1	45.9
Suicide[e]				
All youth age 15 to 19	3.6	5.9	8.5	11.3
White males	5.9	9.4	15.0	19.4
Black males	3.4	5.4	5.6	10.3
White females	1.6	2.9	3.3	4.5
Black females	1.5	2.9	1.6	2.3
Homicide[e]				
All youth age 15 to 19	4.0	8.1	10.6	13.7
White males	3.2	5.2	10.9	9.6
Black males	27.6	59.8	48.8	92.7
White females	1.2	2.1	3.9	3.3
Black females	7.0	10.1	11.0	11.6
Idleness[f]				
White males	. . .	18.0	25.0	25.0
Black males	. . .	23.0	44.0	52.0
Teen motherhood (birthrate)[g]				
All females 15 to 19	89.1	63.3	53.0	59.9
Whites	79.4	57.4	44.7	50.8
Blacks	158.2	140.7	100.0	112.8

TABLE 1-1. *(continued)*

Indicator	1960	1970	1980	1990
Single parenthood (child < age 18)[h]				
All children	9.0	11.3	18.9	25.0
Whites	7.0	8.1	14.0	19.0
Blacks	22.0	33.6	50.2	55.0
Employed mother[i]				
Child < age 6	11.5	30.3	45.1	58.2
Whites	11.2	35.0	43.5	57.8
Blacks	13.6	56.4	63.4	73.1

a. National Center for Health Statistics, *Monthly Vital Statistics Report*, vol. 41 (January 7, 1993), table 22, p. 40; and vol. 42 (May 13, 1994), table 5, p. 16.

b. U.S. Department of Health and Human Services, *Vital Statistics of the United States, 1960, 1970, 1980,* vol. 1, *Natality,* tables 1-39 and 1-81. Data for 1990 are from National Center for Health Statistics, *Monthly Vital Statistics Report*, supplement, vol. 41 (February 25, 1993), table 14, p. 32.

c. Robert Kominski and Andrea Adams, "School Enrollment—Social and Economic Characteristics of Students: October 1991," *Current Population Reports*, Series P-20, no. 469 (Department of Commerce, Bureau of the Census, 1993), table A-4, pp. A-20–26. Data in last column are for 1991. Data for 1960 are from Bureau of the Census, *U.S. Census of Population: 1960, Subject Reports: Educational Attainment: Data on Years of School Completed by Age, Ethnic Origin, Occupation, Income, Etc.* (Department of Commerce, 1961), table 1, p. 1. It is the percent not finishing high school in this cohort.

d. Bureau of the Census, *Current Population Reports*, series P-60, no. 181. "Poverty in the United States: 1991" (Department of Commerce, 1992).

e. National Center for Health Statistics, *Vital Statistics of the United States, 1960, 1970, 1980* (Department of Health and Human Services, 1963, 1974, 1985), vol. 2, *Mortality*, part A, table 1-8, p. 13. Data in last column are from *Vital Statistics of the United States, 1989*, table 1-8, p. 13 (Department of Health and Human Services, 1993).

f. Sara McLanahan and Gary Sandefur, *Growing Up with a Single Parent* (Harvard University Press, 1994). Not calculated for 1960.

g. National Center for Health Statistics, *Vital Statistics of the United States, 1960, 1970, 1980,* vol. 1, *Natality,* tables 1-E and 1-6. Data for 1990 are from *Monthly Vital Statistics Report*, supplement, vol. 41(S), table 3, p. 20.

h. Bureau of the Census, *Current Population Reports*, series P-20, "Household and Family Characteristics," various years (Department of Commerce).

i. Bureau of the Census, *Statistical Abstract of the United States, 1985, 1993*, tables 634 and 637 (data for married women with husband present). Data for 1960 are from *U.S. Census of Population, Subject Reports: Employment* (Department of Commerce, 1961), table 5.

do so. Infants are especially at risk for being cared for in settings that do not conform to professional standards.

Similarly, teacher qualifications vary widely across different types of settings. While about half of all teachers in center-based settings have completed college, only 12 percent of providers in family day care settings have a college education, and 11 percent have not even finished high school. Finally, the annual turnover rate for teachers in child care centers is 25 percent for the country as a whole and 50 percent in about half of all centers, suggesting that many children are being cared for by people whom they have had no time to become attached to and who are unfamiliar with their special needs.[26]

Are All Children Affected Equally?

Nearly all of the indicators discussed so far illustrate the most extreme conditions facing children. Infant death, high school failure, suicide, and homicide are relatively uncommon events, affecting only a few children. It is therefore useful to ask whether trends in the most severe problems that affect only a few children resemble trends in less severe problems to which more children are potentially exposed.

In some instances, the answer is yes: the acute forms of stagnation or decline in children's well-being reported in table 1-1 mirror broader, more diffuse trends among Americans of all ages. Increasing poverty among children is consistent with the decline in living standards among families and households more generally.[27] Similarly, the employment problems facing young men, while more extreme, parallel those facing a majority of male workers in the United States. Back-to-back recessions during the early 1980s brought the most severe unemployment since the Great Depression, and the economic restructuring of the past two decades, while hitting new entrants to the labor market the hardest, has affected men of all ages and nearly all occupations.[28]

In other instances, our indicators are unique to children but are widespread among them. The suicide rate has remained constant among adults over twenty-five, even as it has increased dramatically among our youth. Similarly, the rising homicide rate among young men is at odds with broader trends in murder and violent crime. Murder rates among those between fifteen and twenty-four have risen since the early 1980s, whereas they have remained steady or declined among persons over age twenty-five.[29] Children in all conditions of life face parental divorce, mothers working outside the home, and an insufficiency of good child care facilities.

Growing Inequality among Children

Nevertheless, the conditions of children not only sometimes diverge from those of adults, but also they sometimes diverge from those of other children. Although a majority of children experienced declines in economic status during the 1970s and 1980s, a nontrivial portion of children simultaneously became better off. Children living in two-earner families with college-educated parents, for example, experienced an increase in family income during the 1980s.

Children are also becoming more unequal in arenas other than income. Although children in general, and those in single-parent families especially, have lost time with their parents, children at the top of the income distribution have acquired more of their fathers' time, as married fathers have recently increased the amount of time they spend attending at childbirth and caring for their children.[30] Similarly, since homicide and other forms of violence are highly concentrated in a few neighborhoods in a few cities, most children have become safer during the past decade, while some have experienced an increased risk of violent crime.[31]

Race and Gender Differences

Most of the adverse indicators discussed here are more common among low-income populations, and since people of color are overrepresented among the poor, we would expect minority children to exhibit more problems than white children, on average. And indeed, this is the case. As table 1-1 shows, black children have higher rates of infant mortality and homicide, and their risk of unemployment, idleness, and teen motherhood is much greater than that of whites. The racial difference in homicide rates is nothing less than extraordinary: in 1990, young black men were nearly nine times as likely to be murdered as young white men. The only indicator on which white children are worse off than black children is suicide.

While these racial differences are deeply disturbing, the gap between blacks and whites is not increasing for all indicators, and in some instances it is decreasing. The race difference in high school graduation rates has virtually disappeared during the last two decades. More important, the racial gap in academic achievement is narrowing. White students' reading and mathematics scores on standardized tests improved somewhat between 1971 and 1990, but black students of all ages showed significant improvement. A weaker version of the same pattern obtains for science and civics.[32] Finally, as measured by the black-to-white ratio, the racial disparities in single parenthood and the likelihood of mothers being in the paid labor force have also declined. (See table 1-1.)

We are seldom surprised to find that poor children have more problems than affluent children or that extraordinarily poor blacks have more problems than extraordinarily wealthy whites. But poverty is not the only entry into problems of childhood: gender also plays a role. As table 1-1 shows, boys are more likely than girls to drop out of high school, kill themselves or get killed, and be unemployed. Indeed, as young men's connection to the labor force has weakened over the past two decades, young women have increased their labor force attachment.

Not all indicators favor girls. The gender wage gap, while narrower in 1990 than in 1980, remains favorable to men.[33] At the same time, an increasing proportion of teen mothers are responsible for supporting their children, with at most informal help from the fathers.

We have, then, ample evidence for the first criterion needed to promulgate social policies for children—clearly identified and urgent problems. But the existence of urgent problems is no guarantee that solutions will be found, or even sought. To make that step possible, we must satisfy another criterion: specifying policies that offer reasonable solutions to problems and that can garner support from many political and analytic perspectives. Each proposal in this volume addresses that second criterion.

The Papers

Judging by their reception at our conference, all the proposals will generate significant political and analytic support, though none will escape criticism—warranted or not. Together, the proposals, points of agreement, and grounds for criticism described below give a fair picture of the road ahead for proponents of new social policies for children.

Income Security for Children

Irwin Garfinkel examines income transfer policies for American children in "Economic Security for Children: From Means Testing and Bifurcation to Universality." While public education provides nearly equal benefits to children from all income classes, he argues that the rest of our income transfer system is bifurcated, with means-tested or welfare programs providing benefits to poor, mostly single-parent families and tax subsidies providing benefits primarily to well-off and wealthy families. Working poor and marginally middle-class families are left out. This system is not only inequitable, it also undermines work and marriage among those at the bottom of the income distribution.

Garfinkel recommends replacing major welfare programs and tax subsidies with a set of universal policies: national health insurance, a national child support assurance system, refundable tax credits for children, refundable housing tax credits for adults, and a universal child care system. In lieu of the current aid to families with dependent children program, he recommends a noncategorical, time-limited, cash relief program, followed by work relief.

Because existing public expenditures are already large and would be reallocated, Garfinkel argues that health insurance and child support assurance would require very little additional public spending. For similar reasons, the net cost of replacing tax deductions with refundable tax credits would be moderate—about $6 billion per year.[34] Replacing welfare with work relief could cost an additional $10 billion to $20 billion. Universal child care would be the most expensive part of his proposal—nearly $60 billion per year.

Participants at the conference were impressed by Garfinkel's evidence that families in the second income quintile receive much less support from government than families in the first quintile (and much less than families in the top two quintiles in areas like health care and housing subsidies). There was also general agreement that more consistent child support enforcement was an idea whose time had come.

Participants also had important criticisms. Gary Burtless of the Brookings Institution noted that universal programs create their own work disincentives through a higher tax burden and might therefore create more inefficiency than current income-tested programs. Burtless also argued that the stigma associated with means testing is a virtue because it promotes self-targeting and encourages people to become economically independent. Lawrence Mead of New York University questioned whether economic incentives affected work and marriage, arguing instead that the poor need morally based requirements to enforce work, and, to the extent possible, stable marriages.

Most of the discussion, however, focused on political objections and barriers to Garfinkel's proposal. Gary Burtless argued that Garfinkel's universal proposals would be prohibitively expensive and noted that the scope of the welfare state is shrinking in Europe, suggesting that those countries may be having second thoughts about the wisdom of such expansive (and expensive) programs. Burtless proposed as an alternative a narrower set of universal in-kind (not cash) benefits focused on children (not parents).

Hugh Heclo of George Mason University reinforced Burtless's political concerns by arguing that public support for universal benefits is too low to allow legislative passage, for several reasons. The working poor do not want what people on welfare are getting; they want welfare recipients to work as they are doing. In addition, there is no constituency for giving more money to all parents; voters are not convinced that social problems would disappear if parents were given $1,000–$2,000 more in cash each year. Finally, there is a constituency for limited assistance through means testing for the poor.

Barbara Bergmann of the American University advocated a different form of targeting: employment incentives would be best enhanced by ensuring equal opportunity for those facing barriers to economic independence, namely white women and minority men and women. Bergmann also argued that the level of wages (assuming access to jobs) is as severe a problem as the level of welfare benefits and that Garfinkel's program would leave out the people most in need of help.

Bergmann's last comment, in the context of Heclo's reading of the political scene, underscores the dilemma facing liberals: should they urge legislators to devote limited resources to the poorest families or to provide more help to working poor and near-poor families? Whereas Garfinkel wants to do more for the latter, the three discussants were most concerned about the former.

Schooling

In "Somebody's Children: Educational Opportunity for *All* American Children," Diane Ravitch argues that the country's vision of public schools should follow John Dewey's standard: "What the best and wisest parent wants for his own child, that must be what the community wants for all of its children. Any other ideal for our schools is narrow and unlovely; acted upon, it destroys our democracy." In theory the public education system embraces ideals of equality, excellence, and pluralism; in practice these ideals are approximated for the vast majority of American children. But children in low-income urban neighborhoods attend schools that not only fail to achieve these ideals but also fail to provide children even with basic education in a safe environment.

To address this problem, Ravitch calls for publicly funded vouchers to allow poor children in designated inner-city neighborhoods to choose their own schools, whether public, private, or parochial. Means-tested scholarships, she argues, would create a pluralistic school system dedicated to assuring equity and excellence, because poor students could leave inferior schools in favor of schools with higher quality or programs in line with their own values. Those schools so physically decrepit, educationally bankrupt, or morally vacuous that they could not attract students with other options would simply shut down.

All participants in the conference shared Ravitch's outrage at atrocious schools and her conviction that a good education is essential to all children. Most also shared her conviction that "a good education" includes moral training and a decent environment as well as conventional schooling—an important point of convergence among liberals and conservatives of various stripes. Many were also intrigued by the way her proposal used conservatives' favorite educational reform—market-oriented vouchers—in the service of communitarians' favorite goal—small communities oriented around values and moral commitments.

Like the others, however, Ravitch's proposal elicited questions and concerns. Some participants raised the empirical and interpretive question of whether a poor home or social environment, rather than poor schools, was the underlying factor in children's poor school achievement. If poor schools are largely at fault or if good schools can make a real difference, then subsidized choice might well improve the education of the poor. But if even very good schools can make only slight headway against educational failures stemming from social factors such as poverty, family instability, or racial discrimination, then these questioners feared that choice would be too narrow a solution to promote equality effectively or even to improve public education.

Nomi Maya Stolzenberg of the University of Southern California raised the deepest political concern about parental selection of a child's school. She worried about the extent to which some moral visions can encroach on individual liberties and equality. What is to be done, she asked, when a group charters a school that rejects the principle of equality among genders or races as a matter of faith? Even if certain pedagogical choices are made illegal, someone must set and enforce the standards for the content of acceptable teaching—a political and philosophical quagmire. Thus, Stolzenberg worried, means-tested vouchers may succeed in equalizing choice and thereby promoting equal cultural autonomy of disparate groups, but they increase the risk of undermining the foundations of liberal democracy.

Other participants focused on details of implementation that would necessarily grow out of Ravitch's proposal. For example, although many praised the proposal because it would give more power to parents, others feared some of the consequences of that move. What must or may the government do to ensure that some children are not made even worse off by means-tested vouchers, say by parents who face high information or linguistic barriers and therefore leave their children in already bad schools made even worse by the exit of most other students? Or, how much should the vouchers be worth? As John Witte of the University of Wisconsin put it, "the devil is often in the details," and the ability of a school choice program to achieve equality, excellence, and pluralism depends on how the program is structured. Ravitch pointed out that there have been few trials of this proposal (except in higher education, where it is well proven) and that the details of implementation would vary from district to district, depending partly on what is learned from experience. Participants agreed that such issues would form a large part of future political and analytic disputes over means-tested vouchers.

Child Care

In "Child Care: The Key to Ending Child Poverty," Barbara Bergmann calls for near-universal child care to replace the piecemeal subsidies currently allocated to the very poor. Bergmann considers child care to be a merit good, which all children deserve to have in a decent society regardless of income. She points to child care, of all possible programs to assist children, as "unique in giving parents the ability to help themselves and their children through paid work, thus achieving the status of contributors to society." High-quality subsidized child care directly alleviates poverty and its consequences, relieves women of an anxiety and a source of dependence that is less often shared by men, and enhances the nutritional, cognitive, and emotional well-being of children. Hence it promotes, and is constitutive of, equality.

Child care also promotes efficiency, for two reasons. First, only if most welfare recipients work full time outside the home can the United States make great strides in eliminating poverty. Free child care would give many welfare recipients incentives to get jobs and make it easier for them to hold a job once they enter the labor force. Second, women who stay at home rather than enter the paid labor force because they cannot find good and affordable child care are wasting talents and energy that could be put to good social and economic use.

Bergmann rejects blanket subsidies for the whole population as too expensive. Instead she argues that by providing free care for the bottom quintile of the income distribution and subsidies for the next two quintiles everyone would in fact have the means to obtain satisfactory child care. She suggests sliding-scale fees for those above a certain income level.

The critical question in the child care debate—what kind of child care is best for children?—is both empirical and normative. Conference participants divided into several camps on these issues. Some agreed with Bergmann empirically; they pointed out that the scientific evidence, on the whole, indicates that with the possible exception of infants, children's academic achievement and emotional adjustment are not adversely affected by the mother's working outside the home or by the use of (at least high-quality) child care. They also agreed with her normative claim that women deserve equal treatment, which is best manifested through their participation in the paid labor force. As Andrew Cherlin of the Johns Hopkins University argued, child care is needed not only to alleviate poverty (since it is increasingly difficult for one worker to support a family) but also to promote gender equality (since it is inequitable to require women to curtail their own well-being in the name of children).

Others, however, disagreed with Bergmann empirically as well as normatively. The evidence cited above on the effects of day care did not settle the debate for social conservatives because it pays insufficient attention to the proper inculcation of values, which is just as important an indicator of successful child rearing as is cognitive and emotional development. Furthermore, Lawrence Mead argued, government financing and regulation of child care would not work; it would simply raise costs and increase interference without improving quality or satisfying the need for authoritative redirection of the poor.

Patrick Fagan of the Heritage Foundation argued the normative case against Bergmann's position. In his view, the shared goal of respect for and equality of women is best achieved when women realize their potential by staying at home and raising their own children. No other task is more important, and no commercial service can provide the nurturance and training that a conventional nuclear family usually ensures.

Finally, some participants sought to remain in the middle of this empirical and normative disagreement: they expressed uneasiness about the effects on families and children of extensive child care outside the home, yet argued that because women are choosing to work and because many women on welfare will soon be obligated to work, we must improve access to and quality of child care for the worst off.

Deborah Phillips of the National Research Council addressed an issue underlying much of the previous discussion: the potential conflicts of interest that child care raises between women and children, wealthy and poor, and people of different races. She pointed out that Americans' ambivalence over who should care for children reflects these conflicts, as does the fact that women are paid nothing to care for their own children and very little to care for the children of others.

While Phillips supported Bergmann's call for greater public financing of child care, her main concern was its quality rather than its extent and cost. She worried that Bergmann's proposal would expand the amount of care at the expense of improving quality and ultimately child development. She therefore endorsed a policy that would create fewer new child care slots but would concentrate on ensuring that the children who occupied those slots would receive the education and emotional services they need.

Transition to Work

Robert Lerman, in "Building Hope, Skills, and Careers: Creating a Youth Apprenticeship System," offers a proposal to reshape the educational system at the later stages of secondary school. Lerman suggests that we give young people a greater stake in society by enabling them to be productive workers in the economy while still in high school. The independence of secondary education from the labor market in the United States makes it difficult for non-college-bound teens, about half of all students, to plan careers. And the lack of formal job contacts is a severe barrier in job searches, especially for low-income and minority youths, who have the highest school dropout and unemployment rates.

To address this problem, Lerman proposes an apprenticeship program modeled after the German system of contractual arrangements between employers, workers, and schools. Such a program would enable high school juniors and seniors to spend time both in school and in the workplace. Such apprenticeship programs would provide a merit-based system for youths to acquire credentials for stable, skilled employment before high school graduation, thus increasing their productivity and income. These programs could at the same time lower levels of frustration and boredom among students not well served by schools, enhance self-esteem and incentives to learn, provide more adult role models, and give an alternative to illicit activities with peers. In all of these ways they would reduce the inequalities between well-off and poor children, thus enabling the public education system to be more effective in its universal mission of enhancing all children's social and personal resources.

Lerman argues that a full-scale program of school-to-work apprenticeships would enhance efficiency as well as equality. New workers would acquire training suited to their positions rather than wasting their time and public resources with no training or training ill-suited to available jobs. Employers would be able to try out new workers before investing in a full-time hire, thus ensuring a better fit between worker, job, and setting. A large-scale program, rather than a mere demonstration project, would benefit employers in general because the prepared young workers would not be confined to a certain city or industry. Government sponsorship of the program would reduce employers' incentives to poach skilled workers from other firms, since all employers would receive funding for training.

Lerman's apprenticeship proposal drew little ideological fire. Virtually all participants agreed with his claim that school-to-work linkages need to be dramatically strengthened, and most were enthusiastic about at least the general outlines of his solution to the transition problem. More concretely, Steven Hamilton of Cornell University reviewed the limited U.S. experience with apprenticeships and concluded that the record to date was promising.

Lerman's proposal did not escape scot-free, however. Cecilia Rouse of Princeton University raised the broadest concerns by questioning Lerman's claims that apprenticeships would increase the efficiency of the labor market. She disputed his analogy between the U.S. and German labor markets, since German workers are heavily unionized, have a narrow wage distribution, and are less likely to have attended college. American workers also enjoy higher job mobility and greater flexibility. Do we, she asked, really want more rigid tracking in schools and workplaces? Rouse also pointed out that although individual youths need more skills, it is not clear that businesses in the aggregate face a lack of skilled labor. After all, the United States had a subminimum wage for training new workers that was rarely used and that expired in 1993 with barely any notice. Furthermore, community colleges already offer training in many technical jobs, and they are reasonably effective in attracting students and in increasing their human capital.

Ronald Mincy of the Ford Foundation asked how Lerman's program would help disadvantaged minority youth, who often live in cities with high rates of unemployment, who lack access even to those jobs that do exist, and who are least attractive to employers. Jennifer Hochschild inquired how apprenticeship programs could reach high school dropouts, those most in need of training and direction. Others pointed out that historically apprenticeships in skilled crafts and technical trades have created rather than torn down barriers to entry for women and minorities; they argued for the need to change jobs and hiring patterns to make apprenticeship programs truly effective and equitable.

Health Care for Children

Julia Graham Lear, in "Health Care Goes to School: An Untidy Strategy to Improve the Well-Being of School-Age Children," advocates school-based health centers in low-income schools in order to ensure basic health services for an underserved population. A multidisciplinary team of professionals would provide an array of primary physical and mental health services, as well as substance abuse counseling; parents and local school authorities would choose the specific services appropriate for their community. The centers would also be linked to other health-related programs in the school, such as sex education and programs designed to prevent drug and alcohol abuse and violence. Finally, school-based clinics would be encouraged to develop links with managed-care organizations in the community, thereby allowing referrals for specialized care and health care when schools were closed.

Approximately five hundred school-based health centers have opened during the past decade as small-scale demonstrations. They have brought health care services to a variety of students, many of whom had received no health care for up to two years previously. Lear proposes to expand these centers to include 7,500 schools across the country, including elementary schools as well as secondary schools. To take advantage of scale efficiencies, her clinics would be located in schools with more than five hundred students. To increase equality of health care among children, they would be placed in low-income public schools.

Many participants in the conference were enthusiastic about Lear's proposal on its own terms. Auditors were impressed with the effectiveness of the clinics that currently operate, and few disagreed with Lear's proposals for how and where to expand them, if they are to be expanded.

There was, however, vigorous debate about the importance of school-based clinics relative to other health care policies and much discussion about how clinics should or can fit into a broader program for health care. Lorraine Klerman of the University of Alabama argued that both efficiency and equality dictate that limited resources be focused on infants and women of reproductive age, rather than on adolescents. In her view, providing family planning, abortion, prenatal care, and care for infants and toddlers would do more to improve the health status of children and the population as a whole than would school clinics. Furthermore, Klerman argued that Lear's proposal to expand school-based clinics to include younger children was inappropriate since children in elementary schools are less likely than adolescents to take their health problems into their own hands and seek treatment.

Paul Starr of Princeton University argued that school-based clinics did not fit into a system of universal health care coverage based on managed care, such as the one proposed by the Clinton administration. School clinics would quickly become redundant, since under managed care families would choose a primary health care provider who would then determine the source of services for adolescents and other family members. While providers might choose to develop cooperative arrangements with school-based clinics, they should not be saddled with an obligation to do so. In addition, claimed Starr, a school-based health clinic may provide inferior services compared to a primary provider since its hours, personnel, and equipment are more restricted than those of other clinics. While the Clinton health care reform proposal itself has been sidelined for the time being, the "managed-care movement" is gaining momentum, which means that proponents of school-based health clinics will need to address Starr's concerns if they hope to gain public and private support.

Patrick Fagan raised a more philosophical concern. He noted that several moral communities are served by public schools, that each community has distinct beliefs about sexuality, and that government ought not to elevate one set of beliefs over another. Kristin Luker of Princeton University disagreed with Fagan, arguing that individuals, including adolescents, have the right to decide sensitive personal issues, including those regarding sexuality. In her view, the state has a responsibility to protect their right, and the health clinics proposed by Lear are one way to do so. This unresolved and sensitive debate, as Lear notes in her paper, is a major barrier to implementing reproductive health services for adolescents.

As with most of the other papers, conference participants raised narrower but troublesome implementation questions, which would surely surface in a legislative debate. Robert Johnson of the University of Medicine and Dentistry of New Jersey noted that school-based clinics have limited access even for the targeted group since they are generally not open at night and during the summer, they exclude dropouts, and students need parental consent to use them. Irving Harris of Chicago suggested a two-door model, with one entrance from the school during the day and another from the street when schools are not in session. But other problems of access are not so simple; requiring parental consent may make clinics more palatable to parents, but it erodes adolescents' right to confidentiality and may inhibit some students from even trying to use a clinic.

Physical Security for Children

In "Saving the Children: Crime and Social Policy," John DiIulio argues that the biggest problem facing a small group of the nation's children is physical insecurity. For children of color in violent inner-city neighborhoods, life is, in Hobbes's phrase, "solitary, poor, nasty, brutish, and short."

DiIulio recommends using both private and governmental resources to get tough on crime, through more stringent criminal justice policies and dramatic social measures. On the criminal justice side, he cites the need for more police in poor urban minority neighborhoods where most crime is concentrated. He recommends "saturation community policing," which would include a four- to fivefold increase in the number of police officers in inner cities and a change in policy for police officers that would emphasize foot patrols and help communities solve their own problems. DiIulio argues that saturation community policing is a better strategy for strengthening community security than police crackdowns or auto patrols.

DiIulio also argues for stricter enforcement of jail sentences for violent and repeat criminals. Although many such convicted criminals are black, DiIulio rejects the claim that such enforcement policies would be racially discriminatory; after all, those who would benefit most from stricter enforcement of the laws are the poor black residents of inner cities, who are more likely than other Americans to be victimized by violent and property crime.

On the social side, DiIulio believes that full-scale intervention into the schools and homes of a small group of severely at-risk children is warranted. He contends that some inner cities have become "criminogenic" communities in which the social forces that produce criminals are stronger than those that produce law-abiding citizens. One way to prevent children from succumbing to these forces is to remove from their environment altogether those who have been abused or whose parents have demonstrated their inability to care for them.

Participants at the conference applauded DiIulio's commitment to addressing one of the nation's most volatile and vexing problems. Almost all agreed with his call for saturation community policing in the most violent neighborhoods, and many accepted (albeit with some unease) his insistence that stricter jail sentences for repeat violent criminals would benefit the black community. However, some participants disagreed with DiIulio's argument that more social services would not significantly alleviate the problems of criminogenic communities. Why not, they asked, seek to improve inner-city neighborhoods by providing them with resources to attain middle-class amenities, rather than spending scarce resources on police, jails, or boarding schools? In this view, full employment, good schools, apprenticeships into the work force, high-quality child and health care, and simply more money for poor families to live on might do more to reduce crime than even the best measures to punish criminals or to prevent them from further wrongdoing.

Peter Reuter of the University of Maryland raised a more practical worry, that saturation community policing would be too expensive for most state and local governments. He also cautioned about the combined fiscal and administrative effects of DiIulio's prison and policing proposals and admonished DiIulio to pay more careful attention to the costs of arresting and incarcerating low-level drug dealers.

Most controversy revolved around DiIulio's proposals to "place children in orphanages." Barbara Bennett Woodhouse of the University of Pennsylvania worried that DiIulio's proposal insufficiently respected the rights of families or the preferences of children and that it exaggerated the extent to which severely abused or neglected children are currently forced to remain with parents or guardians who harm them. She also argued that a good program must protect children not only from parental harm and abuse but also from the harm of long, forced separation from their families. Finally, she rebuked DiIulio for linking "boarding schools" to such popular anticrime measures as truth-in-sentencing and "three strikes, you're out" laws. Despite these and other concerns about how DiIulio's proposals would be interpreted and implemented, Woodhouse agreed with his core contention that any placing-out policy, whether administered under current or new laws and policies, should remove children only from parents or guardians whose past actions demonstrated serious future threats.

A final set of concerns focused on the racial implications of DiIulio's proposals. Emily Martin of the federal Office of Juvenile Justice and Delinquency Prevention (OJJDP) asserted that DiIulio understated evidence of racial disparities in the sentencing process of both juveniles and adults. Although DiIulio cited studies that found no evidence of racial disparities when relevant variables were controlled, Martin cited OJJDP analyses that did find such disparities, particularly in juvenile adjudications and postconviction dispositions. To DiIulio's citation of public opinion surveys showing that clear majorities of African Americans favor stronger criminal justice sanctions, Martin responded with skepticism. Her fear that, however well meant and well implemented, DiIulio's proposals would produce racial bias in the criminal justice system sent a clear signal about the political obstacles his proposal would face—just as his responses suggested the possibility of unexpected allies among African Americans for his suggestions.

Child Abuse

In "Child Abuse Reporting: The Need to Shift Priorities from More Reports to Better Reports," Douglas Besharov argues that current child abuse reporting laws and practices encourage overreporting of abuse. Between 1976 and 1993, the number of reports of abuse and neglect more than quadrupled—from 700,000 to 3 million. While the data are admittedly weak, Besharov argues that it is doubtful that abuse has increased this much. Moreover, the best estimates suggest that about 60 to 65 percent of reports are unfounded. Since investigations are time consuming and costly, inappropriate and excessive reporting stretches available resources too thinly. Thus too much concern about child abuse has the paradoxical effect of providing too few resources to detect, investigate, and ameliorate serious abuse and neglect cases.

Investigations also cause harm of their own, argued Besharov. They necessarily invade privacy and usually require interviews of friends, relatives, and professionals who know the family in order to determine the justice of a claim of child abuse. Any such investigation attaches suspicion to parents, and it may result in lasting harm to the reputation and sense of security of innocent parents.

Although he recognizes that some abuse still goes unreported and that many children have been saved from injury and even death by the new attention to child abuse, Besharov recommends that the policy of reporting shift toward better rather than more reporting. To this end, he recommends that states clarify child abuse reporting laws, provide continuing public and professional education, screen reports, modify liability laws, and give feedback to persons who report. In addition, social service agencies should adopt explicit agency policies for reporting abuse. Clarification of what kinds of reports should be rejected short of a full-scale investigation is as important as clarification of what kinds of cases should be reported and investigated.

Conference participants agreed with Besharov that too much attention to potential cases of child abuse can backfire, particularly if poor (and disproportionately black or immigrant) parents are accused of child abuse when their real problem is poverty or unfamiliarity with (or rejection of) American child-rearing norms. And they appreciated the wealth of data he brought to bear on this issue, which is notorious for its dearth of systematic, reliable data. But here as in all other cases they found grounds for disagreement as well as praise.

Rose Firestein of the Legal Aid Society of New York City argued that Besharov underestimated the evidence supporting the claim that abuse is widespread and growing. In her view, government is probably doing too little, not too much, to curb abuse and neglect. Firestein feared that if Besharov's proposals were adopted, children would not be adequately protected from abuse and neglect. She also moved from empirical claims to normative pleas by pointing out the special need for government intervention on behalf of citizens who have the fewest resources and whose rights are most severely violated.

Marva Hammons of the New York City Human Resources Administration shared Firestein's concerns about the greater dangers of under- than of overreporting child abuse and neglect. She also made the more focused argument that, just because most growth in reported cases is of neglect rather than abuse, this is not grounds for minimizing its seriousness. After all, she claimed, the worst forms of neglect can be more harmful than the mildest forms of abuse.

Much discussion in this session focused on the questions of whether poverty causes child neglect and abuse, whether poverty is frequently confused with child neglect or abuse, and whether the apparent association is actually an artifact of biased or incomplete reporting.[35] Sheila Kamerman of Columbia University argued that a great deal of child neglect and child abuse is the consequence of poverty. She thus urged a broad program of income support and services to attack the destitution and insecurity that so often underlie parents' maltreatment of their children. If we are serious about getting government out of the child abuse business, she argued, we must provide the resources families need to manage their own lives.

Patrick Fagan, however, rejected the hypothesized causal link between poverty and child abuse and neglect, citing family structure as the key factor in child abuse. He thus argued for child rearing within a stable marriage as the best way to reduce the incidence of abuse. In his view, government policies, if necessary at all, should focus on inducing people to marry and stay married and on reinforcing parental authority.

Summary

The conference produced a mix of strong enthusiasm and considerable disagreement—a foretaste of the allegiances and disputes to come when these proposals enter the public arena. Some of the dissension was ideological. Proposals that came closest to the sensitive issues of gender roles and racial interactions—such as child care and boarding schools for inner-city youths—produced the hottest debate and the least consensus. Disparate values about parental authority and children's rights also underlay intense discussions of school-based health clinics and child abuse.

Other disputes reflected frustration with crucial but unanswered empirical and analytic questions. Resolution of some of these disputes through bipartisan support seems more likely if appropriate and convincing research data became available. School vouchers for low-income children and apprenticeships for non-college-bound youths appealed to participants on both the left and right. The strength of their appeal depended on interpretations of the relative importance of environmental factors such as poverty and peer pressure compared with institutional factors such as high-quality schools and well-designed transitional programs. But the fact that these proposals did not directly encroach on issues of gender and race made them politically palatable even to those who disagreed on their likely efficacy. Moreover, both proposals envision a joint role for public and private agents in implementing reform—a feature that also can be expected to appeal to both liberals and conservatives.

Yet other disputes centered on judgments about political feasibility. The possibility of public and politicians' support for expensive programs to help the working poor was the chief ground for disputes over family support policies. Prognoses about the likelihood of broad national health insurance shaped much of the discussion of the desirability of school-based health clinics.

As a consequence of the November 1994 election, the debate over how to help children will be driven, for the next few years at least, more by the political and ideological consequences of a new conservative dominance of Congress than by the analytic questions of what really causes or could reduce child abuse or poor schooling. (That point would hold equally if liberals suddenly took control of a Congress that had long been dominated by conservatives.) But as we pointed out above, "conservatism" encompasses at least two rather different stances: a libertarian strand that seeks to minimize any governmental involvement in families and a social-conservative strand that seeks to use government to reinforce traditional family values and practices. Thus we can expect political and ideological disputes among conservatives almost as great as those between liberals and conservatives.

That fact offers some hope, as well as much complexity, for the proposals in this book. Many of the proposals here appeal across party and ideological lines because they outline new institutions that unite market and state, or because they both call on families to be more responsible for children's welfare and call on government to provide resources to help families be more responsible. Possibilities for new alliances exist, and the most imaginative proposals—such as those in this book—will take full advantage of those possibilities.

Another feature of the post-1994 political scene similarly offers both hope and complexity for the proposals in this book. Whatever else conservatives do not agree on, they share the view that the federal government should do less in the arena of social policymaking and that state governments should have more leeway to do whatever they deem best—possibly including more social policymaking. Thus Barbara Bergmann's proposal for a large new federal program subsidizing out-of-home child care is not likely to be enacted by Congress in the next few years. On the other hand, however, if Congress substantially strengthens work requirements for welfare recipients, many states may decide that subsidies for child care are an essential component of their welfare package. So many mini-Bergmanns can be anticipated almost as surely as no full-scale Bergmann.

Similarly, Garfinkel's call for federally funded child support assurance will, we confidently predict, not soon be enacted by Congress. But the fact that the Republican Contract with America calls for stricter child support enforcement and a $500 per child tax credit suggests ongoing support for redressing the bifurcation of the income transfer system and for doing more for working poor families and children. Perhaps more states will adopt elements of his proposal.

Finally, the proposals in this book were not written, and should not be read, as blueprints for immediate passage that become outmoded by any given set of election returns. They focus on basic, unfortunately unchanging concerns: How can poor parents ensure a better education for their children? How can poor communities be protected from excessive crime? How can non-college-bound children be inducted into the adult world? How can abused children be protected without causing harm to nonabusing parents? And so on. These questions will not go away soon, and responsible citizens and public servants must grapple with them. Our hope is that the proposals in this book, and the discussion of the underlying conflicts attendant on each one, will be useful in the coming decade to policymakers as well as advocates—regardless of party or ideology—as they debate, design, and implement new and better social policies for American children.

Notes

1. President Clinton, "Proclamation 6626—National Children's Day, 1993," in *Weekly Compilation of Presidential Documents*, November 22, 1993, vol. 29, no. 46, pp. 2393–94.

2. Chris Graves, "Jackson Urges Youths to Look to the Future," *Star Tribune*, February 13, 1994, p. 7b.

3. William Bennett, "Speech before Catholic School Alumni," March 18, 1991, as cited in M. David Goodwin, "Bennett Calls Catholic Schools Model for Country," *The Courier-Journal*, March 19, 1991, p. 1b.

4. Judy Mann, "Sen. Hatch on Child Care," *Washington Post*, December 23, 1987, p. B3.

5. LH Research, Inc., *A Survey of the American People on Guns as a Children's Health Issue*, prepared for the Harvard School of Public Health (June 1993), p. 3.

6. See Jason DeParle, "The Nation: Despising Welfare, Pitying Its Young," *New York Times*, December 18, 1994, sec. 4, p. 5.

7. On child care, see Gallup/CNN/*USA Today* Poll, Dec. 2–5, 1994. On increased spending, see Times Mirror Center for the People and the Press, Dec. 1–4, 1994. Both surveys are cited in *The Polling Report* (Dec. 26, 1994), pp. 2, 4. For similar levels of public support for government spending on job training and education, see Gallup/CNN/*USA Today* Poll of Jan. 16–18, 1995, cited in *The Polling Report* (Jan. 23, 1995), p. 2.

8. While physical security is not ordinarily thought of as a part of social policy, the recent explosion of homicide among youths in inner-city neighborhoods suggests that government is failing in this most basic of all responsibilities. Child abuse, while narrower than the other domains, is particularly important because it highlights the vulnerability of children and provides a sharp illustration of controversies over the role of government vis-à-vis the family.

9. Charles A. Murray, *Losing Ground: American Social Policy, 1950–1980* (Basic Books, 1984).

10. See Lawrence Mead, *Beyond Entitlement: The Social Obligations of Citizenship* (Free Press, 1986).

11. See David T. Ellwood, *Poor Support: Poverty in the American Family* (Basic Books, 1988).

12. That is, about 45 percent of the respondents chose each answer in each year. In both years, about 10 percent volunteered "both." For the 1993 poll, see Gerald F. Seib, "Politics and Policy," *Wall Street Journal*, June 11, 1993, p. A12. The 1994 data are in *The Polling Report* (June 27, 1994), p. 1.

13. Bureau of the Census, *Statistical Abstract of the United States: 1993* (Washington: 1993).

14. Department of Education, Office of Educational Research and Improvement, *Youth Indicators 1988: Trends in the Well-Being of American Youth* (Washington: 1988), pp. 58, 60, 62. *Average* achievement scores have been more or less flat since 1970, whereas rudimentary and basic skills have risen. See *Statistical Abstract of the United States: 1993*.

15. However, 1960 was during the baby boom, so that while birth rates for teens were higher, they were also higher among all women. For comparisons with other countries, see Timothy Smeeding and Barbara Torrey, "Poor Children in Rich Countries," *Science*, November 11, 1988, pp. 873–77; and

Alan Guttmacher Institute, *Teenage Pregnancy in Industrialized Countries: A Study* (Yale University Press, 1986).

16. Frank Levy and Richard J. Murnane, "U.S. Earnings Levels and Earnings Inequality: A Review of Recent Trends and Proposed Explanations," *Journal of Economic Literature*, vol. 30 (September 1992), pp. 1333–81, especially pp. 1354–64.

17. Kristin A. Moore, Nancy Snyder, and Dana Glei, "Facts at a Glance," (Washington: Child Trends, February 1995).

18. Larry L. Bumpass and James A. Sweet, "Children's Experience in Single-Parent Families: Implications of Cohabitation and Marital Transitions," *Family Planning Perspectives*, vol. 21 (December 1989), pp. 256–60.

19. Sara McLanahan and Gary Sandefur, *Growing Up with a Single Parent: What Hurts, What Helps* (Harvard University Press, 1994).

20. Nicholas Zill and Mary Jo Coiro, "Assessing the Condition of Children." *Children in Youth Services Review*, vol. 14, no. 1/2 (1992), pp. 7–27. Sara McLanahan and Karen Booth, "Mother-Only Families: Problems, Prospects, and Politics," *Journal of Marriage and the Family*, vol. 51 (August 1989), pp. 557–80.

21. Declines in fertility, however, have increased the amount of time parents have for each child. Diane J. Macunovich and Richard A. Easterlin, "How Parents Have Coped: The Effect of Life Cycle Demographic Decisions on the Economic Status of Pre-School Age Children, 1964–1987," *Population and Development Review*, vol. 16, no. 2 (June 1990), pp. 301–25.

22. Sheila B. Kamerman and Alfred J. Kahn, "A U.S. Policy Challenge," in Kamerman and Kahn, *Child Care, Parental Leave and the Under 3s: Policy Innovation in Europe* (New York: Auburn House, 1991), p. 6.

23. Suzanne M. Bianchi, "The Changing Economic Roles of Women and Men," in Reynolds Farley, ed., *State of the Nation: America in the 1990s, Volume One: Economic Trends* (Russell Sage Foundation, 1995), pp. 107–54, especially 110–17.

24. John P. Robinson, "Caring for Kids," *American Demographics*, vol. 11 (July 1989), p. 52.

25. Lynne M. Casper and others, "Who's Minding the Kids? Child Care Arrangements: Fall 1991" (Bureau of the Census, Current Population Reports, 1994).

26. Ellen Eliason Kisken and others, *A Profile of Child Care Settings: Early Education and Care in 1990*, volume 1 (Department of Education, 1991).

27. The elderly are an exception; their poverty rate declined from 24.5 percent in 1979 to 12.2 percent in 1990. Sheldon Danziger and Daniel Weinberg, "The Historical Record: Trends in Family Income, Inequality and Poverty," in Sheldon H. Danziger, Gary D. Sandefur, and Daniel H. Weinberg, eds., *Confronting Poverty: Prescriptions for Change* (Harvard University Press, 1994).

28. The only group of men to experience increases in earnings over the past decade were men with a college degree or more. James R. Wetzel, "Labor Force, Unemployment, and Earnings," in *The State of the Nation*, pp. 59–105.

29. Bureau of Justice Statistics, *Sourcebook of Criminal Justice Statistics, 1992* (Department of Justice, 1993).

30. Michael E. Lamb, *The Father's Role* (Hillsdale, N.J.: Lawrence Erlbaum, 1987); and Kathleen Gerson, *No Man's Land: Men's Changing Commitments to Family and Work* (Basic Books, 1993).

31. Large American cities range from under 300 violent crimes per 100,000 residents annually (Honolulu, Virginia Beach) to over 3,500 per 100,000 persons (Atlanta, Miami, and Newark). Kathleen Maguire and Ann L. Pastore, eds., *Sourcebook of Criminal Justice Statistics, 1993* (Department of Justice, Bureau of Justice Statistics, 1994), p. 368.

32. National Center for Education Statistics, *Report in Brief: NAEP 1992 Trends in Academic Progress* (Department of Education, 1994). See also, from the same office, *Youth Indicators 1988*, pp. 58, 60, 62.

33. Bianchi, "Changing Economic Roles of Women and Men."

34. In December 1994, more Americans (33 percent) supported "a tax credit for parents of $500 a year" than supported any other proposed tax reduction. NBC *News/Wall Street Journal* Poll, Dec. 10–13, 1994; cited in *The Polling Report* (Dec. 26, 1994), p. 2.

35. This issue does not appear in Besharov's chapter in this book. But it was raised by the draft paper for the conference and will certainly be part of any discussion in the political arena of Besharov's proposals. Thus we address it here.

Chapter 2

Economic Security for Children: From Means Testing and Bifurcation to Universality

Irwin Garfinkel

THE UNITED STATES is in the midst of a great national debate about the appropriate amount and form of public investment in children. Ronald Reagan argued that the taxes required to fund existing government programs were seriously undermining incentives and thereby despoiling the wellsprings of capitalism. He proposed dramatic reductions in federal expenditures for children, which were not adopted by Congress.[1] Toward the end of President Reagan's second term, the bipartisan National Commission on Children, chaired by Senator Jay Rockefeller, recommended, with very little dissent, equally dramatic increases in federal public benefits for children. The recommendations included universal health insurance coverage for all citizens, a refundable tax credit of $1,000 for every child in the nation, expansion of the earned income tax credit, expansion of child care funding, a child support assurance system, and once all the other provisions were in place, time-limited cash welfare assistance to be followed by eligibility for work relief.[2]

In 1992 a Democratic president was elected for the first time in twelve years. President Bill Clinton proposed many parts of the agenda of the National Commission on Children, but Congress enacted only the earned income tax credit (EITC) expansion and explicitly rejected the centerpiece of the president's domestic agenda: universal health care coverage.

In 1994, the Republican party won a majority in the Senate and (for the first time in fifty years) a majority in the House of Representatives. In 1995, the House and Senate enacted welfare reform legislation that would have substantially reduced benefits for children. In January 1996, President Clinton vetoed the legislation.

The debate may be even more fundamental. The new Republican Speaker, Newt Gingrich, describes himself as a radical who is opposed to the welfare state and favors its replacement with what he calls the "opportunity state."

Does the U.S. welfare state do too much or too little to reduce the insecurity of children? Is capitalism being overdosed or undernourished? Equally important, are we administering the correct medicine? Do the agenda of the National Commission on Children and President Clinton's proposals take the nation in the right direction? Or was President Reagan right after all?

This chapter focuses on one critical aspect of the modern welfare state: the public income transfer system for families with children, in which income is transferred from one household via some public agency to another household with children.[3] Both cash and in-kind transfers are included. I argue that capitalism generates both extraordinary gains in average living standards and extraordinary insecurity and inequality. The welfare state, by socializing selective aspects of consumption, not only reduces insecurity and inequality, but also generally enhances the productivity of unbridled capitalism. At the same time, overdoses or the wrong doses can undermine productivity. We cannot afford the ideological blinders of either the left or the right. Each case must be judged on its own merits.

The U.S. public income transfer system for families with children is already quite large: we are doing a lot already to reduce the insecurity of American children. Doing somewhat more, however, would be productive. The U.S. capitalist system, rather than overdosed, is a bit undernourished.

Even more important, the structures of several major domains of our income transfer system must be changed. Except for public education and social insurance, the transfer system for children is bifurcated, with means-tested benefits going to families at the very bottom of the income distribution and tax subsidies going primarily to families in the upper-middle and upper parts of the income distribution.

Furthermore, the bulk of means-tested benefits are targeted at the poorest of the poor by limiting them to single-parent families. The very poor and very rich derive the greatest benefits, respectively, from means-tested benefits and tax expenditures. The near poor, lower-middle class, and even the middle class pay the price. This system is not only inequitable, it also undermines work and marriage at the bottom of the income distribution.

To increase both the equity and efficiency of the system of transfers to families with children, I propose a reform agenda that replaces welfare programs and their complementary tax subsidies with universal programs. The transformation requires the following:

—A universal health insurance system;

—A universal child care system;

—Refundable income tax credits for children and refundable housing tax credits for adults (in lieu of child and adult exemptions, the food stamp program, and all housing subsidies);

—A national child support assurance system; and

—A noncategorical relief program consisting of time-limited cash assistance and services that promote independence, followed by work relief (in lieu of the current aid to families with dependent children [AFDC] program).

With two major exceptions, this reform agenda is nearly identical to the agenda of the National Commission on Children. The commission did not propose refundable housing tax credits for adults or the elimination of the food stamp program and all housing subsidies.

One final note: although this chapter focuses on the role of public income transfers in promoting the economic security of children, it must be pointed out that macroeconomic policy plays an even more important role. In a capitalist system, unemployment is the principal source of insecurity. Promoting full employment is the most efficient and equitable way to make families financially secure.[4]

Capitalism, Productivity, Insecurity, and the Welfare State

Capitalism, as even Marx wrote, is the most productive economic system known to humankind.[5] Under capitalism, competition rules, incentives elicit behavior, businesses are allowed to fail. Bankruptcies and unemployment are not just endemic to capitalism, they are essential parts of the creative destruction that makes capitalism so productive.[6] As a consequence, the dynamism of unbridled capitalism breeds economic insecurity.[7]

Economic insecurity, arising from low or irregular income, is inimical to human growth and development. Within human populations there is ample correlational evidence that children who grow up in families with very low income do worse—get less education, earn less, commit more crime—than children who grow up in more fortunate families.[8] There is also experimental evidence with monkeys that an irregular environment is even more damaging than a poor environment.[9]

As capitalism emerges, therefore, it is not surprising that nations adopt public policies to reduce economic insecurity.[10] All capitalist nations first enacted Poor Laws. As countries grew wealthier, they adopted more universal programs. In the first and second halves of the nineteenth century, respectively, American states pioneered free public education and Germany pioneered social insurance. As we near the end of the twentieth century, all advanced capitalist nations provide not only public assistance to their poorest citizens but free elementary and secondary education and a variety of social insurance programs to all citizens. Except for the United States, all industrialized nations provide health insurance or health services and child allowances.[11]

In short, the modern welfare state moderates capitalism by socializing selective aspects of consumption.[12] While total socialization of consumption would eliminate economic incentives and thereby have disastrous consequences for productivity, socialization of selective aspects of consumption may increase not only equality but also productivity. Indeed, I believe a balanced assessment would reveal that most welfare state programs improve productivity. Virtually all people agree that public education increases the productivity of the labor force. Although the United States has lagged behind other capitalist nations in the twentieth century in developing a full-blown welfare state, in the nineteenth century we were the first nation to socialize elementary and secondary education, and increases in productivity were and remain the principal justification. Virtually no one questions the productivity of public health measures such as sanitation and immunization. Even welfare programs can increase productivity. At the very least, by relieving abject poverty and preventing malnourishment during childhood they increase mental and physical abilities in adulthood. In addition, by helping both the innocent victims of capitalism and those with the least capacity to succeed in a competitive market system, welfare programs increase the fairness of the system and quell discontent.

Welfare programs increase productivity minimally because they invest only in the poorest children. They do nothing to prevent failures.[13] In contrast, cash and in-kind benefits provided on a more universal basis without regard to income reduce the economic insecurity of all citizens. Public education; health insurance; children's allowances; and old age, survivors, disability, and unemployment insurance are examples of universal programs that prevent both destitution and resort to welfare.

Just because public spending programs can increase productivity does not mean that all public spending programs do increase productivity. Any gains from spending must be weighed against the productivity losses that come from higher taxes. Moreover, the spending side of the program itself may have negative side effects, such as discouraging work or family formation. If the share of consumption that is socialized is very large, further increases are likely to reduce rather than increase productivity. Overdosing capitalism with too much socialism can kill the goose that lays the golden eggs.

Efficiency and Equity of the U.S. Economic Security System

To convey a comprehensive picture of current public efforts to increase the economic security of children, table 2-1 presents estimates for 1992 of the amounts of publicly sanctioned redistribution to families with children. Some of the benefits, such as elementary and secondary education, are targeted explicitly on children, while others, such as health care, go to parents as well as children. The table includes state as well as federal expenditures; tax expenditures, such as the earned income tax credit, as well as explicit expenditures; in-kind transfers, such as education and health care, as well as cash transfers. From the beneficiary's point of view, benefits from tax expenditures are equivalent to benefits from a government subsidy. In-kind benefits are an alternative to cash transfers. Following Robert Lampman, the table also includes private health insurance benefits for families with children.[14] Employer-provided health insurance is a form of so-

TABLE 2-1. *Public Transfers to Families with Children, by Type, 1992*

Billions of current dollars

	Family structure		Funding authority		
Type of transfer	All families	Single parent	Federal	State	Private
Total	594	198	219	272[a]	103
Universal	280	70	44	236	0
Cash	50	12	25	25	0
Social insurance/ social security	18	7	18	0	0
Unemployment insurance	18	3	3	15	0
Workers compensation	10	2	1	9	0
Other	3	1	3	0	0
In-kind	230	58	19	211	0
Elementary and secondary education	222	56	11	211	0
Medicare	8	2	8	0	0
Tax expenditures	85	14	85	0	0
EITC	12	6	12	0	0
Child care tax credit	3	1	3	a	0
Personal exemption for children	22	2	22	a	0
Personal exemption for adults	21	2	21	a	0
Homeowner deduction	26	2	26	a	0
Government regulated and subsidized	103	18	0	0	103
Third-party health care	89	9	0	0	89
Private child support	13	9	0	0	13
Welfare	127	96	90	36	0
Cash	32	25	19	14	0
AFDC and emergency assistance	24	22	13	11	0
SSI	6	4	5	1	0
General assistance/other	2	0	0	2	0
In-kind	95	70	71	22	0
Medicaid	38	34	22	16	0
Other medical	5	1	2	3	0
Food stamps	20	14	19	1	0
Other nutrition	8	4	8	0	0
Housing	10	9	10	0	0
Child care and Head Start	6	4	4	2	0
Employment	5	3	4	0	0
Foster care	3	2	2	1	0

Source: See appendix A.
a. Underestimated category.

cialization. Insurance is risk sharing and risk spreading. Health insurance redistributes from the well to the sick. When families make decisions about whether to get medical care or not, it makes no difference if they have been insured via their employer or their government. Finally, we also include private child support payments from nonresident fathers to their children. While child support payments redistribute only within the biological family, they redistribute across households from fathers to mothers and children, which usually means from richer to poorer families. And some level of government has always had the responsibility in the United States and elsewhere for regulating and enforcing private child support. These transfers are especially important to this generation of American children because more than half of them will spend part of their childhood living apart from one of their parents.

Perhaps the most striking feature of our system of public transfers to families with children is its size. In 1992 these transfers amounted to $594 billion, or 9.8 percent of GDP. Only a bit more than a third—or 3.6 percent of GDP—is provided by the federal government. By comparison, the federal government spent 6.5 percent of GDP on the aged, 4.9 percent for defense, and 7.8 percent for all other government functions.[15]

The wealthier we are, the more we can afford the costs of reducing economic insecurity. As standards of living increase, we and other nations spend more to reduce insecurity. Between 1950 and 1970, American productivity grew by 42 percent, and per capita social welfare expenditures grew by 74 percent. Between 1975 and 1990 productivity grew by only 13 percent, and per capita income security expenditures grew by only 33 percent.[16]

Are current expenditures on children so large as to constitute a threat to the functioning of capitalism? That is, is the sum of the selective doses too large? Surely not by themselves. Most western European nations spend more. But investing in the current and future security of children is not the sole objective of public policy. The cumulative effect of all public expenditures must be considered. In the United States, all public expenditures in 1990 accounted for 35 percent of GDP. With third-party health care payments, the figure is 39 percent. In comparison, the figures for France, Germany, Italy, the United Kingdom, and Sweden are 46 percent, 42 percent, 47 percent, 38 percent, and 57 percent, respectivley.[17]

That we spend less than the western European nations despite our greater wealth may be an indication that we spend too little. Though some conservatives assert that the western European nations are poorer than the United States because they spend more than we do, their evidence is weak.[18]

Another indication that U.S. transfers to children may be too small is the high poverty rate of children in this country. Twenty percent of all American children live in families with incomes below the poverty line. International comparisons indicate that U.S. poverty rates are substantially higher than those in western European nations, whose better records are attributable primarily to more extensive government transfers.[19]

A second feature of the current system depicted in table 2-1 is that the bulk of the transfers to families with children—public education, half of aid to families with dependent children (AFDC) and medicaid costs, private health insurance, and private child support—do not appear in the federal budget. Thus there should be no natural presumption that increases in investments in children must come in the form of increases in federal expenditures. On the other hand, if the federal government were to adopt more universal programs such as national health insurance, the federal budget might increase appreciably even though there was only a small increase in the overall proportion of income devoted to public purposes.

If the doses are not too large, are they of the right kind? The third feature of the system is that nearly three-quarters of the total spending on children is for in-kind transfers. Expenditures for elementary and secondary education and for medical care—$214 billion and $131 billion, respectively—account for 58 percent of all public benefits for children. Public education is an efficient in-kind transfer because, as compared to a cash transfer, it leads to larger gains in human capital and it confers on society at large very large external benefits.[20] We all benefit from a well-educated society. Similarly, health care transfers are efficient because they lead to larger gains in human capital than would a cash transfer. While the external benefits of health may not be as large as those of education, they are certainly greater than zero. Because they build and preserve future human capital, education and health transfers also promote equality of opportunity more than a cash redistribution of equal magnitude. The more equal the distribution of young adult human capital the greater the equality of opportunity in a society.

In short, that education and health account for nearly 60 percent of total transfers suggests that for the most part the doses are of the right kind. However, food stamps and housing subsidies, which together account for $56 billion, or 9.4 percent of public transfers for families, are more questionable.

A fourth feature of the nonuniversal part of the system is its bifurcation. Universal benefits, which constitute nearly half of the entire system, go to citizens of all income classes. Tax expenditures and government-regulated or -subsidized private benefits, which account for about one-third of total benefits, go principally to upper-middle- and upper-income families. Lower-middle-income, near-poor, and poor families get little to nothing from tax subsidies and private health insurance. Welfare program benefits, accounting for one-fifth of the total, go nearly exclusively to very poor families, most of whom are headed by single mothers.

Some evidence of bifurcation appears in table 2-1. Single-parent families, which are predominantly poor and near poor, receive 25 percent ($70 billion) of universal benefits, which is about equal to the percentage of children who live in single-parent families. In stark contrast, children in single-parent families receive only 10 percent ($9 billion) of health care benefits and 16 percent ($14 billion) of tax expenditures, while, on the other hand, they receive 75 percent ($96 billion) of all welfare benefits.

To convey a clearer picture of the degree of bifurcation in the system and its ill consequences, figure 2-1 reconfigures the data in table 2-1 into six major policy domains: education, health care, housing, social insurance cash transfers, all other public cash transfers, and private child support. A miscellaneous category consisting of other in-kind transfers is omitted from figure 2-1 but included in figure 2-2, which aggregates across domains. The benefits from each of the policy domains and the total overall policy domains are allocated to families according to their position in the income distribution of families with children. The income distribution is divided into fifths. Because somewhat more than 20 percent of all children are poor, the bottom fifth corresponds roughly with poor families.[21] Similarly, the second fifth corresponds roughly to near-poor and lower-middle-income families, the third fifth to middle-income families, and the fourth and fifth fifths, respectively, to upper-middle- and upper-income families.

FIGURE 2-1. *Distribution of Public Transfers within Major Policy Domains to Families with Children, 1992*

Billions of dollars

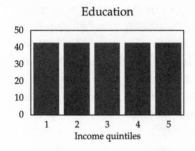

Education

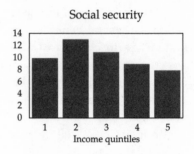

Social security

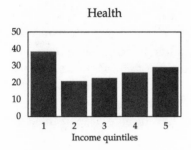

Health

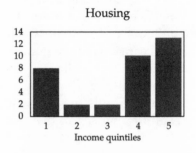

Housing

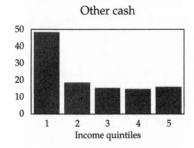

Other cash

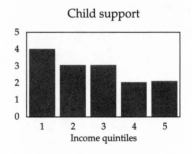

Child support

FIGURE 2-2. *Aggregate Distribution of Public Transfers to Families with Children, 1992*

Billions of dollars

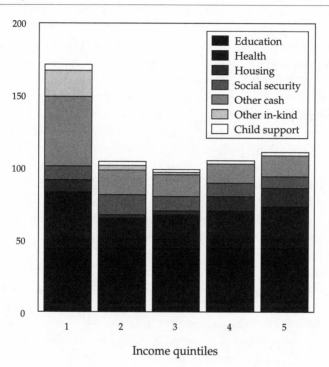

Income quintiles

The estimates of the distribution of benefits come from a variety of sources, described in appendix B, and should be thought of as rough first approximations. In the absence of any good estimator, I assumed that education benefits are distributed equally to all families with children. This estimate takes no account of either higher wealthy suburban expenditures on public education or greater use of private schools by upper-income groups. Given the assumption of equal distribution, figure 2-1 shows each quintile receives one-fifth of total benefits, or $44 billion. My guess is that the overall distribution is somewhat more pro-rich than shown.

Cash social insurance benefits—including unemployment, disability, survivors insurance, workers compensation, and veterans' benefits—like education benefits, are universal, but they are somewhat more redistributive because less-well-off families are more likely to be disabled, unemployed, and widowed and therefore more likely to receive benefits. On the other hand, because benefits are related to previous earnings, better-off families tend to receive higher benefits.

Health care benefits are distributed far more unevenly. The distribution is U shaped. Poor families receive $39 billion of health care transfers. Upper-income families receive the next most, $29 billion, and near-poor and lower-middle-income families receive the least—$21 billion and $23 billion, respectively. Middle- and upper-middle-income working families get health insurance through their employer.[22] Very poor families, including virtually all poor single-parent families receiving AFDC benefits, are covered by medicaid. Who gets left out? The working poor and near-poor two-parent families. They are not eligible for medicaid, and many low-wage employers do not provide health insurance as a fringe benefit. These families fall through the huge crack created by our bifurcated medical care transfer system. A sensible nation would provide health care security to all its children, including those in near-poor and lower-middle-income working families.

The distribution of housing benefits produced by our bifurcated housing transfer system is also U shaped but is even more perverse. Poor families get the bulk of the $10 billion in low-income housing benefits: $8 billion. This amount is less than the $11 billion and $13 billion that upper-middle-income and upper-income families get from housing tax expenditures. Once again, as in the case of health, the two-parent near-poor or lower-middle-class family gets practically nothing. Unlike with health care, however, even middle-income families fall between the cracks of the bifurcated housing transfer system. They receive only $3 billion, not much more than lower-middle-income families.

In the federal income tax, exemptions for parents and children and deductions for mortgage interest and property taxes are deducted from income before taxes are computed. Because the federal income tax is progressive—tax rates increase with income—these deductions are worth more to higher-income families. The tax subsidy for homeownership is the most regressive of all the tax expenditures not only because it is a deduction, but also because the amount that taxpayers can deduct is unlimited and expenditures on housing increase with income.[23] The most persuasive rationale for the homeownership subsidy is that widespread homeownership makes citizens property owners, thereby giving them a share and a stake in the capitalist system of private property. But surely it is the poor rather than the rich who have the smallest stake and thereby, for both efficiency and equity, need the most encouragement.

Low-income housing subsidies are also inequitably distributed. Only one out of four families eligible for subsidies receives them. The rest receive nothing. A minimum test for equity or fairness is that people in equal circumstances be treated equally. Economists refer to this as horizontal equity. The need to phase in a program gradually because of fiscal constraints can justify a temporary horizontal inequity. But providing large benefits to one portion of families and no benefits to another, identically situated portion of families over a long period—as we do in our low-income housing programs—is a violation of this minimum test of equity.

The $10 billion that is currently spent on low-income housing subsidies and the $26 billion spent of the mortgage and property interest tax subsidy would be better spent paying for a refundable tax credit for housing in the federal income tax.

Non-social insurance cash and near-cash benefits combine benefits from welfare programs—AFDC, supplementary security income, and food stamps—with benefits from tax expenditures—the EITC and child and adult exemptions in the income tax. The poorest families get the largest amount of other cash and near-cash benefits: $48 billion. Unlike the housing and health care domains, near-poor and lower-middle-income families get slightly more benefits than middle-, upper-middle-, and upper-income families. This is because child and adult exemptions do not favor the upper-income groups as much as the homeowner deduction does, and the smaller tilt in favor of the upper-income groups is offset by some leakage of income-tested benefits to the near poor and by the EITC, which concentrates benefits on near-poor and lower-middle-income families.

Tax credits are subtracted from taxes owed, rather than from income. Thus the value of a tax credit does not increase as tax rates increase. If the tax credit exceeds the amount of tax owed and, as is the case for the earned income tax credit, the government pays the difference to the citizen, the tax credit is refundable. Because the EITC is refundable and is gradually phased out as income increases, unlike all of the other tax expenditures it concentrates aid on the bottom two-fifths of the income distribution.[24] The expansion of the EITC as part of the 1993 budget agreement will provide more benefits to near-poor and lower-middle-income families.

The distribution of private child support receipts is at first puzzling. Children in poor families receive twice as much child support as children from upper-income families. This is not because rich fathers pay less child support than poor fathers. Just the opposite is true. Private child support increases as the income of nonresident fathers increases. When children from middle-, upper-middle-, and upper-income families live apart from their fathers, however, most of these children live in poor, near-poor, and lower-middle-income families headed by single mothers. The proportion of families headed by single mothers that achieve middle-income status is much smaller. Even smaller are the proportions in the upper-middle- and upper-income groups.

Actually, although this is not apparent from figure 2-1, the overall child support system—public plus private—is as bifurcated as the health and housing systems and produces the same kind of U-shaped curve. Children from families that would have been upper income if they were intact receive much larger private child support than children from upper-middle-income families, who in turn receive larger amounts than children from middle-income families. Children from families that would have been lower middle income receive very little and children from families that would have been near poor or poor receive practically no private child support. But the children from the families that would have been poor and near poor receive a huge amount of public child support in the form of welfare.

The traditional system of government enforcement of private support is grossly inadequate for families from all income classes, but the consequences for lower-income families are particularly pernicious.[25] More than 60 percent of fathers who live apart from their children pay no child support. As table 2-1 shows, fathers now pay about $13 billion. According to newly adopted state child support guidelines, they should pay $48 to $53 billion.[26] Full payment would reduce the poverty and welfare dependence of children in single-mother families by about one-quarter.[27] Furthermore, failure to establish paternity and enforce private support eliminates incentives for men to assume responsibility for birth control and thereby contributes to out-of-wedlock births.[28]

When all benefits are added together, the distributional picture that emerges is again U shaped. Poor families get the largest benefits: $172 billion. But upper-income families get the next largest amount: $112 billion. Upper-middle-income families get the third largest amount. Lower-middle-income and middle-income families get the least: $105 billion and $99 billion, respectively. Providing the most to poor families is equitable. But providing the least to near-poor, lower-middle-income, and middle-income working families and the next most to the richest families is, on its face, inequitable. No wonder so many near-poor, lower-middle-, and middle-income families resent the American welfare state.

Providing so much to poor families and so little to those slightly better off also discourages marriage and work at the bottom of the income distribution. Although the disincentives to work and marry have been reduced substantially by the food stamp and earned income tax credit programs and by recent extensions of eligibility for the medicaid program, they are still serious. The inequitable treatment of the working poor and the severe disincentives to work created by too much targeting by income are well documented and now widely acknowledged.[29] Thus the focus here is on the disincentives to marriage that arise from too much targeting on single-mother families.

Tables 2-2 and 2-3 illustrate the effects as of 1993 of some major parts of the family income transfer system on the rewards for marriage. The top panel of table 2-2 depicts the income a single mother with two children residing in Texas would receive from AFDC, food stamps, and medicaid and the income the same family would receive if the mother were married to a man with annual earning of either $8,500 or $15,000. The bottom panel is identical to the top, except that the mother resides in New York. Texas has low AFDC benefits, and New York, high AFDC benefits.

Consider the Texas case, where the prospective husband can earn only the minimum wage, or $8,500 a year. Column 1 indicates that a single mother with two children residing in Texas could receive $2,208 in AFDC benefits, $3,504 in food stamps benefits plus medicaid benefits, valued at the average national medicaid payment for a single mother and two children, or $4,060.[30] The total value of this welfare benefits package is $9,772. The second column indicates that a single man earning $8,500 would qualify for $91 in food stamps and pay $769 in taxes, for a total income of $7,822. The third column pre-

TABLE 2-2. *Effects of 1993 Income Transfer System on Gains from Marriage in Texas and New York, Couples with Two Children*

Current dollars

State and program	Single female parent	Single male	Combined income		Gross dollar gain (loss) from marriage	Savings from economies of scale	Net dollar gain (loss) from marriage
			Living separately	Living together			
TEXAS							
Minimum wage $4.25							
Wage	0	8,500	...	8,500	...	...	...
AFDC	2,208	0	...	0	...	...	...
Food stamps	3,504	91	...	3,199	...	...	...
Medicaid	4,060	0	...	2,155	...	...	...
Tax	0	(769)	...	0	...	...	...
EITC	0	0	...	1,511	...	...	...
Total	9,772	7,822	17,594	15,365	(2,229)	4,138	1,909
Minimum wage $7.50							
Wage	0	15,000	...	15,000	...	...	...
AFDC	2,208	0	...	0	...	...	...
Food stamps	3,504	0	...	1,639	...	...	...
Medicaid	4,060	0	...	0	...	...	...
Tax	0	(2,372)	...	(1,173)	...	...	...
EITC	0	0	...	1,124	...	...	...
Total	9,772	12,629	22,401	16,590	(5,811)	5,268	(543)

NEW YORK

Minimum wage $4.25

Wage	0	8,500	⋮	8,500	⋮	⋮	⋮
AFDC	6,924	0	⋮	0	⋮	⋮	⋮
Food stamps	2,226	91	⋮	3,199	⋮	⋮	⋮
Medicaid	4,060	0	⋮	2,155	⋮	⋮	⋮
Tax	0	(769)	⋮	0	⋮	⋮	⋮
EITC	0	0	⋮	1,511	⋮	⋮	⋮
Total	13,210	7,822	21,032	15,365	(5,667)	4,946	(721)

Minimum wage $7.50

Wage	0	15,000	⋮	15,000	⋮	⋮	⋮
AFDC	6,924	0	⋮	0	⋮	⋮	⋮
Food stamps	2,226	0	⋮	1,639	⋮	⋮	⋮
Medicaid	4,060	0	⋮	0	⋮	⋮	⋮
Tax	0	(2,372)	⋮	(1,173)	⋮	⋮	⋮
EITC	0	0	⋮	1,124	⋮	⋮	⋮
Total	13,210	12,629	25,839	16,590	(9,249)	6,077	(3,172)

Source: Author's calculations.

TABLE 2-3. *Effects of Changes in the EITC, Food Stamps, and Medicaid on Gain (Loss) from Marriage in Three States*

State and program	Earning $8,500	Earning $15,000
Texas		
As of 1993	1,909	(543)
1985 EITC and medicaid	(1,280)	(1,265)
1970 AFDC, no food stamps or EITC	(4,242)	(2,011)
EITC—1996	3,118	861
1996 EITC, no food stamps at $15,000	3,118	(778)
Illinois		
As of 1993	629	(1,823)
1985 EITC and medicaid	(2,760)	(2,745)
1970 AFDC, no food stamps or EITC	(7,063)	(4,832)
EITC—1996	760	(419)
1996 EITC, no food stamps at $15,000	760	(2,058)
New York		
As of 1993	(721)	(3,172)
1985 EITC and medicaid	(3,888)	(3,872)
1970 AFDC, no food stamps or EITC	(8,642)	(6,411)
EITC—1996	(589)	(1,768)
1996 EITC, no food stamps at $15,000	(589)	(3,407)

Source: Author's calculations.
a. Families with two children.

sents the combined income of the couple if they live separately, which is just the sum of columns 1 and 2, $17,594. Column 4 shows their income if they married. Note that the couple is eligible for $3,199 in food stamps, $2,155 worth of medicaid, and a $1,511 earned income tax credit. (Many readers may be surprised that the two-parent family is eligible for so much aid; I certainly was. The surprise is the result of very rapid change in the system.[31]) For now, note that the total income of the married couple is $15,365.

As displayed in column 5, the couple gives up $2,229 worth of income if they marry and live together. They lose about $2,200 in AFDC benefits, $1,905 in medicaid benefits, and $400 in food stamps benefits. The couple loses the AFDC benefits because two-parent families with full-time work cannot receive AFDC benefits. Similarly, they lose medicaid benefits because only the children in two-parent poor families are covered by medicaid; the parents must fend for themselves. But working poor, near-poor, and lower-middle-class two-parent families are the most likely to fall through the cracks of our bifurcated medical care system. Finally, note that these losses are offset by a gain of $1,511 from the earned income tax credit. Because only families with children and with earnings are eligible for the EITC, the couple can only get the EITC if they marry.

Although the couple must give up $2,229 to live together, two can live more cheaply together than apart. Marriage leads to savings that arise out of economies of scale. Column 6 presents an estimate of the savings from economies of scale based on the equivalency scales embodied in the official measure of poverty. The saving from living together for this couple amounts to $4,138.

Fortunately, in this case, the $4,138 gain from living together is greater than the $2,229 loss in benefits. Attempts by the government to target aid on the most needy by limiting benefits to single-parent families "tax" away only half the gain from marriage. If the government wants to encourage marriage, it is counterproductive to tax away even half the gain from marriage. But as illustrated in the second panel of table 2-2, as of 1993, in the Texas case where the prospective husband earns $15,000, we were taxing away more than 100 percent of the gain from marriage. Indeed, policy imposed a $543 marriage penalty. The bottom panel of table 2-2 indicates that in New York, whether the prospective husband earned $8,500 or $15,000, more than 100 percent of the gains from marriage were taxed away, resulting in marriage penalties of, respectively, $721 and $3,172.

Why is there a bigger marriage penalty for the higher-wage worker? Most important, medicaid benefits for two-parent families are limited to families with income below the poverty line. Earnings of $15,000 place the family above the poverty line.[32]

Why is the penalty higher in the state with higher AFDC benefits? One obvious answer is because AFDC benefits are higher in the high-benefit state. If AFDC benefits in New York were reduced to the level of AFDC benefits in Texas, the marriage penalty in New York would be reduced to the Texas level. Indeed, as Charles Murray so fondly points out, if AFDC benefits were eliminated entirely, the marriage penalty would be eliminated.[33] What Murray neglects to mention is that there is another, perhaps less obvious, answer to the question. If

AFDC and medicaid benefits were offered to two-parent families on the same terms as they are offered to single-parent families, there would be no marriage disincentive. The marriage penalty arises from excessive targeting of benefits on single-parent families. The excessive targeting can be reduced (or eliminated) either by reducing (or eliminating) benefits to single mothers and their children or by extending benefits now available to single mothers and their children to two-parent families. That single-mother families are already quite poor and that half of the current generation of American children will spend part of their childhood growing up in a family headed by a single mother suggests that it would be wiser to extend benefits to two-parent families.

Table 2-3 presents only the bottom-line gain (or loss) from marriage for a variety of other policy scenarios designed to highlight the importance of recent improvements in the EITC and medicaid programs and the importance of the stigma that accompanies food stamp benefits. In addition to Texas and New York—low and high AFDC benefit states, respectively—results are also presented for Illinois, a medium-benefit state. The first rows in each state report the gains (or losses) for the two different prospective husbands' earning levels—$8,500 and $15,000 in 1993. All subsequent rows deviate from the first row.

In the second row for each state, EITC and medicaid benefits for 1985 are substituted for 1993 benefits. In 1985 the EITC was worth only $726 (in 1993 dollars) to a parent with earnings of $8,500 and nothing to a parent with earnings of $15,000. Children in working two-parent families were not eligible for any benefits from medicaid. As a consequence, the marriage penalty was much greater in 1985 than it was in 1993.

As the third row of table 2-3 indicates, the marriage penalty was even higher in 1970 when there were no food stamps or EITC programs and medicaid benefits were available only for single-parent families. Indeed, the size of the marriage penalties in 1993 dollars that are associated with the 1970 policies are astounding. For the minimum-wage worker case they range from a low of $4,242 in Texas to nearly $7,063 in illinois and $8,642 in New York! These huge marriage penalties pertained roughly to the situation between 1965, when medicaid was enacted, and 1974, when the food stamps program was made a permanent national program and the EITC program was enacted.[34] A comparison of the entries in rows 1, 2, and 3 indicates that extending aid to two-parent families by enacting the food stamps and EITC programs and by liberalizing eligibility for medicaid has played a critical role in reducing the penalty for marriage among poor persons.

The fourth row for each state, in which the 1993 EITC benefit is replaced by the much higher legislated benefit for 1996, indicates that the expansion of the EITC proposed by President Clinton and enacted by Congress in 1993 will reduce the marriage penalty even further. In some cases, the penalty is eliminated entirely. But even in these cases we will still be taxing away large chunks of the gains from marriage that come from economies of scale.

The fifth row of table 2-3 gives added cause for concern. The fifth row for each state, like the fourth, replaces the 1993 EITC with the 1996 EITC, but it also eliminates the food stamp benefit for the married family earning $15,000. The rationale for eliminating the food stamp benefit for this family is that although some families with income above the poverty line are eligible for substantial food stamp benefits, only 17 percent collect them.[35]

As income-tested programs go, the food stamp program seems ideally suited to provide benefits to two-parent working families. Families with no other income are entitled to receive approximately $100 per person per month in food stamps. Unlike AFDC, the food stamp program does not try to capture the gains from economies of scale of living together. Moreover, work is not taxed so harshly. Benefits are reduced by only 24 cents for each dollar earned in excess of at least $220 per month.[36]

Unfortunately, food stamps are paid in a debased currency. Virtually all income-tested benefits are, to a greater or lesser degree, stigmatized. Food stamps must be the most stigmatized. Recipients must reveal themselves not only in the process of applying for benefits, but again and again, in the process of spending them. Unless they are reduced to desperation, most working two-parent families entitled to food stamps do not claim them. Research indicates that families would spend very little less on food if they received cash rather than food stamps.[37] Of course, the stigma that accompanies the stamps is yet another cheap method of targeting the most needy. Those who are truly desperate will apply. Like most cheap fixes, however, it breaks down. Many two-parent working families are left out and marriage is thereby undermined. Former presidents Richard

Nixon and Jimmy Carter proposed substituting cash payments for food stamps. It is about time we did so.[38]

Finally, housing and child care assistance further reduce the gains to marriage for poor single mothers because both benefits are in scarce supply and single-parent families tend to be given priority. As indicated by table 2-1, single-parent families receive 66 percent of income-tested child care subsidies and 90 percent of income-tested housing subsidies.

The unfairness to working-class two-parent families and the resulting marriage penalty in the public transfer system arise from excessive targeting on the poorest families—those headed by single parents. Limiting benefits to single-parent families discourages marriage. Limiting benefits to poor single-parent families discourages work among mothers with low earnings capacity. Yet marriage and work convert poor families to near-poor and lower-middle-income families.

Of all the possible inefficiencies arising from transfers, reducing incentives to work and marry is probably the most important. (I use the term *marriage* to refer to long-term coresidence.)[39] Viewed in terms of consumption, work and marriage decisions overwhelm virtually all other choices. Only education choices have similarly large implications in terms of investment. Work generates the income that makes other consumption possible. Work experience is also a critical component of human capital and thereby a critical component of productivity. Marriage enhances consumption possibilities through economies of scale, specialization, and the creation of social capital.[40]

Marriage is also a critical factor in producing security for children. Children who grow up in single-parent families have dramatically lower and more irregular incomes and dramatically lower achievement rates than children who grow up in two-parent families. Differences in levels and regularity of income account for about half the difference in achievement.[41]

The poor earn less in the market than the nonpoor. How can we expect them to make it the way Americans are supposed to make it—by working hard and raising their children to do likewise—when in the process of aiding them on the cheap, we stack the deck against work and marriage? To reduce the rewards for work and marriage more for the poor than for the rest of the population—by limiting benefits to single-parent families and steeply income-testing those benefits—is a violation of equality of opportunity. Universal programs that are not limited to single-parent families or to poor families discourage neither marriage nor work.

While universal programs buy us more, they also cost more. That is, they require higher taxes—but not of everybody. In general, universal (as opposed to categorical means-tested) programs provide greater benefits to the near poor and the lower middle class at the expense of the top two-fifths of the income distribution.[42] The higher tax rates faced by the upper two-fifths may decrease productivity more than the increases in productivity from universal benefits. But the opposite may be true. For as we have seen, by reducing benefits substantially as income increases—either through work or marriage—categorical means-tested programs impose very high taxes on the poor, the near poor, and even the lower middle class. Universal programs decrease these very high tax rates. Is it more efficient to have low tax rates for the rich or the poor? It is a complicated question. The little research that has been done, however, suggests that universal programs are more efficient.[43]

Proposed Reforms: Costs and Benefits

The previous section found much that is right as well as much that is wrong with the public transfer system for children. Public investment in children is substantial, but by no means excessive. The heavy investments in in-kind transfers in the form of education and health insurance are both efficient and equitable. Housing subsidies, on the other hand, are inefficient and inequitable. Food stamps, though admirably structured in many respects, would be more efficiently provided as cash. The biggest weakness of our current system, however, lies in its bifurcated nature: extreme targeting of categorical income-tested programs to aid very poor families and perversely targeted tax expenditures and publicly sanctioned private transfers to aid middle- and upper-income families. Most near-poor and lower-middle-income working two-parent families are left out. This is both inequitable and inefficient.

Eliminating the bifurcation by replacing welfare programs and their complementary tax subsidies with universal programs will increase the efficiency and equity of the transfer system.

Substituting universal transfers for our bifurcated set of income-tested and tax benefit programs and adding work relief to time-limited cash assistance would cure the principal weakness of the existing system, but would also require larger public investments in children. However, because public investments are already much greater than most people think, the extra investments required would be much smaller than most people think. In my judgment the benefits exceed the costs for all of the components proposed.

Universal Health Care and Child Support Assurance: Low-Cost, High-Benefit Reforms

Most Americans now believe that one objective of policy should be to achieve equal access to health care. Indeed, a year ago we appeared to be on the verge of adopting some form of universal health care system.[44] Providing universal health care coverage is essential to eliminating the current inequitable treatment of near-poor, lower-middle-income, and even middle-income families and the resulting marriage disincentive. Some estimates indicate that a universal health care system would reduce child poverty by nearly 20 to 30 percent and welfare caseloads by up to 20 percent and increase the probability of marriage by up to 2.6 percent.[45]

Providing universal coverage is also a prerequisite to controlling costs and achieving the objective of equal access in an efficient manner.[46] Costs have exploded because consumption of care has been largely socialized. From consumers' point of view cost is no object because they do not bear the costs. The Congressional Budget Office estimates that if the Clinton administration's health proposal were adopted and the proposed methods for constraining the rate of growth of premiums were perfectly effective, the federal government's budget for health care would increase by $681 billion in 2004. At the same time, total spending on health care would decrease by $150 billion.[47] In other words, a universal health care system would increase the federal budget but decrease true economic costs.[48]

Public enforcement of private child support is particularly interesting from both an analytic and practical point of view because it gets to the heart of the socialization question. In a world in which all of the costs of child rearing were socialized, there would be no role for private child support and therefore no child support enforcement. No major political parties or figures in the United States or western

Europe advocate full socialization of child-rearing costs. As a consequence, private child support is publicly enforced in all of these nations.

To redress the failings of the child support system, the United States should add a new child support assurance system (CSAS) to our menu of social security programs. CSAS is based on a partnership of responsibility between parents and government. Parents are responsible for sharing income with their children. Government is responsible for enforcing private support and for ensuring a steady flow of income to all children with an absent parent.

The essential mechanics are easy to understand. Child support awards are set by a legislated formula—based on a percentage of the nonresident parent's income—and payments are deducted from the parent's earnings, just like social security deductions. The government guarantees a minimum level of child support—an assured benefit—just like minimum benefits in old age and unemployment insurance. The assured benefit is financed from welfare savings and from a very small addition to the social security payroll tax.

Child support assurance would increase the economic security of all children who live apart from a parent, rich and poor alike. Withholding a fixed percentage—17 percent, for example—from the paychecks of all nonresident parents would increase the amount and regularity of private payments. Even so, private support payments for many poor children would continue to be low and irregular, just as the incomes of their fathers are often low and irregular. The assured benefit would compensate by providing a steady, secure source of income for these children. It would more than double the reduction in poverty and welfare dependence achieved from private support alone. In short, child support assurance would facilitate the movement of poor and near-poor single-parent families into the lower middle and even the middle class.

The cost of child support assurance would depend on the level of the assured benefit, whether the assured benefit offset welfare benefits or added to welfare, whether it were taxable, and how much the system increased private support payments. Microsimulation analysis indicates that with a medium-run improvement in private support payments achievable perhaps in 15 to 20 years, a $2,000 assured benefit for the first child, which offset welfare benefits and was taxable, would reduce the poverty gap of children potentially eligible for child support and the proportion dependent on welfare by about one-fifth at no extra cost to the government.[49]

How can a government program not limited to poor families be so cheap? There are four reasons. First, because most children living with poor parents are already receiving AFDC, an assured benefit that offset welfare would entail little additional cost for this group. Second, the collection parts of the system would lead to increases in private child support payments by the fathers of children now receiving welfare, leading to savings in welfare costs. Third, despite the fact that it would insure children of all income classes, the assured benefit per se would not be very costly. For the most part men and women tend to mate with people from similar backgrounds. This assortative mating guarantees that only a small proportion of government expenditure for the assured benefit would go to a child living with a wealthy parent, because in the overwhelming majority of such cases, the nonresident parent would be equally wealthy and there would be no public subsidy. In rare cases, of course, there would be a poor nonresident parent of a child residing with a wealthy parent. Fourth, taxing the public portion of the assured benefit substantially reduces this already small leakage.

Refundable Tax Credits: A Moderate-Cost, High-Benefit Reform

Refundable tax credits for children are, from an economic point of view, identical to child allowances. Both provide the same benefit to all children, irrespective of income.[50] As such, credits or allowances are more progressive than the child exemption in the federal income tax. They are also an essential ingredient of a universalistic public transfer system. A credit or allowance for children of $1,000 per year per child would permit elimination of the child benefits in the food stamp program. The very poorest would be no worse off—so long as cash welfare benefits were increased as explained below—and the working, near-poor, two-parent family would be substantially better off.

Similarly, a refundable tax credit for adults would be more progressive than adult exemptions in the federal income tax. A credit of $850 would permit elimination of the food stamp program entirely. A politically appealing way of achieving adult refundable credits is to cast them as housing tax credits and to give a larger credit for home-ownership costs than for rental costs. A refundable housing tax credit would be of help to all adult citizens, including the homeless. A larger credit for ownership costs would increase ownership at the bottom of the income distribution and thereby increase the property and wealth of the poor and their stake in capitalism.

At the same time, the institution of a refundable tax credit for housing would make it easier politically to gradually get rid of all other public subsidies for housing—including both low-income subsidies and deductions for homeowners in the income tax. While these subsidies constitute some of the most glaring inequities in our current tax-transfer system, their precipitous elimination would itself create inequities. Eliminating homeowner deductions would reduce the value of homes. Similarly, eliminating rent subsidies would entail a large loss of income for many low-income families. In both cases, elimination should proceed gradually and by equalizing both up and down. The creation of a refundable housing allowance credit in the income tax would facilitate such a gradual transition.

To equalize up, rent subsidies would be capped at their current nominal level and the homeowner deduction also would be capped at a relatively generous level in nominal terms—say $6,000 per adult. The value of the refundable credit would be indexed to the cost of living and also increased gradually in real terms until it became as valuable as the credit. Increases in the real value of the refundable credit would be a form of tax reduction—an extension of President Clinton's proposal during the campaign for a middle-class tax cut. To equalize down, initially taxpayers would be allowed to use either the deduction or the new credit. In subsequent years, however, taxpayers would be able to deduct a declining proportion of the excess value of their deductions. If the proportion declined by 5 percent each year, within twenty years deductions would be entirely eliminated. The value of rent subsidies in excess of the housing credit could be reduced gradually over the same period.

Refundable tax credits for children and refundable housing tax credits for adults in lieu of food stamps, all housing subsidies, and child and adult exemptions would eliminate one of the most glaring inequities of the current bifurcated transfer system and substantially reduce poverty and insecurity. Surprisingly, because the costs of food stamps, housing subsidies, and child and adult exemptions are quite large, the net additional costs of a refundable tax credit of $1,000 annually per child and a refundable housing tax credit of $850 per adult would be only $6 billion.[51] Thus this reform could easily be reclassified as a low-cost, high-benefit reform. But even a small increae in the value of the child and adult credits would lead to large increases in net costs. A child credit of $1,200 per year and an adult credit of about $1,000 would yield a net cost of $47 billion.[52]

Universal Child Care: A High-Cost, High-Benefit Reform

Government provision of child care is discussed in detail in another chapter. For my purposes two issues are critical: Should there be any public subsidization of child care and should it be universal or bifurcated? Nothing is more vital to future productivity than child rearing. This argues for high-quality child care. The traditional method of providing child care—full-time care by the mother—is of very high quality and very expensive. The forgone market earnings of mothers are enormous, so most mothers of pre-school-age children now work. It is in the national interest to make certain that modern forms of substitute child care are as high in quality as the traditional form.

A second and closely related justification for public subsidization of child care is to promote gender equity and thereby efficiency. In modern industrial societies, the responsibility for child rearing falls principally on the mother. The forgone labor market experience stunts her human capital growth. This is not only inequitable but also inefficient. A nation that relies only on its men for market work squanders half its human potential.

A third justification for public subsidization is that it would be unwise as well as unfair to insist that poor single mothers work and not to pay for high-quality care for their children. To make poor single mothers bear the costs of child care out of their meager earnings would substantially reduce their family's well-being.

To the question of whether we should substitute some form of universal provision for the current bifurcated system, my answer is clearly yes. It is a mistake to provide disproportionate child care assistance within the bottom half of the income distribution to single-mother families. It is a mistake to shortchange working near-poor and lower-middle-income families.

The benefits of universal child care are likely to be enormous. In addition to the long-term investment benefits in the children, child care reduces poverty and insecurity at the same time that it rewards work and independence. France and Sweden have the most universal systems of child care in the world, practically no child poverty, and lower rates of dependence than the United States.[53]

Unlike the other universal reforms, however, because we currently spend so little publicly on child care, universal high-quality child care cannot be done cheaply from public funds. Assuming that child care costs $4,800 per child, a universal system to cover children age two through five would cost an additional $56 billion.[54] In addition, no account is taken of the first year of the child's life. I and many others believe that parental care during the first year of life should be encouraged via paid parental leave. This would further increase costs.

Finally, there is no reason to believe that child care should be a federal responsibility. Education has traditionally been a state responsibility. A strong argument can be made that the best way to achieve a universal child care system is to extend the age of school downward.[55]

Residual Public Assistance: A Low- to Modest-Cost, Moderate-Benefit Reform

The universal benefit system advocated above is designed to increase both equity and efficiency. It would substantially reduce poverty and insecurity, provide benefits to working poor and near-poor families, and reinforce work and marriage. The cash benefits are not sufficient to bring a family out of poverty in the absence of work or marriage. Child and adult credits together equal only 31 percent of the poverty level in 1993 for a family of four. Providing poverty-level benefits universally would be inefficient. Such high benefits are not required to eliminate poverty among the working poor. What they require are benefits to supplement rather than replace earnings. Low benefits combined with low tax rates—universal benefits—are the best method to supplement earnings. At the same time, poverty-level universal benefits would also discourage work and marriage both by providing too generous an alternative and by requiring very high taxes to finance.

Because some adults will be unemployed and others will be unable to work, there will be a need for a residual means-tested public assistance system. To the maximum extent possible, the unemployed should be aided through unemployment insurance. Although the coverage provided by the U.S. system can and should be improved,[56] unemployment insurance cannot provide benefits to those who have not worked or to the very long-term unemployed without compromising the integrity of the program. Similarly, to the maximum extent possible, the disabled should be aided by disability insurance or the supplementary security income program. But there will always be temporary disabilities, necessitating a residual public assistance program.

Unlike AFDC, public assistance should not be limited to families headed by women, but should be available to all adults—single and married, with and without dependents—and their dependents. The benefits should be paid in cash, because that is the cheapest form of transfer. But for those expected to and capable of work, unrestricted cash relief should be time limited, because both cash relief in exchange for activity promoting independence and work relief are superior methods of reinforcing work and family. Cash relief benefits when added to child and adult credits would equal the poverty level. Work relief jobs would pay the minimum wage and provide up to forty hours per week of work, which when combined with child and adult credits would provide a poverty-level income. To create an incentive for regular market work, work relief earnings would not qualify for EITC supplementation.

Such a residual public assistance program would constitute a substantial improvement over the current system. It would sweep up whatever poverty remained after the conversion to a universalistic system. At the same time, like the universal programs it would also reinforce work and family.[57]

How costly would such a system be? That is very hard to estimate. Except for the time limits, the benefits are far more generous and available to a much larger group of people than is AFDC. And both contingent cash relief and work relief are more expensive per recipient than is unrestricted cash relief. Except for the time limit, all of these considerations suggest that the program would be far more costly than the current AFDC program. And in the current environment it would be much more costly. But in an environment with universal health and child care, refundable tax credits for children and adults, and child support assurance, there would be less need for public assistance. Placing relatively short time limits on unconditional cash relief and providing contingent cash relief and work relief will further restrict the demand for relief. My guess is that in such an environment most of the single mothers who now depend on AFDC would find and retain work in the private sector. Public assistance would be providing a much larger share of its resources to young men, fathers or not. Indeed, my guess is that more than half of the work relief jobs would be filled by men.

Finally, the costs of a residual public assistance system would depend on the strength of the macroeconomy. While all of the reforms suggested here would strengthen the macroeconomy by reinforcing work,[58] monetary and fiscal policy have larger effects. It is conceivable that in a universalistic environment combined with an aggregate unemployment in the 4 percent range, the above-described public assistance program would actually cost less than the current AFDC program. My wild guess is that depending on the state of the macroeconomy, the additional costs of the public assistance program would range from close to zero to as much as $20 billion. Needless to say, more research is needed.

Summary

Capitalism generates both high productivity and insecurity. By applying selective doses of socialism, the welfare state reduces insecurity and thereby enhances both the equity and efficiency of unbridled capitalism. As with any medicine, however, it is possible to administer underdoses, overdoses, and the wrong doses. Although the scope of the U.S. welfare state as reflected in its system of public income transfers to families with children is already large, there is no evidence of overdosing, and high rates of child poverty provide some evidence of undernourishment. The major problems of our system can be traced to its bifurcated structure: welfare programs aid very poor families and tax expenditures aid middle- and upper-income families. Near-poor and lower-middle-income working two-parent families are left out. This is both inequitable and inefficient. It discourages work and marriage.

To further reduce the economic insecurity of children and to increase equity and efficiency, welfare programs and their complementary tax subsidies should be replaced with the universal programs proposed here. Although these actions would require larger public investments in children, only universal child care would require a substantial increase in taxes. Universal health care, child support assurance, and even refundable tax credits for children and adults could be financed largely through redirection of existing expenditures. In conjunction with the universal programs, a reformed public assistance program would require only low to modest increases in taxes.

What are the political prospects of this ambitious reform agenda? Given the defeat of President Clinton's health care reform proposal and the Republican capture of both the House and Senate in the 1994 elections, the short-term prospects appear bleak. Yet our politics are now rather volatile. When I began writing this chapter, President Clinton had recently proposed universal health care coverage as the centerpiece of his domestic agenda. Public opinion polls showed strong support for it. One year later, politically it was dead.

As for child support assurance, since 1984 the nation has been taking giant strides toward a new child support assurance system. In 1984 Congress unanimously voted to require all states to adopt numerical guidelines that courts could use to determine child support obligations and income-withholding laws under which employers would withhold the wages of delinquent obligers. The Family Support Act of 1988 went even further. As of 1994 the numerical guidelines determine the presumptive child support award. Judges may depart from the guidelines only if they give a written justification, which may be reviewed by a higher court. In all new cases, unless the parties agree to an alternative arrangement, child support obligations are routinely withheld by employers from the wages of obligers.

In 1984 and 1988, respectively, Congress also granted Wisconsin and New York waivers to use federal funds that would otherwise have been devoted to AFDC to help fund demonstrations of an assured child support benefit. As part of his welfare reform proposal, the president proposed legislation to further strengthen enforcement and provide new federal funds for state demonstrations of an assured child support benefit. There is a bipartisan consensus within the Congress for further strengthening child support enforcement—especially in the areas of paternity establishment and interstate enforcement—and before the 1994 fall elections, bipartisan support for experimenting on the state level with an assured child support benefit.[59] The Republican welfare reform bill, however, contains no provision for demonstrations of an assured benefit.

A year ago, the possibility of a refundable tax credit for children appeared to be declining. Despite its huge gross cost of $40 billion, the bipartisan National Commission for Children unanimously endorsed a $1,000 refundable tax credit for children. A somewhat smaller refundable credit for children was the centerpiece of the middle-class tax cut President Clinton proposed during the 1992 campaign. In the face of large deficits, the president abandoned, at least temporarily, his middle-class tax cut proposal. But in response to the Republican tax cut legislation, which includes a $500 per child nonrefundable tax credit, the president has proposed a more targeted nonrefundable credit.

Government funding for various forms of child care has been increasing fairly steadily at least since 1964. Head Start, a highly targeted federal program, is popular politically and has already been expanded. Of the total additional spending of $9.3 billion over five years in the Clinton administration's welfare reform proposal, $4.2 billion was devoted to additional spending on child care. While such expansions will not lead directly to a universal system and may even retard its development, they increase the public share of the costs and thereby reduce the future additional costs of converting to a universal system. The Republican welfare reform bill would reduce federal funding for child care.

Although President's Clinton's welfare reform proposal would have taken the nation in the direction proposed in this chapter, the Republican welfare reform legislation would take us in the opposite direction, by substantially reducing benefits and shifting responsibility from the federal to state governments. As noted above, the president vetoed the legislation.

Finally, we come to refundable housing tax credits for adults. Unfortunately, as of now, these are not even on the horizon. But many proposed reforms—such as old age and unemployment insurance at the turn of the century—that were at first judged to be politically infeasible are now accepted parts of our modern welfare state. To avoid advocating programs because they are politically infeasible is to engage in a self-fulfilling prophecy. The distribution of the benefits of our current system of housing subsidies is hard to defend.

Appendix A

The expenditures reported in table 2-1 are calculated in two stages. The first involves estimating the total expenditures. The second stage is estimating what part of that expenditure is used for families with children and for single parent families. Table A-1 lists in column 1 the total expenditure figure. Column 2 lists the source of the expenditure and the page number. The abbreviations are explained below. Columns 3 and 4 list the proportion of the expenditure used by family type. Column 5 lists the source of the proportions. Those proportions marked estimates are best guesses. The figures in table 2-1 in the text can be derived by multiplying the expenditures in column 2 by the proportions in columns 3 and 4.

Expenditure Abbreviations (in order of appearance)

SSB-A   Social Security Administration, *Social Security Bulletin*, Annual Statistical Supplement (Washington, 1993).

SSB-F   Ann Bixley, "Table 4.A.1—Public Income-Maintenance Programs: Cash Benefit Payments." *Social Security Bulletin*, vol. 56 (Fall 1993), p. 148.

SSB-S   Ann Bixley, "Public Social Welfare Expenditures, Fiscal Year 1990." *Social Security Bulletin*, vol. 56 (Summer 1993), pp. 70–76.

GB   Committee on Ways and Means. *Overview of Entitlement Programs: 1993 Green Book* (Washington, 1993).

NCC   National Commission on Children, *Beyond Rhetoric: Final Report of the National Commission on Children* (Washington, 1992).

Kim   Yuen Hee Kim, "The Economic Effects of the Combined Non-Income-Tested Transfers for Families with Children: Child Support Assurance, Children's Allowance, and National Health Insurance." Ph.D. dissertation, University of Wisconsin, 1993.

CRS   Congressional Research Service, *Cash and Noncash Benefits for Persons with Limited Income: Eligibility Rules, Recipient and Expenditure Data FY 90-92* (Washington, 1993).

TABLE A-1. *Public Transfers to Families with Children, by Type of Transfer*

Percent unless otherwise specified

Type of expenditure	Expenditure (billions of 1992 dollars)	Source of expenditure data	Families with children	Single-parent families	Source of proportion
Universal					
Cash					
OASDI	286.0	SSB-A-13	0.06	0.02	SIPP-90
Unemployment insurance	39.5	SSB-A-15	0.46	0.07	SIPP-90
Workers compensation	26.1	SSB-A-324	0.39	0.07	SIPP-90
Other					
Black lung	0.1	SSP-A-326	0.04	0.00	SIPP-90
Veterans comp.—no means test	16.3	SSB-F-148	0.21	0.04	SIPP-90
In-kind					
Elementary and secondary education	222.3	SSB-S-98	1.00	0.25	a
Medicare	133.2	SSB-A-14	0.07	0.02	CPS-90
Tax expenditures					
EITC	12.4	94 GB-704	1.00	0.52	CPS-90
Child care tax credit	3.4	91 GB-868	1.00	0.32	b
Personal exemption for children	21.6	NCC-85	1.00	0.10	estimate
Personal exemption for adults	67.5	c	0.31	0.03	c
Homeowner deduction	64.5	d	0.41	0.03	d
Government regulated and subsidized					
Third-party health care	206.4	e	0.43	0.04	e
Private child support	13.4	f	1.00	0.68	f

TABLE A-1. (continued)

Percent unless otherwise specified

Type of expenditure	Expenditure (billions of 1992 dollars)	Source of expenditure data	Families with children	Single-parent families	Source of proportion
Welfare					
Cash					
AFDC and emergency assistance					
AFDC	23.6	CRS-205	1.00	0.90	g
Emergency assistance	0.3	CRS-205	1.00	1.00	estimate
SSI	21.3	CRS-205	0.30	0.17	SIPP-90
General assistance and other					
General assistance	3.4	CRS-205	0.50	0.00	h
Veterans pensions—means tested	3.7	CRS-205	0.10	0.05	SIPP-90
Indian, Cuban, refugee assistance	0.0	CRS-205	0.16	0.00	SIPP-90
In-kind					
Medicaid	90.8	94 GB-802	0.42	0.38	i
Other medical					
GA—medical	4.9	CRS-204	0.50	0.00	h
Medical—veterans	7.8	CRS-204	0.10	0.05	j
Other medical	3.2	CRS-204	0.44	0.33	k
Food stamps	23.3	CRS-206	0.85	0.59	SIPP-90
Other nutrition					
WIC	2.6	CRS-206	1.00	0.45	SIPP-90
School lunch and breakfast	4.7	CRS-206	1.00	0.52	CPS-90
Other food programs	1.3	CRS-206	0.85	0.59	l

Housing					
Public/subsidized housing—Note L	19.9	CRS-207	0.48	0.40	[m]
LIHEAP	1.8	CRS-211	0.49	0.32	SIPP-90
Child care and Head Start					
Social services block grants	0.8	CRS-209	1.00	0.52	[n]
Child care and development block grants	0.8	CRS-209	1.00	0.52	[o]
Child care JOBS and AFDC	0.8	CRS-209	1.00	1.00	estimate
At-risk child care—AFDC	0.6	CRS-209	1.00	1.00	estimate
Head Start	2.8	CRS-208	1.00	0.55	[p]
Employment					
JTPA	1.8	CRS-210	0.85	0.29	[q]
Summer youth employment	1.2	CRS-210	1.00	0.52	[o]
Job Corps	1.0	CRS-210	1.00	0.52	[o]
JOBS—100% FHH	1.0	CRS-210	1.00	1.00	estimate
Foster care					
Foster care	2.1	CRS-205	1.00	0.52	[o]
Social services block grants	1.2	CRS-209	1.00	0.52	[n]

The Proportions

The Housing and Household Economic Statistics Division of the Bureau of the Census made available unpublished computer runs on the expenditures of various federal programs by family type from both the Current Population Survey (CPS) and the Survey of Income and Program Participation (SIPP) for 1990. When these proportions are used, they are noted as CPS-90 and SIPP-90 in column 5.

a. The apportionment for elementary and secondary education to single parent families is based on the proportion of children between six and seventeen reported in Bureau of the Census, "Household and Family Characteristics: March 1993," *Current Population Reports*, series P-20, no. 467 (Department of Commerce, 1993), table 3, pp. 12–16.

b. The proportions for the child care tax credit are taken from Internal Revenue Service, *Sources of Income—1990: Individual Income Tax Returns* (1993), table 1.3, p. 23.

c. The personal exemption for adults is calculated from Internal Revenue Service, *Statistics of Income—1990: Individual Income Tax Returns* (1993), table 1.2, p. 19. First the 1992 income categories and the number of exemptions for each type of filing unit—joint, filing separately, head of household, and single—by income category were adjusted to 1990 dollars using the CPI. The numbers for each income category were estimated using weighted averages. The number of exemptions at each tax rate were then summed. Next the value of the exemption at each tax rate was calculated, the tax rate times the exemption. The number of exemptions at each tax rate was then multiplied by the value of the exemption and the result was summed to gain the value of the adult personal exemption. This is an underestimate because it only gives the exemption to adult filers and not to dependent adults in the household. The value of the exemption to dependent adults is between $0.5 billion and $1.0 billion. The numerator used to estimate the proportion going to families with children first assumes that there are two adults in a married family with children and one adult in a father-only and mother-only family. The number of each family type is taken from Bureau of the Census "Household and Family Characteristics: March 1993," *Current Population Reports*, series P-20, no. 467 (Department of Commerce, 1993), table 3, pp. 12–16. The denominator is the number of adults from the same source. The proportion going to single parents is a working estimate of 10 percent.

d. The homeowner deduction is from the projected tax expenditures for 1992 House Committee on Ways and Means, *Overview of Entitlement Programs—1991 Green Book*, Committee Print, 102 Cong. 1 sess. (Government Printing Office, 1991), table 1, p. 868. It includes deductibility of mortgage interest (38.8 B), deferral of capital gains on sale of principal residence (11.5 B) and the low-income housing credit (1.1 B). While not available from the *1991 Green Book*, the deductibility of property tax on owner-occupied buildings (13.7) and exclusion of interest on state and local government bonds for owner-occupied housing (1.7) are reported in the *1993 Green Book*, table 2, p. 1022. They are deflated to 1992 dollars using the following formula: $(38.8 + 11.5 + 1.1 + (13.7 + 1.7) * 38.8/45.5 = 64.5$.

The proportions of the homeowner deduction applied to families with children and single-parent families are calculated using Bureau of the Census, *American Housing Survey for the United States in 1991* (Department of Commerce, 1993), table 3-9, p. 106. There were 59,796 owner-occupied units, of which 21,937 were families with children, making the ratio 0.367. Those over sixty-five have paid their mortgages down and, in fact, *American Housing Survey for the United States in 1991*, table 3-13, p. 118, reports that while all households make a median monthly mortgage payment of $482, those over sixty-five pay only $273. The ratio of 0.367 is an underestimate. Table 3-9 reports that 15,739 owner-occupied units have a householder over the age of sixty-five. We have corrected the ratio using the following formula: $21,937 / (59,796 - 15,739 + 15,739 * 273 / 482) = 0.414$. This proportion is applied to the deductibility of mortgage interest, deferral of capital gains on sale of principal residence, the low-income housing credit, and exclusion of interest on state and local government bonds for owner-occupied housing. However, senior citizens pay $10 tax on each $1,000 of assessment, while others pay $11 for each $1,000 of assessment (*American Housing Survey for the United States in 1991*, table 3-13, p. 118). Therefore the proportion used for the deductibility of property tax on owner-occupied buildings is $21,937 / (59,796 - 15,739 + 15,739 * 10/11) = 0.376$. To calculate the benefits to single-parent families, the same formula is used, except the number of single-parent households (1,758) from table 3-9 is substituted in the numerator.

e. Private child support is from unpublished data from the 1992 CPS. The proportions come from Bureau of the Census, "Child Support and Alimony: 1989," *Current Population Reports*, series P-60, no. 173 (Department of Commerce, 1991), table 1. We assume that married women are living in two-parent households.

f. AFDC is apportioned using the *1993 Green Book*, table 1, p. 617.

g. Congressional Research Service, *Cash and Noncash Benefits for Persons with Limited Income* (p. 74), reports that half of general assistance goes to families with children. The proportion for GA-medical is the same as that used for GA.

h. Medicaid for families is calculated from the *1993 Green Book*, table 17, p. 1654, by adding the figures for AFDC children, AFDC adults, and other Title XIX, plus adding disability times the proportion by family type from the SSI from the 1990 SIPP data. Single parents' share is calculated using the AFDC method for AFDC and Title XIX medicaid costs. The disability share is from the 1990 SIPP data using the SSI share.

i. Medical care for veterans without service-connected disability uses the family-type proportions from the SIPP Veterans Pensions.

j. Other medical includes Indian health services, maternal and child health, community health and family planning services, and migrant health centers, all taken from Congressional Research Service, *Cash and Noncash Benefits for Persons with Limited Income*, p. 204. Proportions for family type for Indian health services, maternal and child health, community health centers, family planning services, and migrant health centers are the combined medicaid and GA-medical proportions.

k. Other nutrition includes child and adult care food program, summer food program for children, commodities program, food distribution on Indian reservations, and special milk program. These data are from Congressional Research Service, *Cash and Noncash Benefits for Persons with Limited Income*, p. 206. They are apportioned, as are food stamps above.

l. Public and subsidized housing includes section 8, low-rent public housing, rural housing loans, rural rent assistance, rural housing preservation, rural self-help TA grants, farm labor housing loans and grants, section 236 interest payments and homeownership assistance, Indian housing improvement, and home investment partnerships; data are from Congressional Research Service, *Cash and*

Noncash Benefits for Persons with Limited Income, p. 206. Proportions used are those for public housing from the CPS-90.

m. Social service block grants are apportioned to child care and foster care according to Congressional Research Service, *Cash and Noncash Benefits for Persons with Limited Income,* p. 209.

n. The proportions for child care block grants and social service block grants for child care, summer youth employment, Job Corps, foster care, and social service block grants for foster care are based on the 1990 CPS–school lunch proportions.

o. *1993 Green Book,* p. 1690, reports that 55 percent of Head Start children are from single-parent households.

p. The all-families Job Training Partnership Act proportions are from SIPP-food stamps; the single parent proportion is from the JTPA evaluation.

Appendix B

Appendix table B-1 gives the public expenditures from table A-1 by income quintiles used to create figures 2-1 and 2-2.

The quintile break points for families are $16,960, $30,000, $44,200, and $64,300; see U.S. Bureau of the Census, "Money Income of Households, Families, and Persons in the United States, 1992," *Current Population Reports,* series P-60, no. 184 (Department of Commerce, 1992), table 15, p. 46. The proportions for social security, SSI, public assistance, worker's compensation, and child support are "Money Income of Households," table 22, p. 88. Because published data on the distribution of benefits by income class do not correspond exactly to my income quintile breaks, I assigned a weighted proportion of those in an income class to an income quintile. The proportion for public aid is used for medicaid. The proportion for education is equally distributed among the income quintiles. An estimate was made of children among the quintiles; "Money Income of Households," table 18, p. 68. The proportion by quintile was approximately equal.

There are two caveats on assigning the proportion based on the number of children. The first is that wealthier people use more private schools; the second is that public education in communities with wealthier people tends to cost more per student. The proportion for third-party medical care, taken from Jack A. Meyer and Sharon Silow-Carroll, *Building Blocks for Change: How Health Care Reform*

TABLE B-1. *Distribution of Public Transfers to Families, by Income Quintiles*

Summary of categories

Income less than	Quintile	Education	Health	Housing	Cash social security	Other cash	Other in-kind	Child support	Total
$16,960	1	44	39	8	10	48	18	4	172
$30,000	2	44	21	2	13	18	3	3	105
$44,200	3	44	23	2	11	15	1	3	99
$64,300	4	44	26	11	9	14	0	2	106
More than $64,300	5	44	29	13	8	15	0	2	112
Total	. . .	222	139	37	50	110	22	13	594

Detail by expenditure category

Income less than	Quintile	Social security	Unemployment insurance	Workers compensation	Veterans	Education	Medicare social security	Adult & child exemptions	Dependent care
$16,960	1	5	3	1	1	44	2	0	0
$30,000	2	5	4	2	1	44	2	6	1
$44,200	3	4	4	2	1	44	2	11	1
$64,300	4	2	4	2	1	44	1	11	1
More than $64,300	5	2	3	2	1	44	1	14	1
Total	. . .	18	18	10	3	222	8	43	3

	Quintile	Mortgage tax credit	Child support	Third-party health	Public assistance	Supplemental security income	Other health	Housing	In-kind
$16,960	1	0	4	3	37	4	34	8	18
$30,000	2	1	3	14	6	1	5	1	3
$44,200	3	2	3	20	2	1	2	0	1
$64,300	4	10	2	25	1	0	1	0	0
More than $64,300	5	13	2	28	0	0	0	0	0
Total	…	26	13	89	46	6	42	10	22

Affects Our Future (Reston, Va.: Economic and Social Research Institute, 1993), table 1, p. 92, reports the distribution by quintile of employer-paid health premiums net of taxes. The mortgage tax exemption is estimated using the distribution by income class given in the *1993 Green Book,* table 31, p. 1085. Weighted proportions are assigned to income quintiles.

Notes

1. John L. Palmer and Isabel V. Sawhill, eds., *The Reagan Record: An Assessment of America's Changing Domestic Priorities, An Urban Institute Study,* chapters 4 and 6 (Cambridge: Ballinger, 1984). Irwin Garfinkel and Sara S. McLanahan, *Single Mothers and Their Children: A New American Dilemma,* chapter 5 (Urban Institute Press, 1986), pp. 129–63.

2. National Commission on Children, *Beyond Rhetoric: A New American Agenda for Children and Families,* Final Report (1991). The commission recommended state experimentation with an ensured child support benefit before federal implementation.

3. The larger public income transfer system for the aged is ignored.

4. See Alan Blinder, *Hard Heads, Soft Hearts: Tough-Minded Economics for a Just Society* (Reading, Mass.: Addison-Wesley, 1987) for a particularly clear economic exposition of this argument. For a cogent sociological exposition, see William Julius Wilson, *The Truly Disadvantaged: The Inner City, the Underclass, and Public Policy* (University of Chicago Press, 1987).

5. "The bourgeoisie, during its rule of scarce one hundred years, has created more massive and more colossal productive forces than have all preceding generations together." Karl Marx and Friedrich Engels, "Manifesto of the Communist Party," reprinted in Lewis S. Feuer, ed., *Marx and Engels: Basic Writings on Politics and Philosophy* (Anchor Books, 1959), p. 12. See also the entire discussion on pp. 8–13.

6. Joseph A. Schumpeter, *Capitalism, Socialism, and Democracy* (Boston: Unwin Paperbacks, 1987).

7. If capitalism is so productive, how can incomes be low as well as irregular? Indeed, as conservatives are fond of reminding us, the absolute standard of living of many poor American families exceeds that of most families in the world. But low income is a social as well as an economic phenomenon. If inequality at the bottom of the income distribution is so severe that a family's income is substantially below the average living standard in the community—even if its absolute standard of living is high by historical and cross-country standards because the family lives in the wealthiest nation in the world—such a family will be insecure. Such a family lives on the margin, scrambling to make ends meet. Bills mount. Rent payments are missed. Sinking even deeper is an omnipresent threat.

8. Sara McLanahan and Gary Sandefur, *Growing Up with a Single Parent:*

What Hurts, What Helps (Harvard University Press, 1994). For evidence on crime, see Ross L. Matsueda and Karen Heimer, "Race, Family Structure, and Delinquency: A Test of Differential Association and Social Control Theories," *American Sociological Review*, vol. 52 (December 1987), pp. 826–40.

9. Leonard A. Rosenblum and Gayle S. Paully, "The Effects of Varying Environmental Demands on Maternal and Infant Behavior," *Child Development*, vol. 55 (1984), pp. 305–14. The monkey infants randomly assigned to environments in which their mothers had to work very hard to get enough food did worse than the infants of mothers assigned to the richer feeding environment. The offspring assigned to an extremely irregular or insecure environment—which alternated randomly between the poor and rich conditions—did the worst. It would be useful to have more animal research on this topic.

10. Families also change their adaptation strategies, and the changes should be discussed in relation to one another. I leave this topic for a future paper.

11. Through its federal tax system, the United States provides a tax benefit for children in the form of personal deductions for children and encourages the provision of employer-funded health insurance by not taxing this fringe benefit. The universality of child allowances has been challenged in the other major English-speaking nations—Great Britain, Canada, and Australia.

12. Many, following Marx, identify socialism with ownership of the means of production. But to achieve a society with a distributional principle of "From each according to their ability, to each according to their need," it is not logically necessary to socialize the means of production. An economy that provided all goods publicly and taxed 100 percent of income—that is, an economy that completely socialized consumption—would achieve this distributional ideal and be just as disastrous as the East European economies, which completely socialized production. Complete socialization of consumption eliminates economic incentives.

13. Furthermore, in a capitalist economy, it is impossible to disguise the fact that welfare programs are for economic failures. As a consequence, welfare programs provide only minimal increases in fairness and quelling of discontent.

14. Robert Lampman, *Social Welfare Spending: Accounting for Changes from 1950 to 1978* (Academic Press, 1984).

15. The source for federal expenditures on the elderly is House Committee on Ways and Means, *Overview of Entitlement Programs—1993 Green Book*, Committee Print, 100 Cong. 1 sess. (Government Printing Office, 1993), p. 1564, table 1. We begin with the weighted average of the 1990 and the 1995 estimates to derive an estimate for 1992 of $389 billion. To this we add $4.4 billion, which is a rough estimate of the value of the increased standard deduction for senior citizens ($900 for those filing singly or as head of household in 1992; *1994 Green Book*, table 16-17, p. 719). These estimates are calculated in the manner described in appendix A, note c. The source for the defense and other government spending is *Economic Report of the President* (GPO, 1993), table B-75.

16. The productivity data are taken from U.S. Bureau of Labor Statistics, *Handbook of Labor Statistics* (1989), table 98, p. 348, for the period 1950–70. For the period 1975–90, the productivity data are from *1993 Economic Report of the President*, table B-44, p. 397. The social welfare expenditure series is taken from Ann Bixley, "Public Income-Maintenance Programs: Cash Benefit Payments," table 4.A.1, *Social Security Bulletin*, vol. 56 (Fall 1993), p. 148.

17. Organization for Economic Cooperation and Development, *OECD in Figures—1991* (Paris: 1991). Tax expenditures are not included.

18. See Torsten Persson and Guido Tabellini, "Is Inequality Harmful for Growth?" *American Economic Review*, vol. 84 (June 1994), pp. 600–21. They find that inequality reduces growth and there is no significant relationship between transfers and growth. Persson and Tabellini cite Nordstrom Hakan, *Studies in Trade Policy and Economic Growth Monograph No. 20* (Stockholm: Institute for International Economic Studies, 1992).

19. Timothy Smeeding, Barbara Boyle Torrey, and Martin Rein, "Patterns of Income and Poverty: The Economic Status of Children and the Elderly in Eight Countries," in John L. Palmer, Timothy Smeeding, and Barbara Boyle Torrey, eds., *The Vulnerable* (Urban Institute Press, 1988), pp. 89–119.

20. Of course, the positive effects of the externalities and human investment must be weighed against the negative effects of the distortion of consumer choice. For an example of such an analysis see Robert J. Lampman, *Social Welfare Spending: Accounting for Changes from 1950 to 1978* (Orlando: Academic Press, 1984).

21. The correspondence is not exact because the income quintiles are not adjusted for family size.

22. This fringe benefit form of employee compensation is not taxed. The subsidy is worth more to those at the top than those at the bottom of the distribution—a violation of equity. This system was spurred by the decision during World War II to disregard employee compensation in the form of health insurance and other fringe benefits in terms of both wage and price control regulations and by the federal income tax. The tax subsidy for health insurance is not shown as a tax expenditure because the value of this tax expenditure is already reflected in the value of third-party health care payments.

23. Homeowners are allowed to deduct mortgage interest and property tax payments from their income before they compute their federal taxes. While these costs of homeownership are deducted, the value of homeownership—the rent not paid—is not reported as income.

24. Because the child-care tax credit is not refundable and its value depends on actual child care expenditures, which increases with income, its value does go up as income increases.

25. Irwin Garfinkel, *Assuring Child Support: An Extension of Social Security* (Russell Sage Foundation, 1992).

26. Cynthia Miller, Irwin Garfinkel, and Sara McLanahan, "Child Support: Can Fathers Pay More?", paper presented at RAND Conference, Reshaping the Family: Social and Economic Changes and Public Policy, January 20–21, 1994; and Elaine Sorenson, "Noncustodial Fathers: Can They

Afford to Pay more Child Support?", unpublished manuscript, Urban Institute, 1993.

27. Donald T. Oellerich and Irwin Garfinkel, "Distributional Impacts of Existing and Alternative Child Support Systems," *Policy Studies Journal*, vol. 12, no. 1 (September 1983), pp. 119–30.

28. Robert J. Willis, "A Theory of Out-of-Wedlock Childbearing," paper presented at the Workshop on Expanding Frameworks for Fertility Research, National Research Council, Woods Hole, Mass., September 22–23, 1994.

29. Irwin Garfinkel, *Income Tested Transfer Programs: The Case For and Against* (Academic Press, 1982); Garfinkel and McLanahan, *Single Mothers and Their Children*; and David T. Ellwood, *Poor Support: Poverty in the American Family* (Basic Books, 1988).

30. This is the average national cost of medicaid for a mother with two children in 1991 adjusted to 1993 dollars (*1993 Green Book*, p. 1659, table 20).

31. Indeed, the table overstates the extent to which the system has already changed. To be eligible for medicaid in 1993, a child had to be no more than twelve years of age. Each year since 1987, the maximum age of the child is scheduled to increase by one year from a base of age six.

32. In addition, the $15,000 earner gets a smaller EITC benefit than the $8,500 worker, because $15,000 places the family in the tax-back range of the EITC.

33. Charles A. Murray, *Losing Ground: American Social Policy, 1950–1980* (Basic Books, 1984).

34. No adjustment is made for the lower values of the standard deduction and personal exemptions in the income tax in the earlier periods, thus understating the true marriage penalty in the earlier periods. In addition, the estimate are understated because of our calculation of the value of medicaid benefits. We could not find figures for family medicaid benefits for 1970. We began with 1975 figures and discounted them by the aggregate growth of medicaid expenditures between 1970 and 1975. Because the bulk of the growth in expenditures in this period is due to growth in caseloads rather than growth in per family expenditures, our estimate of the 1970 value of medicaid is too low. Using the 1975 figure for medicaid would increase the marriage penalties reported in table 2-3 by about $900.

35. Carole Trippe and Pat Doyle, *Food Stamp Participation Rates, January 1989* (Food and Nutrition Service, Department of Agriculture, 1992).

36. Child care deductions of up to $160 per month per child are also permitted.

37. Thomas M. Fraker and others, "The Effects of Cashing-Out Food Stamps on Household Food Use and the Cost of Issuing Benefits," *Journal of Policy Analysis and Management* (forthcoming).

38. An even more limited reform that would probably reduce the stigma somewhat would be to substitute a food stamp electronic credit card for the stamps.

39. Cohabiting relationships without marriage are generally of shorter duration than marriages. Larry L. Bumpass and James A. Sweet, "National Estimates of Cohabitation," *Demography*, vol. 26 (November 1989), pp. 913–27.

40. Gary S. Becker, *A Treatise on the Family* (Harvard University Press, 1991); James S. Coleman, *Foundations of Social Theory* (Harvard University Press, 1990); and McLanahan and Sandefur, *Growing Up with a Single Parent.*

41. McLanahan and Sandefur, *Growing Up with a Single Parent.*

42. Gordon Tullock, "Income Testing and Politics: A Theoretical Model," chapter 4, in Garfinkel, ed., *Income Tested Transfer Programs: The Case For and Against.* See also the comments by Anthony Downs, Larry Orr, and Benjamin Page, and chapters 1, 12, and 13.

43. Garfinkel, ed., *Income Tested Transfer Programs;* see especially chapters 1, 6, 7, 8, and 13.

44. Whether the Clinton administration proposal is the best method of achieving universal coverage is beyond the scope of this chapter.

45. Yuen Hee Kim, "The Economic Effects of the Combined Non-Income-Tested Transfers for Families with Children: Child Support Assurance, Children's Allowance, and National Health Insurance." Ph.D. dissertation, University of Wisconsin, 1993; Robert Moffitt and Barbara L. Wolfe, "The Effect of the Medicaid Program on Welfare Participation and Labor Supply," *Review of Economics and Statistics,* vol. 74 (December 1992), pp. 615–26; and Aaron S. Yelowitz, "Will Extending Medicaid to Two Parent Families Encourage Marriage?" UCLA Department of Economics, July 1994, mimeo.

46. Irwin Garfinkel, "Financing Medical Care: A Welfare Economics Analysis." Ph.D. dissertation, University of Michigan, Ann Arbor, 1970; and Henry J. Aaron, *Serious and Unstable Condition: Financing America's Health Care* (Brookings, 1991).

47. Congressional Budget Office, *An Analysis of the Administration's Health Proposal* (February 1994), p. 26.

48. The federal budget increase includes the health alliance budgets. The bulk of this increase represents a shift from existing third-party payments to the health alliances. If one assumes that health insurance premiums are equivalent to taxes from an employee's point of view—a reasonable assumption—the total "tax" burden of the system will not increase much and may even decrease.

49. The medium-run improvement entails an increase in award rates (the proportion of cases with child support awards) and collection rates (the proportion owed that is collected) halfway between the current level and perfection and an increase in awards to the level of the Wisconsin child support guidelines—17 percent of gross income for one child, and 25 percent, 29 percent, 31 percent, and 34 percent for two, three, four, and five or more children. The assured benefit would be increased for the second and third child by $1,000 per child and for the third, fourth, and sixth child by $500 per child. For cost estimates of the Assured Child Support benefits, see Daniel R. Meyer and others, "Who Should Be Eligible for an Assured Child Support Benefit?", in Irwin Garfinkel, Sara S. McLanahan, and Philip K. Robins, eds., *Child Support Assurance: Design Issues, Expected Impacts, and Political Barriers as Seen from Wisconsin* (Urban Institute Press, 1993).

50. From an administrative point of view, however, child allowances are superior. Child allowances could be deposited by electronic transfer in the accounts of all children on a monthly basis. No extra income verification is required. Whereas income taxes are filed only on a yearly basis, low-income families need to receive benefits during the course of the year. Thus with tax credits a way must be found to provide the benefits during the course of the year.

51. There are 64.8 million children and 186.2 million adults in 1993. Bureau of the Census, "Household and Family Characteristics: March 1993," *Current Population Reports,* series P-20, no. 477 (Department of Commerce), table 3, pp. 12–16. The child credit would have cost (64.8 * $1,000 =) $65 billion, or $43 billion more than the exemption for children in the federal income tax. A refundable housing tax credit or $1,000 per adult will cost (186.2 * $850 =) $158 billion. In lieu of adult exemptions, costing $68 billion, the refundable housing tax credit cost an additional $90 billion. The total cost of both tax credits is $133 billion. This estimate is conservative—a bit too high—in that it does not eliminate the double exemption for the aged. Eliminating the food stamp program, housing subsidies for the poor, and the homeowners tax subsidy in the income tax would save $23 billion, $22 billion, and $65 billion, respectively, for a total of $110 billion. Child and adult allowances, in conjunction with a universal health care system, would also lead to a reduction of AFDC costs, over and above the savings from CASA, of probably at least $10 billion and more likely $15 billion and an SSI saving of $2 billion. That leaves a net cost of (133 − (110 + 15 + 2) = $6 billion.

52. The cost sensitivity results from the large gross costs of universal benefits combined with the fixed costs of the current system. Increasing the adult credit by $150 increases gross and net costs by $28 billion. A $200 increase in the child credit increases gross and net costs by $13 billion.

53. Irwin Garfinkel and Sara McLanahan, "Single Mother Families, Economic Insecurity, and Government Policy," in Sheldon H. Danziger, Gary D. Sandefur, and Daniel H. Weinberg, eds., *Confronting Poverty: Prescriptions for Change* (Harvard University Press, 1994).

54. In 1992 there were 8 million two- and three-year-old children, 3.8 million four-year-olds, and 3.8 million five-year-olds. I assumed that all of the five-year-olds were in half-day kindergarten and therefore cut the cost in half for them. I also subtracted $10 billion in current expenditures.

55. For a related argument for a division of responsibility between the states and the federal government, see Alice Rivlin, *Reviving the American Dream: The Economy, the States, and the Federal Government* (Brookings, 1992).

56. Only about one-third of the unemployed receive benefits from unemployment insurance. One way to extend coverage of the system is to make entitlement to benefits a continuous rather than a discontinuous function of previous attachment to the labor force. Every day worked should entitle the worker to some portion of a day's unemployment insurance should (s)he become unemployed.

57. For a discussion of how work relief reinforces family as well as work, see Garfinkel and McLanahan, *Single Mothers and Their Children*.

58. Reinforcing work reduces the nonaccelerating inflationary rate of unemployment. Irwin Garfinkel and John L. Palmer, "Issues, Evidence, and Implications," in John L. Palmer, ed., *Creating Jobs: Public Employment Programs and Wage Subsidies* (Brookings, 1978).

59. On the Democratic side, see Senator Bradley's proposal, the *Interstate Child Support Enforcement Act*, S.689, 103 Cong. 1 sess., and the proposal by Senator Dodd and Senator Rockefeller, *Child Support Assurance Act of 1994*, S.1962, 103 Cong. 1 sess. On the Republican side, E. Clay Shaw, Nancy L. Johnson, and Fred Grandy, members of the House Ways and Means Committee, recommended a demonstration of a child support assurance program in their position paper "Moving Ahead: How America Can Reduce Poverty Through Work" (June 1992), unpublished. However, by the time the proposal was written as legislation (H.R. 741, *Responsibility and Empowerment Support Program Providing Employment, Child Care, and Training Act*, 103 Cong. 1 sess.), the demonstration of the assured benefit had been dropped.

Chapter 3

Somebody's Children: Educational Opportunity for *All* American Children

Diane Ravitch

CERTAIN VALUES are paramount in any discussion of education in the United States: equality, excellence, and pluralism. We are all committed to the principle of equality of educational opportunity. We are all committed to the principle of educational excellence. These principles are sometimes counterpoised rather than juxtaposed, but I believe that our pursuit of equality and excellence must be joined, because educational opportunity—if equal—should be equal in excellence, not equal in mediocrity. And finally, we are all committed to the liberal democratic ideals of diversity and pluralism, for we recognize that in a free society healthy differences of opinion and practice not only promote progress but are required for it.

In the United States today, we have an education system from kindergarten through twelfth grade that embraces these ideals in theory, but fails to achieve them in reality. Whether one looks at the results of international assessments, standardized tests, or performance-based assessments, our students do not achieve high levels of excellence, and despite considerable progress over the past generation, there continue to be large gaps in achievement between children from different social classes and different racial or ethnic groups.[1] For many children, especially children who are poor and are racial minorities, both equality and excellence in education remain out of reach. In addition, while our public schools honor diversity and pluralism by bringing together students from many different backgrounds, they simultaneously dishonor diversity and pluralism by requiring conformity to state-imposed policies on controversial issues about which reasonable people differ and by prohibiting the use of public funds in schools that differ from the majoritarian consensus (for example, single-sex schools and schools for those with strong religious convictions).

The proposal that I offer faces substantial political opposition because it challenges a powerful status quo. Yet there are many indications of growing interest in this policy. Over the next several years, many cities, states, and perhaps even the Congress are likely to authorize demonstration projects to gauge its feasibility. The ultimate test of any educational program should be not whether it satisfies political constituencies, but whether it measurably improves the education of children.

On February 15, 1994, Secretary of Education Richard Riley delivered a speech at Georgetown University on the "State of American Education" in which he noted, "Some schools are excellent, some are improving, some have the remarkable capacity to change for the better, and some should never be called schools at all."

I was struck by the reference to schools that "should never be called schools at all." Who attends them? Chances are, these students are African American and Hispanic; chances are, they are from very poor families, in which a single parent is struggling to make ends meet. These are the children who are compelled to attend schools that most teachers shun, if they can, in neighborhoods that people of means avoid, if possible.

The secretary closed his speech with the famous quote from John Dewey, "What the best and wisest parent wants for his [and, may I say, her] own child, that must be what the community wants for all of its children. Any other ideal for our schools is narrow and unlovely; it destroys our democracy."[2]

The question must arise, Who are the best and wisest parents and what would they do if their children were assigned to one of those places that are not fit to be called schools?

Somebody's children are compelled—one might say condemned—to attend schools that should never be called schools at all. Somebody's children go to those schools. Not mine. Not yours. Not the secretary's. Not the president's or the vice president's. Surely not the mayor's or the superintendent's or even the teachers'. What would the best and wisest parents do if their children were zoned into schools that are physically unsafe and educationally bankrupt? They would move to a different neighborhood or put their children into private schools. That's what the president and the vice president did. That is what well-to-do and middle-class parents do.

But somebody's children are required to go to those schools. Some parents who do not have the money to move to a better neighborhood or to put their child into a private school have been told that their child must stay there no matter how bad the school is. If they are parents with motivation and energy, they are told by school officials and policymakers that they must stay right where they are, because they are the kind of parents who might someday help to improve that dreadful school. The people who tell them this would not keep their own child in that school for even a day.

What should we do about those children and those schools? Many people say, "We must reform those schools." Of course, they are right. For policymakers and academics, this is the appropriate response to clearly inadequate schools. But as parents, this is an outrageous proposition, for our own children live this day, in the here and now, and they cannot wait around to see whether the school will get better in five or ten years. I suggest that we project our passion for our own children's welfare—as Dewey suggested—onto those parents who lack our money, power, and education; they love their children as much as we love ours. Their desperation about their children's future is greater than ours because they know that the odds are stacked against them. They should not be expected to wait patiently for the transformation of the failing institutions where their children are required to go each day, the places that the secretary of education says do not deserve to be called schools at all. We surely would not be willing to make the same sacrifice of our own children; why should they?

Dewey was right: what the best and wisest parents want for their children is what the community should want for all its children. Not the promise of good education someday, maybe, but the reality of good education today.

So the problem to which I address my essay is, How can we quickly improve the educational opportunities available to those children who are now attending schools that should not be called schools?

I suggest that states, cities, or the federal government should provide means-tested scholarships to needy families, who may use them to send their children to the school of their choice, be it public, independent, or religious. The size of the scholarship should vary in relation to family income; the needier the child, the larger the grant. Children with disabilities should receive the full amount of financial aid to which they would be entitled under state and federal law, because their education is expensive, no matter who provides it. Since funds will necessarily be limited, highest priority for such scholarships should go to children who are presently enrolled in schools that have been identified by public authorities (for example, the state commissioner of education or the city superintendent) as the lowest performing in the district. The number and size of such scholarships can be strictly controlled by public authorities in order to gauge the cost and consequences (although care should be taken to assure that public authorities do not make the number and size so small as to render the program meaningless). In higher education there are Pell grants for needy students that can be used to attend any accredited institution, regardless of its sponsorship. In effect, I am suggesting Pell grants for elementary and secondary education.

The beneficiaries of these scholarships should be those who are poorest, without regard to ability, with priority for those whose schools are acknowledged by public authorities to be the lowest performing by objective measures. Usually these schools are well known to officials, parents, and the press. In New York State, for example, the state commissioner of education has identified seventy-seven schools as "schools under registration review" because of extremely poor pupil performance and high dropout rates. It would not be difficult to select objective criteria to identify such schools, including attendance rates for students and teachers, dropout rates, and various measures of pupil performance. Parent education and family income obviously contribute to pupil performance, but we must take care not to build into public policy a sense of resignation that children's socioeconomic status determines their destiny. Public policy must relentlessly seek to replicate schools that demonstrate the ability to educate children from impoverished backgrounds, instead of perpetuating (and rewarding) those that use the pupil's circumstances as a rationale for failure.

When allowed full choice among public schools, parents help identify the least effective by voting with their feet. If allowed the opportunity for their children to receive scholarships to attend the school of their choice, whether public or nonpublic, parents of poor children would become empowered consumers rather than hapless clients ignored by an unresponsive bureaucracy. In addition to providing immediate assistance to the neediest students, this strategy would help to transform or even close those schools that have been unchanged by all previous reform efforts.

Of course there is the danger of perverse incentives. Dropouts should not be eligible for such scholarships, in order not to encourage or reward dropping out. It is possible that parents might send their children to a school with a terrible reputation in hopes of winning a scholarship, but that seems unlikely.

There are many different ways to structure a scholarship program for needy students and many different policy considerations involving criteria for eligibility, size of individual scholarships, cost, transportation, support services for parents, evaluation, and so on. As cities and states seek to implement school choice, many different approaches will be tried. I do not offer a single solution to any one of these questions, because experience to date is too limited to provide definitive answers. The issue at hand is not the specific details that should be adopted in a given program but the general principles that should guide the development of such programs in the future.

Of one thing I am convinced: the big, anonymous comprehensive high school that was the hallmark of American education for most of this century is incapable of meeting the needs of endangered youngsters in the cities. The "shopping mall high school," as it was appropriately called by Arthur Powell, Eleanor Farrar, and David Cohen, offers something for everyone, cafeteria style, but it cannot provide the individual support and nurturance that most of these young people need. The typical comprehensive high school is large and impersonal, with a studied air of neutrality toward all students. But that is exactly what these children do not need. They need schools that work closely with each student and his or her family; they need schools that are designed to be intensely engaged with each child as a unique person. Children need to be in schools where there are many adults who know their names and care about them, know when they are absent, know when they have a problem, think about their futures, and expect to talk frequently to their parents or guardians.

I am persuaded that the most successful urban schools are those that have a sense of purpose, a mission, an identity of their own.

Some of these schools are public, some are not. Paul Hill and his colleagues describe them as "high schools with character." Theodore R. Sizer writes, "Good schools are thoughtful places. The people in them are known. The units are small enough to be coherent communities of friends." Anthony Bryk, Valerie Lee, and Peter Holland analyze the way Catholic schools create a strong sense of community, with a coherent philosophy, shared values, and common purpose.[3] Hill and his colleagues call such places focus schools.

> Focus schools resemble one another, and differ from zoned comprehensive public schools, in two basic ways. First, focus schools have clear uncomplicated missions centered on the experiences the school intends to provide its students and on the ways it intends to influence its students' performance, attitudes, and behavior. Second, focus schools are strong organizations with a capacity to initiate action in pursuit of their missions, to sustain themselves over time, to solve their own problems, and to manage their external relationships.[4]

Most children need to be in focus schools, schools with a high degree of autonomy and self-direction, schools with a clear sense of purpose, schools where they are known, schools that are small enough to create a sense of community, schools where no one is anonymous or overlooked. Students in the inner city have the greatest need to attend schools where adults know them, watch over them, watch out for them, and care for them. In today's society, with most parents working, their children need schools that function in loco parentis, with the knowledge and assent of parents who welcome a partnership with the school.[5]

There are two complementary strategies to expand the numbers of focus schools. One is to provide means-tested scholarships to poor children, allowing them to attend any school that accepts public accountability for education standards and civil rights laws. The other is to promote the spread of charter schools and special-purpose public schools managed under contract by public or private organizations. This latter alternative is spreading rapidly, having been adopted by a score of states, under consideration in several more, and endorsed by the National School Boards Association. A charter school is "a public school under contract or charter to a public agency, governed by a combination of administrators, teachers, parents and others."[6] Charter schools are usually freed of burdensome rules, regulations, and mandates in exchange for agreeing (in their charter) to be accountable for educational and fiscal results. The virtue of charter schools is that they encourage innovation with accountability; they are public schools, regardless of who manages them, operating with public funds, open to all who apply. A charter school may be a new school or an existing public school that wishes to gain greater autonomy in managing its own affairs.

The charter/contracting strategy is politically practical and avoids the inevitable constitutional problems that will accompany any choice plan that includes private and religious schools. The scholarship strategy empowers poor parents to choose the school their child will attend. These two paths will create a more diverse, pluralistic system of good schools from which parents and students may choose. One creates demand for special-purpose schools by supplying scholarships; the other creates a new supply by encouraging the creation of additional special-purpose schools.

Both strategies should be pursued at the same time. Both are necessary if there is to be any prospect of large-scale change, because otherwise supporters of the status quo may severely restrict the number of charters granted and may seek to marginalize charter schools as appropriate only for a tiny minority of students with special interests. Taken together, both strategies would expand educational opportunities for poor children. Wherever specialized magnet schools or choice programs have been made available, parents have responded enthusiastically, largely because of their perception that their child may be neglected in the anonymity of the typical large comprehensive school, as well as the implicit (and usually explicit) promise that the new, small schools offer an individualized education, in which no child is overlooked.

Although it is tempting to support public choice only, because it is less controversial, I argue the case for full choice involving both state and nonstate schools because, first, opening choice to all schools will rapidly expand the supply of places available, and second, I support the inclusion of private and religious schools, so long as they are willing to comply with state education standards, as a matter of justice. I do not contend for full choice solely on grounds that competition is good, although I do think that competition is good. There may be one somewhere, but I have difficulty thinking of any monopoly that effectively serves the public and simultaneously meets individual needs. Nor do I argue for full choice on the grounds that private schools are by their nature better than public schools; I do not believe that. On the contrary, I know that there are many excellent public schools, as there are many mediocre private schools.

No, what I argue is that it is unjust to compel poor children to attend bad schools. It is unjust to prohibit poor families from sending their children to the school of their choice, even if that school has a religious affiliation. It is unjust to deny free schooling to poor families with strong religious convictions, equally as unjust as it would be to prohibit the use of federal scholarships in nonpublic universities (like Notre Dame, Marymount, Yeshiva, or Princeton). It is unjust that there is no realistic way to force the closure of schools that students and their parents would abandon if they could.

For the following reasons, the policy of means-tested scholarships would benefit low-income children and their families, while encouraging pluralism.

A means-tested choice program would strengthen the role of parents and families in children's lives. Public policy should aim to enhance the role of parents in their children's lives. There is clear evidence that parent participation is much greater in Catholic schools than in public schools, and it is probably greater in focus public schools than in ordinary public schools. Parents of children in Catholic schools are twice as likely as public school parents to belong to and participate in the PTA. Parents of poor black students in Catholic schools participate in the PTA at much higher levels than do their counterparts in public schools.[7] It is possible that the act of choosing a school makes parents feel more responsible and become more involved, as does belonging to a community of shared values.

A means-tested choice program would allow low-income students to move to a better school—public, private, or religious. As the charter school movement spreads across the country, there are increasing opportunities for students to move to small, purposeful schools. A model school created by Wayne State University in Detroit was heavily oversubscribed. Rice University in Houston was inundated with applications for a new school near its campus. Disadvantaged urban students in Catholic schools have a lower dropout rate and higher test scores than their peers in public schools.[8] One reason for the difference is the fact that students in Catholic schools are much likelier to be placed in college preparatory programs, regardless of their race or social class. So, for example, in 1990, 63 percent of high school sophomores in Catholic schools were on a college track, compared with 39 percent of public school sophomores.[9]

A means-tested choice program would enable students to attend schools where teachers and parents agree on a code of conduct. Participating in a close, consensual community would help to protect and nurture youngsters and to buttress them against the dangers of the street. Most public schools operate on the basis of hierarchical, bureaucratic rules and regulations. Such schools fail to engage students as members of a community. Under a program of choice, eligible students would be able to attend a school where there is focus, mission, and identity. It is only in such a setting that students who are now alienated will begin to see themselves as responsible participants, surrounded by adults and other students who are affected by their decisions and actions. Under the current system there is no incentive to establish new focus schools. In a choice program there would be encouragement to create many such schools.

A means-tested choice program would minimize conflict within school systems by giving options to people with conflicting values. Some parents prefer a school that requires uniforms; others do not. Some may want progressive pedagogy; others may not. Although some individual schools of choice may be homogeneous in their basic values, the system as a whole would foster greater pluralism and diversity.

A means-tested choice program would help school districts use every educational resource in the community to meet a surge in enrollments. The United States is once again in the midst of a large increase in school enrollments. The National Center for Education Statistics projects that enrollment in grades kindergarten through eight will increase from 35.2 million in 1992 to 39.7 million by 2004, an increase of 13 percent, and that enrollment in grades nine through twelve will grow from 12.9 million in 1992 to 16 million in 2004, an increase of 24 percent.[10] Increases of this magnitude will force public officials either to invest billions of dollars in constructing new schools or to use all existing facilities fully.

The best response to these enrollment increases is to take advantage of all schools through a choice system that is well organized, well supervised, and coordinated with existing public schools.

A means-tested choice program would encourage individual decision-

making, a fundamental value in a democratic society. It is hard to think of any other part of American life in which choice is portrayed as an evil. Having the ability to choose among competing products and services allows us to exercise control over our lives; the absence of choice means that someone else has made a vital decision for us, as though we were incompetent to manage our own lives. It is possible to argue that life is unfair and that poor people have no right to demand the kind of mobility available to people of means. But the example of higher education suggests a workable model for providing scholarships for poor students in elementary and secondary schools.

My proposal is not new; many others have made similar suggestions.[11] It is, however, new for me. I have reconsidered my views on the relationship between public and nonpublic schools. I do so not because of any animus toward public education. I attended public schools in Houston, Texas, for thirteen years. I have always considered myself a friend and supporter of public education; I still do. From July 1991 until January 1993, I was an assistant secretary of education in the administration of President George Bush, which strongly endorsed the principle of school choice, and it might have been reasonable to suppose that I did too. In truth, I was unresolved about the issue. Indeed, in 1983 I argued in the *New Republic* that tuition tax credits were a bad idea because they might undermine the independence of nonpublic schools. During my time in the federal government I devoted my energy to advocating the creation of voluntary national standards and seldom spoke about choice. Frankly, I avoided the topic because I knew that I could make the argument for both sides. I was impressed by the research about Catholic schools by Coleman, Greeley, and others, but I had not made up my mind and did not intend to be pushed, for political reasons, to say something that I was not sure about.

Many events and ideas have caused me to change my mind about choice. Not least of the reasons is that many years have passed in which the problems of the most desperate inner-city schools have remained fundamentally unchanged, despite wave after wave of reforms and programs. Trying harder has helped some schools, but the worst are untouched. Certain personal experiences also changed my perspective. I recall, in particular, a visit to Britain in the fall of 1992, when I went to learn about that nation's efforts to create a national curriculum and national assessments. I was also curious to learn about "grant-maintained" schools, and I asked to visit a typical one. These are schools where parents have voted to leave the jurisdiction of the local board of education and to receive public funding directly from the national government.

To my surprise, I was sent to a Roman Catholic girls' school in London, where most of the students were members of racial minorities. The nun who showed me around was in street dress, as were the teachers. The money that previously was consumed by the local school board (about 15 percent of the school's budget) was now contributed directly to the school. The school used a capital grant from the government and its additional funds to build a new science laboratory, make long-deferred repairs, and hire additional teachers. For the first time, the staff was allowed to select the school's food supplier; competitive bids were solicited. The local school board (which previously held a monopoly) was unable to submit a bid, because it did not know how much its food services cost. The school selected a caterer after comparing price and quality among bidders. In other words, instead of acting as the last link in a bureaucratic chain, the staff in the school became free to act as adults, making responsible decisions. As I went from classroom to classroom, I saw teenage girls preparing for the national examinations, in an atmosphere that was orderly, cheerful, and well maintained. What I most vividly recall is the comment of my guide, who said, "You can always tell a grant-maintained school by the smell of fresh paint."

Not only do the British provide public funds for religious schools, they insist that religious and moral education is a regular part of the national curriculum, whatever the student's belief. So do many other nations. This is obviously not the practice in the United States. Opposition to funding nonpublic schools, especially religious schools, is powerful here, and admitting any demonstration of religious faith into the public school is anathema. We have been told for many years that the use of any public funds in a religious school violates the constitutional principle of separation of church and state and that it amounts to an illegal establishment of religion.

Yet when we look at other developed democracies, we find that our so-called "wall of separation" is anomalous. Every other western nation provides state aid to religious and other private schools. Denmark, for example, provides direct government funding for nongovernmental schools so that parents can exercise religious and political freedom. These state-funded nonpublic schools attract only about 5–6 percent of the total enrollment, a testament both to popular support for state schools and to Denmark's commitment to religious and political pluralism. Like Denmark, other nations act on the principle that it would be a denial of religious freedom to distribute public funds only to state schools. After the fall of communism, many parents and teachers in eastern Europe demanded alternatives to state schools, which had proved themselves to be instruments to impose ideological and political conformity.[12]

The more I learned about schooling in other democracies, the more I wondered about the roots of our own practices. Why do we insist that public funds go only to state schools when other western nations do not? Why do we adamantly refuse any public funding for those who attend religious schools, but only at the primary and secondary levels? Why is Mary Jones—a young woman from an impoverished family—ineligible for public funds when she is an eighteen-year-old senior at St. Mary's Academy, yet eligible for a federal Pell grant when she is an eighteen-year-old freshman at St. Mary's College? Is it fair to deny free education to needy citizens whose sincere religious convictions make it impossible for them to send their children to secular state schools? Why is public funding available only to schools that exclude religious values? Why is there free speech in public schools for all controversial views except religious ones? Why would it be an "establishment of religion" if students with public grants attended schools sponsored by scores of different religious groups? Does the Constitution require hostility to religion or neutrality toward all religions?

Public schools are defined as "only those schools owned and operated by the government," yet places of public accommodation (hotels, restaurants, buses, theaters, and so on) are defined as public not on the basis of who owns and operates them but by whom they serve.[13] Thus the paradox: a school in an exclusive suburb that educates affluent students at a cost of $15,000 a student a year is "public," while an inner-city parochial school that educates impoverished minority students at a cost of $2,000 a year is not "public."

I am a historian of education, and my first book—*The Great School Wars: New York City, 1805–1973, A History of the Public Schools as Battlefield of Social Change*—dealt at length with the issues of public and nonpublic schools. I thought that I had adequately examined the evolution of the secular public school. But the more I questioned my own views, the more I began to doubt what I once knew. I looked again at familiar literature with a fresh eye and found answers that I had not seen or had not wanted to see before.

The rise of the American common school during the nineteenth century cannot be understood without reference to the dominant influence of evangelical Protestantism in their formation and, more specifically, to the relentless efforts by evangelical Protestants to deny public funds to Catholic schools. Historian David Tyack has documented the extensive role of evangelical Protestant clergymen as leaders of the common school movement and as state superintendents who "spread the gospel of the common school in their united battle against Romanism, barbarism, and skepticism."[14] Historian Lloyd Jorgenson has described the close ties between the Protestant common school movement and nativism, embodied by the Know-Nothing party. The object of the common school movement was not to establish nonreligious, secular schools but to establish schools that were state controlled, nonsectarian, and Christian. Jorgenson writes,

> In state after state during the [eighteen] fifties, with Know-Nothing leaders in the forefront of the battles, state school officers and Protestant denominational bodies were able to obtain legislation denying public funds to non-public schools and requiring Bible reading in the public schools. There was no mistaking the motivation behind these campaigns; the leaders openly and boastfully made anti-Catholicism the dominant theme of their attacks. At the best, the campaigns were brutal; at the worst they begot violence and bloodshed. But they achieved their objectives. By the end of the fifties, the principle of denying public aid to non-public schools had been firmly established in almost all states. . . . Much later the disinheritance of the church-related schools, a doctrine largely born of bigotry at the state level, was transmuted by the U.S. Supreme Court into high constitutional principle.[15]

The goal of the common school movement was not to create secular schools but to ensure that all public funds were devoted solely to nondenominational Protestant schools and that no public funds could be used for "sectarian" schools. Catholic schools were, of course, sectarian schools, as were denominational Protestant schools.

The common school reformers achieved their purpose: throughout the nineteenth century and well into the twentieth century, students in nonsectarian public schools read the Protestant Bible, sang Protestant hymns, recited Protestant prayers, and learned a Protestant version of European history.[16]

As Jorgenson notes, political leaders did not claim that it was unconstitutional to spend public funds in Catholic schools; instead, they passed laws in the states to prevent it and even attempted to pass a constitutional amendment to make sure that no public money could be allotted to the schools of the "papists." The leaders of the common school movement did not justify this policy by invoking the principle of separation of church and state; their argument was "simple and blunt: the growth of Catholicism was a menace to republican institutions and must be curbed." Over the years rioters, clergymen, voters, and politicians have tried to suppress Catholic schools as an affront to "American" values. Jorgenson finds it "ironic that policies born of religious intolerance should today be regarded with reverence."[17]

The philosophy of public education that we now celebrate was shaped by evangelical Protestant ministers and nativists who believed that the Catholic Church was anti-American and dangerous. Put simply, the idea of the common school was rooted firmly in anti-Catholic bigotry.

Over the years we have developed a theory of public education that is unnecessarily constricted. Public education, in current theory, occurs only in schools operated and controlled by the government. Yet it is the education of the public—all the public—that should concern us. When public officials use the phrase "all our children," they often do not literally mean *all* our children; they mean, "all our children who attend state schools." This seems fundamentally unfair and undemocratic. If there were an epidemic of polio, would public officials vaccinate all children, or only those who attend state schools? If public funds are made available to educate children with severe disabilities, should they be used for all children with severe disabilities or only those who attend state schools? If ignorance is to be vanquished, should it be vanquished among all our children or only among those children in state schools?

With this conceptual background, I return to the questions that must be seen as central to the reform of education. How can we expand educational opportunity for poor children in urban areas, where academic achievement is lowest and where social conditions are worst? How can we provide them with access to schools that have a strong sense of community, shared moral values, and a commitment to their success? How can we do this now rather than someday? My answer is that those children who are most at risk of failure should receive scholarships, to be used in the schools of their choice. If the scholarships are generous enough, and if enough students receive them, many schools will welcome scholarship students, and new schools will open to supply the demand for good education.

Interestingly, Theodore Sizer and Phillip Whitten offered a similar program in 1968, which they called "A Proposal for a Poor Children's Bill of Rights." They suggested that poor children should receive a coupon equivalent to about three times the average national expenditure, to be used in the school of their choice, and that the value of the coupon would be so attractive that schools would compete to enroll poor children. Among the benefits that they saw were the empowerment of parents of poor children and the elimination of inferior schools; the largest benefit, they predicted, would be the eventual savings on the cost of police, welfare, prisons, and other conditions associated with poverty. In response to the fear that poor parents were unequipped to choose the right school for their children, the authors wrote, "We feel, unhappily, that giving parents more power can only be seen as the least of evils. We trust them little, but still more than we trust the present monopoly of lay boards and professional schoolmen."[18]

Since Sizer and Whitten offered their proposal, social conditions in which poor and minority children live have worsened in many respects. Fundamental changes in the family over the past generation have added new disadvantages to those who are neediest. From 1960 to 1991 the proportion of poor children living in female-headed households grew from 23.7 percent to 59 percent. Among poor black children, the proportion living in female-headed households during that period increased from 29.4 percent to 83.1 percent.[19] At the same time that female-headed households became the predominant family structure in poor black communities, other social indicators went from bad to worse: the suicide rate for youngsters of all races ages fifteen to nineteen nearly tripled, and the homicide rate for this group more than tripled. During the same three decades the arrest rate for youngsters fourteen to seventeen nearly tripled.[20] When we add to

these dire statistics the other conditions of social distress—teen pregnancy, drug and alcohol abuse, AIDS, and homelessness—we must
recognize that many young people, particularly those who are poor
and members of racial minorities, are living in cruel, desperate, and
frightening circumstances.

What can schools do to support and protect young people from the
pressures that threaten them? There are many things that schools can
do, and there are many things that they cannot do. They cannot by
themselves end poverty, although children who do not get a good education are likely to be condemned to a lifetime of poverty. They
cannot by themselves create jobs or improve housing conditions or
stop the violence on the streets. There are other public and private
agencies with these purposes, and the schools must collaborate with
them. But schools in big cities can and must make changes that enable
them to nurture and guide the young people who are growing up in
a milieu fraught with peril.

There are strong objections to full school choice. I will review the
main objections in order to suggest why I think that a system based
on choice is preferable to a system built on compulsion.

*"A choice program—even if means tested—would destroy the public
school system."* Some people oppose even public school choice, on the
ground that those running the system know best what is in everyone's interest. Opposition is even stronger to choice programs that
allow families to use public funds to send their children to nonpublic
schools. Critics fear that if nonpublic choice were available, huge
numbers of families and children would flee from their local public
schools or leave public education altogether. Yet there is no evidence
for such fears. According to a poll commissioned by the Carnegie
Foundation for the Advancement of Teaching, only 19 percent of
public school parents would like to send their children to a private
school.[21] The same poll shows that most parents—87 percent—are
satisfied with their children's public schools. The Carnegie
Foundation interpreted these figures as evidence that few people are
interested in choice; I interpret them to mean that 19 percent of families would leave the public schools if they could afford to. Assuming
that many of these families would not qualify for means-tested scholarships, I conclude that in a system that permitted means-tested
choice of all schools, the public schools would continue to enroll 80

percent or more of all students, instead of today's 90 percent. There is no reason to fear a wholesale exodus from what is a fundamentally sound institution. Not only would the public school system not be destroyed, it would be strengthened by the ability to shut down bad schools.

"There is no precedent for allowing students to use government funds for education in private or religious institutions." For many years, the federal government has provided scholarships to college students (Pell grants) to attend the college or university or proprietary school of their choice. Students may use their Pell grants to attend Princeton or Georgetown or the local state university. The federal government does not care whether students attend public, private, or religious institutions, so long as the institution is accredited and approved by its state. Eighty percent of students enroll in public institutions, no doubt because public universities cost less than private ones. The same dynamic would hold in primary and secondary education, and the overwhelming majority—80 percent or more—would continue to attend state schools. Public higher education has not been destroyed by a system that allows students to use federal scholarships at non-public institutions; on the contrary, most people believe that the United States has the best and most pluralistic system of higher education in the world.

In addition, private and sectarian organizations currently receive public funds to manage Head Start centers, special education programs, hospitals, nursing homes, social service agencies, and a variety of other public activities.

In 1993 a unanimous U.S. Supreme Court made clear (in *Florence County School District Four* v. *Carter*) that a school district must reimburse parents who educated their learning-disabled child in a private school, after the parents rejected the school district's "individual education plan" as inadequate. The Court held that the usual state requirements "do not apply to private parental placements." The school district set as a goal for Shannon Carter that she would progress four months in reading and mathematics for every year of schooling; in her private placement, she progressed three grade levels in three years. The state complained that the private school selected by Shannon's parents did not have the approval of the state education agency; in response, the Supreme Court quoted a lower court approvingly: "It hardly seems consistent with the Act's goals to forbid parents from educating their child at a school that provides an appropriate education simply because that school lacks the stamp of approval of the same public school system that failed to meet the child's needs in the first place." In short, the Supreme Court approved paying public funds to a nonpublic school when it is freely chosen by parents and when—as in the case of Shannon Carter—it meets needs that are not met in the public schools.

"An education finance system that includes religious schools would be unconstitutional." There is no question that under current law it would be unconstitutional for a public authority to provide funds directly to religious schools. However, financial assistance that goes directly to parents, to spend at the school of their choice, would not violate the principle of separation of church and state. The 1971 *Lemon* v. *Kurtzman* ruling established a three-prong test to determine the constitutionality of legislation affecting church-state issues: (1) the statute must have a secular legislative purpose, (2) its principal effect must neither advance nor inhibit religion, and (3) it must not foster "an excessive governmental entanglement with religion." A law that grants funds to parents, not to religious schools, would meet all three constitutional requirements.

So, for example, the Supreme Court in 1983 (in *Mueller* v. *Allen*) upheld a Minnesota state law that allowed all parents of school-age children to deduct expenses for tuition, textbooks, and transportation from their state taxes, regardless of where their children attended school, even though most of the benefits were likely to flow to parents of children in sectarian schools. In 1986 a unanimous Supreme Court (in *Witters* v. *Washington Department of Services for the Blind*) upheld the grant of state aid to a blind student who was attending a Bible college, preparing to be a minister. Justice Thurgood Marshall wrote the opinion, stressing the importance of individual choice: "[A] State may issue a paycheck to one of its employees, who may then donate all or part of that paycheck to a religious institution, all without constitutional barrier; and the State may do so even knowing that the employee so intends to dispose of his salary. . . . In this case, the fact that aid goes to individuals means that the decision to support religious education is made by the individual, not the State." In 1993 the Supreme Court (in *Zobrest* v. *Catalina Foothills*

School District) found no conflict with the establishment clause when a public school district was asked to provide a sign language interpreter for a deaf student in a Roman Catholic high school. Again the Court relied on the fact that the decision was made by the parents: "By according parents freedom to select a school of their choice, the statute ensures that a government-paid interpreter will be present in a sectarian school only as a result of the private decision of individual parents."

In his textbook, legal scholar Laurence H. Tribe writes that recent Supreme Court decisions "suggest that the Court would uphold an educational voucher scheme that would permit parents to decide which schools, public or private, their children should attend. The establishment clause probably would not stand as an obstacle to a purely neutral program, at least one with a broad enough class of beneficiary schools and one that channeled aid through parents and children rather than directly to schools."[22]

"A choice system would put an intolerable burden on already strained state and local budgets." Apparently many people voted against the school choice proposal in California's 1993 referendum because they feared that it would cripple the state budget. That proposal, however, was not means tested. A scholarship that was available only for poor children would have measurable, predictable, and limited impact on the budget. It would be available to a limited number of students and could be expanded only as feasible. Such a program would cost the public no more—and if bureaucracy were substantially reduced, possibly less—than the state spends for those children now in public schools.[23] The state would be responsible for monitoring the quality of services provided, instead of acting as the sole provider of services itself.

To be sure, the availability of public transportation would serve as a constraint on choice. Public authorities cannot be expected to create a massive network of minivans. They should, however, supply free bus passes for schoolchildren, which is usually sufficient in big cities to permit many choices. Of course, choice would not be unlimited, but it never is. Students could not "choose" to attend a school ninety miles away, nor could they choose a school that was already oversubscribed. On the other hand, I see no reason to prohibit out-of-district choice, so long as the receiving school has space available and has the programming to meet the needs of the student.

"A choice program would skim off the best students." A means-tested scholarship makes "creaming off" highly improbable, since it is only the neediest students—those who are very poor or those who are now in low-performing schools—who will be eligible for these scholarships.

Good schools in big cities would not be adversely affected by a means-tested choice program, although they are likely to get many more applicants. Their students do not want to leave; their parents know that they are getting a good education and have no interest in removing them. In New York City, a small number of excellent, mixed-ability schools—called education option schools—regularly receive eight or ten applications for every opening; many of their applicants currently attend private and parochial schools. The success of these schools demonstrates that there is a vigorous, unfilled market for good public schools in the big cities.

As cities introduce varieties of public school choice, including charter schools and magnet schools, they expand the number of focus schools that are available to students. The growing number of these new-style public schools reduces still further the number of students who would leave the public school system if offered a means-tested scholarship. Indeed, the spread of full choice is likely to induce cities to increase the number of focus schools to meet the demand from students and parents. In this way, choice is likely to strengthen public education.

"A choice program would worsen segregation in big-city districts." It is hard to see how segregation could become worse if means-tested scholarships were provided to poor students enrolled in inner-city schools with almost exclusively African American and Hispanic populations. If anything, allowing choice to these students may well reduce inner-city segregation; at the very least, it cannot make it worse.

"No evidence shows that choice would increase the academic achievement of poor, inner-city students." Since there have been no large-scale demonstrations that permit full choice to all students, with means-

tested scholarships for poor children, it is impossible to say whether poor children would achieve higher test scores or higher graduation rates under such a plan. Choice is not a panacea, and there is no reason to expect that it would produce miraculous results overnight. But it is at least possible that permitting students to enroll in schools of choice will reduce student alienation and increase parental participation, both of which may contribute to higher attendance rates, improved academic performance, and increased graduation rates.

On the other hand, the existing system of hierarchical, bureaucratic controls must be judged by the same exacting standard; it has been in existence for well over a century. Surely it is fair to ask, Is the existing system capable of raising the achievement of poor, inner-city students? Does anyone expect dramatic improvement in big-city school systems as they are now organized? If the answers are yes, then choice should be rejected; if no, then choice should be explored in meaningful, large-scale, long-term demonstration projects.

"Some parents would not take advantage of a choice program." If a district announced that it intended to provide scholarships for the neediest children in the lowest-performing schools, there would probably be some parents who would not respond to invitations to choose a new school. But since the overwhelming majority of needy children have parents or guardians who care about their education, the number of nonparticipants would be small. In the few cases where no family member stepped forward to choose a school for a scholarship student, the decision could be made by a panel of community-based child advocates, such as representatives of local community organizations, parent associations, and churches. In any event, it would be the responsibility of the school system to ensure that every parent and guardian received good information about the choices available and that each student enrolled in a school with appropriate programs and a commitment to his or her education.

"Public funds might support schools that teach bizarre religious ideas, antiscientific ideas, or racist ideas." During the California voucher controversy, there was concern that public funds might support schools run by religious cults, creationists, or racists. It should not be difficult to avert this problem. First, no school should be eligible to receive

public scholarships if it excludes students on grounds of race or religion. Second, all schools that accept public-scholarship students should be required to prepare their students to pass state subject-matter assessments. The state should require that students are able to pass the city or state's examinations in mathematics, science, history, civics, English, and foreign languages at rates no worse than comparable public schools. Third, schools that teach racial or religious hatred should be barred from participation in the choice program. Nonpublic schools that do not meet these requirements should be excluded from the choice program.

"Nonpublic schools might shun students with handicapping conditions." Students with special needs should be eligible for a scholarship to go where their needs can best be met; if the size of the scholarship is large enough, new schools will be created to cater to the needs of these children. As the Supreme Court has already ruled, the parents of disabled students have the right to obtain a free, publicly financed education in the private sector if the state cannot provide it. Some states already pay private school tuition for students with special needs that cannot be met in the public schools.

"Some public schools would lose most of their students." If a district decides to provide scholarships on the basis of need, as well as to those enrolled in the worst schools, then some schools may have a sharp drop in enrollment. Allowing parents to remove their children would be an important signaling device to public school officials; they would restructure or close schools that no one wanted to attend instead of forcing poor children to remain in them. Very bad schools should be closed and replaced by new schools, with a new principal, new faculty, and new mission. The means-tested scholarship would strengthen the public schools by providing a mechanism that identifies and eliminates the worst schools.

"Public authorities could not hold nonpublic schools accountable if they were not directly controlled and regulated by the state." On the contrary, public authorities would find it easier to ensure accountability of nonpublic schools than they are now able to ensure accountability of public schools. At present there are usually few, if any, consequences for failing public schools. What happens to public schools where the

leadership is poor, teaching is ineffective, and children are not learning? The state cannot punish the school by taking away money because that only makes matters worse; if it gives the school more money, it seems to be rewarding failure, which discourages effective schools that win no rewards for success. The state can take over bad schools or send in monitors, but these strategies have not thus far proved effective.

With nonpublic schools and public charter schools, the state could act decisively and impose real accountability. If such schools failed to meet their contractual obligations or demonstrated their educational inadequacy, the state could cancel their charter or withdraw their eligibility to receive public scholarships. In fact, public authorities would have more power over nonpublic and charter schools than they currently have over public schools, with the ultimate power to exclude them from the choice program. Those nonpublic schools that did not wish to accept public accountability would not participate in the program.

"Schools with different values are socially divisive." Actually, our most divisive school-related conflicts occur because we impose a single set of state-defined values on everyone in public schools. Scarcely a week goes by without the eruption of a bitter controversy in a public school somewhere over social, political, or religious differences. The state board of education and the local board of education are often combat zones where warring groups fight about condom distribution, textbooks, outcome-based education, prayer in the schools, political messages on T-shirts, and other contentious issues. As pluralism in the school and society grows, the conflicts will become more intense. Inevitably, some parents win and some lose. Some families are forced to live with decisions by the school board that are deeply offensive to them. Those of us who are liberal and secular feel comforted when our side wins and frightened when the other side wins. Yet why should people who are not liberal and secular be compelled to submit their children to values that they find deeply obnoxious? Why should those who are liberal and secular be compelled to submit their children to values that they find oppressive and narrow minded? Perhaps they are both right, and each should be in a school in which there is no state-imposed uniformity of opinion. Under a means-tested choice program, schools should differ from each other in a

variety of ways, so long as they respect the Constitution and the laws of the state and comply with the state's education standards.

If we cease trying to impose state-defined values and instead permit diversity of values, there may well be more harmony and less divisiveness. In a review of school choice in other nations, Charles Glenn reports that "choice reduces the level of conflict over the purpose and control of schooling, and thus encourages broad societal support."[24] In schooling, one size does not fit all.

"Newcomers to the United States would not be assimilated into the mainstream if they attended ethnic or religious schools." Most people, including new immigrants, would continue to patronize traditional public schools, because they are free, convenient, and satisfactory to the overwhelming majority of parents. Those parents who do not choose to patronize public schools do not threaten the stability of the nation. There is no evidence that adults who attended religious schools or other private schools are less patriotic, less civic minded, less likely to vote in elections, or less willing to serve their country than those who attended public schools. Nor is there any evidence that those who attended religious or other private schools are less tolerant than those who attended public schools.

The public schools may not be the primary instrument of civic assimilation in our society. American society itself—its laws, its cultural pluralism, its openness, its tolerance for diversity, its encouragement of freedom of expression and enterprise—may be the most effective instrument of social assimilation. Although a few groups, like the Amish or Hasidic Jews, choose to live apart from society, most Americans—regardless of the kind of school they attended—have no trouble assimilating into American society. And even separatist groups like the Amish or Hasidic Jews, it seems to me, should be allowed to use means-tested scholarships, if they wish, to attend the schools of their choice. As a mature democracy, we should be long past the time when we feared that any deviation from the mainstream threatened the stability of our society. Our commitment to pluralism and diversity should be strong enough to tolerate the very small number of devout separatists who do not wish to assimilate.

In 1859, John Stuart Mill considered some of the same questions in his famous essay "On Liberty." In that magnificent defense of freedom of opinion, Mill asserted, "If all mankind minus one, were of one opinion, and only one person were of the contrary opinion, mankind would be no more justified in silencing that one person, than he, if he had the power, would be justified in silencing mankind." When he turned his thoughts to education, Mill argued,

> If the government would make up its mind to *require* for every child a good education, it might save itself the trouble of *providing* one. It might leave to parents to obtain the education where and how they pleased, and content itself with helping to pay the school fees of the poorer classes of children, and defraying the entire school expenses of those who have no one else to pay for them. . . . That the whole or any large part of the education of the people should be in State hands, I go as far as any one in deprecating. All that has been said of the importance of individuality of character, and diversity in opinions and modes of conduct, involves, as of the same unspeakable importance, diversity of education. A general State education is a mere contrivance for molding people to be exactly like one another: and as the mould in which it casts them is that which pleases the predominant power in the government, whether this be a monarch, a priesthood, an aristocracy, or the majority of the existing generation, in proportion as it is efficient and successful, it establishes a despotism over the mind, leading by natural tendency to one over the body. An education established and controlled by the State, should only exist, if it exist at all, as one among many competing experiments, carried on for the purpose of example and stimulus, to keep the others up to a certain standard of excellence.[25]

Mill believed that students should be required to take annual examinations to ascertain whether they had acquired "a certain minimum of general knowledge," but he maintained that examinations on disputed topics—like religion or politics—"should not turn on the truth or falsehood of opinions, but on the matter of fact that such and such an opinion is held, on such grounds, by such authors, or schools, or churches." He saw no danger in students' learning the religion of their parents, but he warned that "all attempts by the State to bias the conclusions of its citizens on disputed subjects, are evil."

Like Mill, I worry about the power of the state to mold opinion and to establish official knowledge. With the current move toward national standards, such a worry is more than theoretical. Yet national and state standards offer a realistic means of public accountability for schools of choice, be they public or private. The public has a right to know that its money is well spent, that the state does not support institutions that violate civil rights laws, and that children are educated to high standards. Those schools that accept students with public scholarships should expect to be reviewed periodically by public authorities, who remain responsible for safety, health, and overall educational quality.

I began this essay with a statement of commitment to the goals of pluralism, equality, and excellence. This proposal promotes pluralism because it would create incentives for a diverse, pluralistic system of schools with many different kinds of sponsors, all dedicated to educating the public. It supports excellence, because public officials would be responsible for setting standards for quality and reviewing the performance of all educational institutions that receive public funds, with the power to withdraw public approval from those schools that failed to meet their stated performance goals. It serves equality, because it would endow poor children with sufficient resources to escape from failing schools and to gain entry to the public or nonpublic school of their choice. The intention is to empower public officials to act as guardians, auditors, and evaluators, while empowering those children and families who are ill served by current institutions.

Nobody's children should be compelled to attend a bad public school. A good school system must offer equal educational opportunity to everybody's children.

Notes

1. For a summary of data about test scores, dropout rates, and graduation rates, see Department of Education, National Center for Education Statistics, *The Condition of Education 1992* (1992), pp. 39–60. For information about performance assessments, see John A. Dossey and others, *Can Students Do Mathematical Problem-Solving? Results from Constructed-Response Questions in NAEP's 1992 Mathematics Assessment* (Office of Educational Research and Improvement, Department of Education, 1993).

2. Department of Education, Public Affairs, "State of American Education," remarks prepared for Richard W. Riley, secretary of education, speech delivered at Georgetown University, February 15, 1994, pp. 2, 13.

3. Paul T. Hill, Gail E. Foster, and Tamar Gendler, *High Schools with Character* (Santa Monica, Calif.: RAND, 1990); Theodore R. Sizer, *Horace's School: Redesigning the American High School* (Boston: Houghton Mifflin, 1992), p. 128; and Anthony S. Bryk, Valerie E. Lee, and Peter B. Holland, *Catholic Schools and the Common Good* (Harvard University Press, 1993).

4. Hill, Foster, and Gendler, *High Schools with Character*, p. vii.

5. There is a large body of research supporting the proposition that students fare better in a small school with a clear mission than in a large, anonymous school where there is minimal engagement between adults and children. In addition to Sizer, *Horace's School*; Hill, Foster, and Gendler, *High Schools with Character*; and Bryk, Lee, and Holland, *Catholic Schools*; see Linda Darling-Hammond, *Standards of Practice for Learner-Centered Schools* (New York: NCREST, Teachers College, 1992), p. 20: "Studies of school organizations, including two massive studies of secondary schools conducted by the National Institute of Education, have found that student achievement, positive feelings towards self and school, and positive behavior (including attendance, retention, and low levels of violence) are higher in smaller settings and those where students have close, sustained relationships with smaller numbers of teachers over their school career."

Fred M. Newmann, "Reducing Student Alienation in High Schools: Implications of Theory," *Harvard Educational Review*, vol. 51 (November 1981), p. 550, comments, "Organizational theory and the literature on the social psychology of organizations suggest six general issues relevant to reducing student alienation: the basis of membership, the nature of organizational goals, organizational size, decision-making structure, members' roles, and the nature of work. My review of the literature on these six issues leads me to propose the following guidelines: voluntary choice, clear and consistent goals, small size, participation, extended and cooperative roles [for teachers], and integrated work."

William J. Fowler Jr. and Herbert J. Walberg, "School Size, Characteristics, and Outcomes," *Educational Evaluation and Policy Analysis*, vol. 13 (Summer 1991), p. 200, noted, "Increased school size has negative effects upon student participation, satisfaction, and attendance and adversely affects the school climate and a student's ability to identify with the school and its activities. Students who are dissatisfied, who do not participate in school activities, who are chronically absent, and who do not identify with the school will achieve less, whether on achievement tests or on postschooling outcomes."

6. Keith A. Halpern and Eliza R. Culbertson, *Blueprint for Change: Charter Schools: A Handbook for Action* (Washington: Democratic Leadership Council, n.d.), p. 1.

7. Unpublished data from the National Education Longitudinal Study of 1988 (NELS: 88), Base Year Data (U.S. Department of Education, 1992).

8. Ibid.; unpublished data from the almanac of the National Assessment of Educational Progress, U.S. Department of Education, for reading and mathematics, 1992. On the National Assessment of Educational Progress tests of reading and mathematics in 1992, disadvantaged urban students in the

eighth grade in Catholic schools scored significantly higher than their public school peers in reading (but not in mathematics). In twelfth grade, disadvantaged urban students in Catholic schools scored significantly higher in both reading and mathematics. See also Anthony S. Bryk, Valerie Lee, and Julia Smith, "High School Organization and Its Effect on Teachers and Students: An Interpretive Summary of the Research," in William H. Clune and John F. Witte, eds., *Choice and Control in American Education: The Theory of Choice and Control in American Education* (Philadelphia: Falmer Press, 1990); James S. Coleman, Thomas Hoffer, and Sally Kilgore, *High School Achievement: Public, Catholic, and Private Schools Compared* (Basic Books, 1982); and James S. Coleman and Thomas Hoffer, *Public and Private High Schools: The Impact of Communities* (Basic Books, 1987).

9. Department of Education, *America's High School Sophomores: A Ten-Year Comparison, 1980–1990* (1992), p. 17.

10. Department of Education, National Center for Education Statistics, *Projections of Education Statistics to 2004* (1993), p. xi.

11. Senator Daniel Patrick Moynihan and Senator Robert Packwood made a similar proposal in the late 1970s. See also John E. Coons and Stephen D. Sugarman, *Family Choice in Education: A Model State System for Vouchers* (Berkeley: Institute of Governmental Studies, 1971); John E. Coons and Stephen D. Sugarman, *Education by Choice: The Case for Family Control* (University of California Press, 1978); and John E. Chubb and Terry M. Moe, *Politics, Markets and America's Schools* (Brookings, 1990).

12. Denis P. Doyle, "Family Choice in Education: The Case of Denmark, Holland, and Australia," commissioned by the National Institute of Education, March 22, 1984. See also Charles Leslie Glenn, *Choice of Schools in Six Nations: France, Netherlands, Belgium, Britain, Canada, West Germany* (Department of Education, 1989).

13. Doyle, "Family Choice," pp. 4, 26.

14. David Tyack, "The Kingdom of God and the Common School: Protestant Ministers and the Educational Awakening in the West," *Harvard Educational Review*, vol. 36 (Fall 1966), p. 450.

15. Lloyd P. Jorgenson, *The State and the Non-Public School, 1825–1925* (University of Missouri Press, 1987), p. 69.

16. This was the case at the public high school that I graduated from in Houston, Texas, in 1956.

17. Jorgenson, *The State*, pp. 216, 221; also see pp. 138–40.

18. Theodore Sizer and Phillip Whitten, "A Proposal for a Poor Children's Bill of Rights," *Psychology Today*, August 1968, pp. 59–63.

19. Department of Education, *Youth Indicators, 1993: Trends in the Well-Being of American Youth* (1993), p. 48.

20. Ibid., pp. 116–17. The rates for suicide, homicide, and arrests are national, not localized to disadvantaged urban communities. They are not likely to be better in those communities and are probably worse.

21. Carnegie Foundation for the Advancement of Teaching, *School Choice* (Princeton, N.J.: Carnegie Foundation, 1992), p. 104.

22. Laurence H. Tribe, *American Constitutional Law*, 2d. ed. (Mineola, N.Y.: Foundation Press, 1988), p. 1223.

23. There are large cost differences between public and nonpublic schools, especially Catholic schools. Some observers attribute the difference solely to labor costs and predict that the cost of Catholic schools would equal those of public schools if they were to pay their teachers the same as public teachers are paid. However, part of the differential is attributable to the overadministered, bureaucratic structure of public education. A report by the Organization for Economic Cooperation and Development found that the United States has a higher proportion of nonteaching personnel than any other OECD nation. See Center for Educational Research and Innovation, *Education at a Glance: OECD Indicators* (Paris: OECD, 1993).

24. Glenn, *Choice of Schools in Six Nations*, p. 218.

25. John Stuart Mill, *The Six Great Humanistic Essays of John Stuart Mill* (Washington Square Press, 1963), pp. 230–33.

Chapter 4

Child Care: The Key to Ending Child Poverty

Barbara R. Bergmann

ALL ASPECTS of child care are remarkably controversial. Some think that all children should be cared for full time by their own mothers and that any other form of care is pernicious and should be discouraged. Others think families should purchase child care if they want to and have the resources to do so, but the government should not be involved in producing it or paying for it. Still others believe that government provision or subsidization of child care in closely regulated facilities is indispensable to progress on certain important problems we face as a community.

I believe a cogent case can be made for a large government role in the provision of child care. The main rationale for such a program is that we are unlikely to make progress against the problem of child poverty in America without it. Such a program would have other beneficial effects. Publicly provided child care would make a major improvement in the position of women, who are, after all, half of the citizens, and who have yet to achieve full and equal participation in society. It could also contribute to the detection and prevention of child abuse.

The opposition to a program of substantial government support for child care has been strong in the past and looks even stronger in the near future. For some, such a policy goes against the grain of their thinking about what is best for children and about the duties they think women owe to their children. Others, far from wanting such an expansion of government activities, believe that the government sector should be shrunk to the smallest size possible. Many consider the large government expenditure that such a policy would entail to be unaffordable.

As this is written, those who would minimize government activities and expenditures for social programs and who are most opposed to out-of-home roles for married women have come into the ascendant in Washington. They would be unlikely to back a large new child care program. However, the penalties we pay in child poverty and in low-quality care for the lack of such a program will grow and are likely to become more obvious in time. The benefits of a subsidized child care program may eventually become apparent to the public, and politicians more friendly to such a program may gain influence. It seems worthwhile, therefore, to lay out the nature of those penalties and benefits and to strip away some of the obfuscatory rhetoric on both sides of the child care debate.

What Is the Problem?

The proponents of government provision or financial support of child care have been accustomed to build their case for government action on a lack of an "adequate supply" of high-quality child care at "affordable prices." Unfortunately, this expression of what the problem is has invited misinterpretation and thus has tended to obscure the real issues. A number of economists have interpreted the proponents' statements in terms of the supply-and-demand model of a competitive market and have tried to assess the validity of what they take to be the proponents' factual claims about such markets.[1] They have interpreted the "shortage" language of the proponents as a claim that there is a gap between the amount demanded and the amount supplied for high-quality care, presumably at "the" price that others are paying.[2] They have interpreted the "price" language of the proponents as a claim that prices are higher than a normally working competitive market would produce.[3]

When one looks about for systematic evidence of persistent discrepancies between the amount of child care supplied and demanded, one can find waiting lists for care at below-market, concessional, subsidized prices. This means that the amount appropriated to provide government subsidies for child care is not sufficient to provide for all those whom the government has defined as eligible. However, this does not count as evidence that the market for private unsubsidized care is not working well. Data are not systematically collected that could document some parents' inability to find high-quality day care places in private facilities at prices currently being charged to those parents whose children are being accommodated. In fact, statistical data of this sort are not collected for most commodities, for the good reason that shortages, while they do occur, are a fairly rare phenomenon in a free-market economy. Occasionally a shortage will be documented in newspaper photographs, such as those of the waiting line for Super Bowl tickets. However, this kind of evidence is not likely to turn up for the day care industry.

Lacking direct data on shortages in the market for private care, we are reduced to examining data on the expansion of supply. The American market economy has in fact responded in the last two decades to the increased demand for purchased child care by increasing the amount supplied. The number of licensed child care centers almost tripled between the mid-1970s and 1990, and four times as many children were enrolled.[4] The evidence of a hefty expansion of supply does not allow us to rule out the existence of shortages as defined above. However, the verdict on shortages has to be that their existence has not been demonstrated and that they are unlikely to be a serious problem in most times and places.

In the matter of prices, economists would argue that prices charged by private day care providers should and normally will cover their costs, plus a reasonable profit, and that there is nothing unhealthy or wrong about that. Economists define prices as being too high only in cases where competition is lacking or very weak, because then suppliers can charge prices that are seriously out of line with costs. Direct evidence on the state of competition in day care, as in most other industries, is lacking. However, the day care industry is composed mostly of small-scale enterprises, and it is relatively easy for new providers to enter. Industries with such characteristics are usually not thought of as suffering from lack of competition.

The failure to document shortages and noncompetitive prices has allowed those opposing government help with child care problems to dismiss as baseless the proponents' justifications for government intervention. I would argue, however, that economists have misinterpreted the proponents' statements of justification. Child care proponents are not making a factual statement about the good or bad workings of the child care market. Rather, they are expressing a value judgment that it is wrong (morally, not economically) for parents to have to pay the prices that are being charged for high-quality care, even though such prices may be justified by the costs. The reference that proponents make to shortage is not a complaint that supply does not match demand at current prices. Rather, it is a lament that, costs being what they are,[5] little or no good-quality care is for sale at the much lower price that it would be right (again, morally, not economically) for parents to have to pay. The clue to the proponents' meaning is the term *affordable*. It does not come up in connection with most commodities—shoes, strawberries, shrimp, or automobiles. Many people would like to consume more of them than they do, or consume better-quality varieties. They complain about the size of their incomes, but they do not complain about the prices or availability of most of the commodities they have to leave out of their budgets. Affordability is an issue only about commodities that have two characteristics: their cost is large relative to a person's wage and their absence or poor quality undermines a person's or a family's entire well-being. When people ask that a commodity be "affordable," they are saying that everybody ought to be able to consume it regardless of income.

We hear about affordability in connection with housing, when the problem of homelessness is discussed. We hear about it in connection with medical care and the situation of those without health insurance. Housing and medical care are sometimes called merit goods, goods that in the common estimation ought to be available to all people in a decent society, regardless of their incomes or their behavior.[6] When we hear about affordability in connection with child care, we are hearing the nomination of child care as a merit good.

Should child care be considered a merit good? Its cost is certainly large as a share of the budget. Employed single mothers with children under five who depend on purchased care spend on average 21 percent of their income for that purpose (table 4-1).[7] If those currently on welfare were to find and take a job, those among them who would be forced to purchase child care would have to spend an even higher percentage of their income for it. Welfare mothers are, of all single mothers, disproportionately black and less well educated, so, partly because of racial discrimination, the jobs they would get would pay less than the average of those currently held by single mothers.

Is out-of-home child care necessary to a decent life? Whose life? The heavy cost of high-quality child care and the low wages available to women cause some mothers who would rather work to remain home, perhaps on welfare, and some mothers to put their children

TABLE 4-1. *Mean Weekly Child Care Expenditures, Employed Mothers Paying for Child Care, Youngest Child Younger Than Age Five, 1990*

Family income	Weekly expenditure (dollars)	Percentage of income
Below poverty	37.27	23
Above poverty	65.45	9
Under $15,000	37.92	25
$15,000–24,999	50.72	13
$25,000–34,999	50.71	9
$35,000–49,999	64.53	10
$50,000 or more	85.11	6

Source: Sandra L. Hofferth and others, *National Child Care Survey, 1990* (Washington: Urban Institute, 1991), pp. 164–65.

into low-quality care. It forces some who decide they cannot do without good child care to spend most of their income on child care and rent. Those who use the affordability rhetoric are saying that confining women to such choices debars them and their children from a decent life and that such debarment ought to be remedied by government action.

Thus the complaint about the supply of affordable child care is not at all a complaint about the workings of the marketplace or about supply or even about prices. Rather it is a plea for the rescue of certain groups through government subsidy for child care or government provision of child care. Whether and for whom one endorses that plea depends on one's views of the alternatives. As I shall argue below, I believe the case for government provision of child care for those who, with their children, would otherwise lead a poverty-stricken life to be very strong. As will be apparent, help with child care for those at the bottom end of the income scale, if it is to be rationally structured, requires some help with child care for those higher up the income scale.

While a significant reduction in child poverty should be a sufficient reason for a program of this sort, there are additional benefits to the provision of child care. It would increase the possibilities of independence for mothers, ensure high-quality care for the children, prepare children for school, reduce child abuse, and aid in its detection. For those such as Nancy Folbre who believe that parents are performing a service to all of society by providing future citizens, and deserve society's help, the provision of child care to a sizable share of parents would be a way of accomplishing that.[8]

Government-Provided Child Care: An Antipoverty Strategy

Under the current structure of social programs, single mothers and their children are highly susceptible to poverty, whether they are on welfare or are off welfare and supported by the mother's wages. Table 4-2 shows the incidence of poverty in such families, according to two methodologies of defining who is in poverty: the official government method, which does not take account of the need a job-holding single mother might have to pay for out-of-home child care or medical insurance, and the Basic Needs Budget (BNB) method, which does.[9] Families on welfare are overwhelmingly poor whichever method of counting is used—97 percent according to the official method, 89 percent according to the BNB method. Of those single-parent families where the mother held a job, 24 percent were counted as poor, using the official method. Using the BNB method, which looked more closely at the special needs of families with employed single mothers, 56 percent were counted as poor. Even in families where the mother held a full-time job for the whole year and suffered no unemployment or time off the job, 23 percent were in poverty according to the BNB method.

There is an urgent need to restructure social programs so as to reduce the incidence of poverty among children. One suggestion, from Charles Murray, would be to cut off all cash aid to single parents.[10] (Of children living with single mothers in 1992, approximately 8 percent were living with never-married mothers; the remainder lived with mothers who were divorced or separated.)[11] Cutting off aid to single parents would presumably force unmarried sex partners to consider the newly rigorous consequences of a birth out of wedlock and force parents contemplating a marital breakup to worry more about how the children were to be supported. Murray's draconian suggestion if implemented might (or might not) reduce the number of out-of-wedlock births and marital breakups. Without doubt it would entail large-scale child destitution and the separation of many children from their mothers. For this reason, it would probably not be likely to find support with a majority.

TABLE 4-2. *Poverty in Single-Parent (SP) Families under the Basic Needs Budget Method, as Compared with the Official Method, 1989*

Percent unless otherwise specified

	Poverty definition	
Demographic characteristic	*Basic needs budget*	*Official method*
Poverty rate of SP families	47	39
Number of poor SP families	4,147,000	3,436,000
Number of poor persons living in SP families	14,057,000	11,905,000
Poverty rate of children under 18 living in SP families	56	48
Number of poor children living in SP families	8,771,000	7,514,000
Poverty rate of SP families with jobs	37	24
Poverty rate of SP families with full-time year-round workers	23	9
Poverty rate of AFDC families (families with 50 percent or more of income from AFDC)	89	97
Poor SP families in which the single parent was employed outside the home	56	45
Poor SP families with more than half their income from AFDC	32	42

Source: Trudi J. Renwick and Barbara R. Bergmann, "A Budget-Based Definition of Poverty, with an Application to Single-Parent Families," *Journal of Human Resources,* vol. 28 (Winter 1993), pp. 1–24.

Leaving aside the Murray position, a solution to the problem of poverty among children requires that more economic resources be mobilized for the support of those children's families, preferably in a way that will not discourage them from making efforts to earn income. Some of the extra resources these families need can come from additional earnings of the mother and from government cash transfer payments that supplement wages. Certainly, some should come from improved child-support enforcement and from a system of child support assurance, such as that proposed by Irwin Garfinkel.[12] I argue, however, that government provision of child care is the most beneficial and most politically acceptable way of providing a large share of the resources that are needed.

To look at the magnitude of additional resources needed to raise single-parent families out of poverty, I have made use of the Basic Needs Budget, which appears in the top panel of table 4-3 for the case of families with two preschool children.[13] For single mothers with jobs, the standard of life envisioned in the BNB includes safe, high-quality full-day care for their preschool children and after-school care for their elementary school children. As Harriet Presser has shown, a considerable proportion of all single mothers do not have relatives capable of giving free high-quality child care, who could provide it at little or no sacrifice to themselves.[14] Accordingly, the family of the mother with a job has been assigned money in the BNB—$400 per child per month in this adaptation—to purchase licensed child care, as well as additional amounts for transportation to work.

Table 4-3 lays out two alternative ways of providing enough extra resources to get single parents out of poverty, as poverty is defined using the basic needs budget. The first column in table 4-3 shows what we can call the full-welfare solution. A mother with two children on welfare in a state with median benefits currently gets $7,094 in aid to families with dependent children (AFDC) and food stamp benefits. She could achieve the BNB standard if given an additional $3,753 in benefits. We may note parenthetically that welfare—provided on condition that there be a child (under age eighteen) in the home and that the mother not hold a job of any substance—is a support for one particular form of child care. This solution of the poverty problem has its adherents. However, prevailing sentiment appears to be that the government should not offer a comfortable life, exempt from job-holding, to women who lack private support for themselves and their children, unless they are widows. In fact, the public apparently no longer wishes to continue providing the far-less-than-comfortable standard of living that is now being given to welfare mothers.

The second column shows a set of benefits that would allow a mother earning the minimum wage full time year-round to meet that standard (assuming she had health insurance under some future scheme providing universal coverage). In addition to the currently mandated earned income tax credit (EITC) and food stamp benefits, she would need additional benefits totaling $9,746. The provision of totally subsidized high-quality child care for the children would

TABLE 4-3. *Alternative Methods of Providing the Level of Living Prescribed in the Basic Needs Budget for a Single-Parent Family with Two Preschool Children, 1993*

Dollars

Item	Full-welfare solution	Wage-plus-child-care solution
Food	3,508	3,508
Housing	4,280	4,280
Clothing, health care, personal care	2,596	2,596
Child care	0	9,600
Transportation	463	1,024
Cost of goods and services	10,847	21,008
Social security tax	0	676
Federal income tax	0	0
Dependent care credit	0	0
Earned income tax credit	0	−1,384
State income tax	0	175
Total required	10,847	20,476
Annual wage	0	8,840
AFDC, 1993 level in median state	4,404	0
Food stamps, 1993 levels	2,690	1,890
Child care provided	0	9,600
Additional cash inflow required	3,753	146
Government benefits less taxes	10,847	12,168

Source: Renwick and Bergmann, "A Budget-Based Definition of Poverty," pp. 1–24.

provide almost all of these benefits. (A suggestion for the structuring of benefits for those with wage levels higher than the minimum wage is discussed in another section.)

The wage-plus-child-care solution would be more costly to the public purse than the full-welfare solution, but it has the selling point with the general public that it requires that the mother hold a job. Another major selling point is that it would deliver most of its benefits directly to the children, with little cash to the parents beyond benefits currently offered, as shown in table 4-3. Programs with government-supplied child care as a centerpiece are in effect in some European countries and in conjunction with national health insurance, child allowances, and child-support enforcement keep poverty among their children low.[15]

Of course the wage-plus-child-care solution requires that single mothers get jobs. It is commonly assumed that they would not be fit to hold any jobs at all without elaborate and expensive training for which billions of dollars of government funds would have to be expended and that, in addition, there are no jobs for them to fit into. These assumptions can be challenged. As table 4-3 shows, the jobs with the lowest wage possible—those at the minimum wage—would suffice to get most families up to the BNB standard, if child care is provided. Teenagers get and perform satisfactorily in such jobs by the millions without special, expensive, government-financed training, and there is no reason to think that single parents are inferior as workers to the general run of teenagers. Obviously one would hope that at least some single mothers would get better-than-minimum-wage jobs immediately on going off welfare or graduate into them from minimum-wage jobs. Concern for poor children should motivate better enforcement of the laws against race and sex discrimination to enable more of them to do so. However, even the poorest job would support a standard of living above that allowed by current welfare grants, as long as child care is provided.

Those who offer the "no jobs" objection assume that new entrants to the labor force must endure unemployment until the number of jobs grows to accommodate them. In fact, there is considerable turnover, particularly in low-wage jobs, and new entrants compete with those previously in the labor force for the vacancies that result. Moreover, the provision of child care to them and to other low-income families would create several million jobs in child care centers. Some jobs in public service employment could be provided in geographic areas with high unemployment rates. Better unemployment insurance coverage for single parents and support for parents disabled from work would also be needed.

The provision of child care, not just on a transitional basis, but for as long as the children were of an age to require it, would crucially affect the incentives of mothers currently on welfare to take jobs. Even without the push of a time limit on welfare, the provision of child care, a guarantee of health insurance, and the beefed-up EITC would make the financial rewards mothers get for taking a paying job far greater than they now are. Without the huge financial drain of child care, an employed mother in a low-wage job would get to keep a far higher proportion of her paycheck.

Child Care: A Better Form of Poverty Benefits

Most economists have favored benefits to the poor in the form of cash, rather than government distribution of goods or services such as child care, on the ground that those receiving cash from the taxpayers will get maximum benefit out of it if they, rather than the taxpayers, choose what it is to be spent on. However, in this case giving the benefit in the form of cash (even with a requirement of jobholding) would probably not be as popular with the taxpayers as giving the service. Since verification of jobholding would be difficult, giving the unearmarked cash would be providing welfare on a better scale than now, since the parent could refrain from work and use the money for living expenses.

Child care services cannot, as cash can, be exchanged for items that do not benefit the child. Single parents are seen by many as having acted irresponsibly by giving birth to children without having adequate private resources to nurture them properly and having aggressed against the taxpayers, who are forced to come to the rescue. Those who think that way will be more likely to favor benefits for services for the innocent children, rather than benefits going to the purse of the delinquent parents to spend as they wish.

More positively, high-quality child care that is free to parents could provide a safe, nurturing, and comfortable daytime environment for the children. Providing such services would put a floor under their quality of care. It could insulate them for most of their waking hours from the stresses of a poverty-stricken milieu and could serve to acculturate them to mainstream values and habits. It should improve children's readiness for school. In public facilities, or publicly regulated facilities, children could receive preventive health care, nutritious meals, and attention to cognitive and behavioral development. Abuse would be more likely than now to be detected.

The Costs of a Child Care Benefit Program

The provision of child care, with the aim of contributing to the solution of the problem of child poverty, could not be restricted to people coming off welfare, since as we have seen, many of the single parents who already hold jobs do not earn enough to attain the Basic Needs Budget standard. Nor could it be restricted to one year per child, nor be a half-day program, as Head Start and most kindergarten programs now are. It could be restricted to single-parent families, but only at the expense of discouraging marriage and ignoring the well-being of poor children of married couples. It would be desirable for at least some child care subsidies to be extended to the middle-income groups, to establish political support for the program and to bring in a constituent group that would be effective in demanding high quality standards. Sliding-scale fees for those above some modest income level could be established, which would gradually reduce benefits as income rose. This would be necessary to prevent "notch" effects—depriving a family of benefits worth thousands of dollars because their income was a dollar over the cutoff point.

One can easily make a rough estimate of the cost of providing care to children of low- and middle-income families. There are 19 million children under five years old in the United States. A study relating current costs of private and public child care centers to measures of quality suggests costs on the order of $4,800 per child per year would be required if good-quality care were to be procured (averaging the costs of providing care for infants and for the older children).[16] Providing the lowest-income quintile with free high-quality child care and the next two quintiles with partially subsidized care on a sliding scale would cost $36 billion annually.[17] There are 29 million children between five and twelve. Providing three-fifths of them with care on the same basis before and after school and in the summer, at a cost of $3,400 each, would cost an additional $39 billion, for a total cost of $75 billion a year.

As more mothers went to work, there would also be a rise in expenditures for the earned income tax credit. Any resultant increase in the unemployment rate would mean somewhat higher outlays for unemployment insurance for the experienced unemployed, who would be competing with an expanded labor force—now including the former welfare mothers—for job vacancies.

Large-scale direct government provision of child care would probably lead to some developments that would raise both quality and costs. Recent surveys of child care centers and family day care homes suggest that at least some of them do a poor job of caring for children.[18] Child care workers employed by government would command pay and benefits greater than are now enjoyed by private sector workers in this field, possibly setting a higher standard for the latter. This would be an entirely welcome development, as it would attract more trained and talented people and would lower the high turnover that is currently endemic to the industry and that does not serve children's need for stability.[19] Lower child-caregiver ratios than are now common might also be mandated. Government help with child care fees (restricted to licensed facilities) would increase parents' demand for higher-quality care. That, and improved oversight, might drive operators of seriously subpar facilities from the industry.

There would be some offsetting savings: costs for AFDC and the food stamps single mothers get, currently running at about $32 billion, would decline. Not all children in the middle-income ranges would be sent to day care; some would certainly continue to be cared for at home by their parents. Furthermore, some of the programs we now have, such as Head Start and half-day kindergarten, could be restructured as full-time programs to serve custodial functions in addition to their cognitive-development functions. As a result, some of the $24 billion governments are already spending on educational programs for young children (table 4-4) would serve child care functions better than they currently do.

The cost estimated here for outright provision of care to children in the bottom fifth of the income distribution, plus partial provision on a sliding scale of fees to those in the next two-fifths, represents a daunting sum in the present political context. The much larger sum that would be required for universal provision of child care by government would be more daunting still. Those opposed to income testing for government programs (with the single exception of the income tax) usually speak in terms of generating political support for the program and for the inclusion in the program of benefits for those citizens able to insist on high-quality services. The current situation of the public schools—universally available but delivering low-quality services to the children most in need of high-quality services—does not lend support to the quality argument for universal provision. Nor does it seem likely that the political difficulty of enacting a program of child care provision that would significantly

TABLE 4-4. *Expenditure for Government Programs Relating to Child Care in the United States, 1990–91[a]*

Billions of dollars

Program	Expenditure
Head Start	2.4
Public kindergarten[b]	15.0
Credit on federal income tax for child care expenses[c]	2.3
Child care and development block grants	0.7
Title XX grants to states used for child care subsidies	2.0
Child care to avert AFDC	0.8
Child care food program	0.5
Foster grandparents	0.1
Total	23.9

Source (except where otherwise indicated): "Cash and Noncash Benefits for Persons with Limited Income: Eligibility Rules, Recipient and Expenditure Data, FY 1990–92," 93-382 EPW (Congressional Research Service, 1993).

a. Data are for the twelve-month period ending September 1991.
b. Derived from material in *Digest of Education Statistics*, 1993.
c. *Statistics of Income Bulletin*, vol. 12 (Spring 1993), p. 12.

better the lives of poor children would be reduced by doubling its cost in the interest of providing a good to the upper-income groups that they can readily supply for themselves.

Roadblocks to a Sizable Child Care Program

An important roadblock in the way of enacting a sizable child care program extending subsidies into the middle classes is that such a program would constitute in the eyes of some an improper and unwise enticement for even more mothers to stop providing full-time care for their children at home. There are those—proponents of the "old-fashioned family"—who think that the use of nonmother care, whether through household purchase or government provision, has pernicious effects. Some who think this way feel that out-of-home child care is inferior to in-home care by the mother, a proposition that is true for an undetermined proportion of children at each age, but cannot be true for all children regardless of age. Others believe that much that is wrong with society springs from the changes in the role of women in society and the economy; they think that legitimation and widening use of out-of-home child care pushes society further in this undesirable direction. The implication of these lines of thought is that government policy should be structured so as to encourage mothers (at least married mothers) to stay at home with their children and to discourage (or at least not encourage) the use of out-of-home child care.

Penelope Leach's 1994 book *Children First*, which extols constant contact between mother and child and preaches that mothers can never do enough for their children and should stay home until the youngest child is eight years old, is the latest volley from the side of those who excoriate mothers who take jobs and send their children to day care.[20] Leach presents herself as one of those who oppose out-of-home care out of concern for children's well-being, safety, and proper development. How serious are such concerns?

A volume produced under the auspices of the National Research Council had the following conclusions about the effects of nonmother care on children: "Child care settings were traditionally viewed as environments that, by comparison with children's own homes, were deficient as contexts for development. [Our review of the evidence] present[s] a different picture. Family day care and center care can be environments that effectively support children's health and development. They can also provide some unique opportunities for enhancing development (for peer interactions, cognitive interventions, cultural affirmation). Yet existing evidence from research and professional practice forces us to face an important caveat: child care supports healthy physical and psychological development only when it is of high quality." [21]

In a recent review of the research that has been done on the effects of out-of-home care on children, Alison Clarke-Stewart comes to similar conclusions. She reviewed the results of two dozen studies carried on between 1971 and 1990. All but two of these studies "showed that children in day care did at least as well—and sometimes better—on tests of mental and intellectual development."[22] The same set of studies showed, however, that children in day care are "sometimes less polite, less agreeable. . . . more irritable and more rebellious." Clarke-Stewart interprets the latter behavior in a benign way: the children who go to day care are developmentally more advanced and therefore more independent and determined to get their own way. Clarke-Stewart is more cautious about the results of day care for infants. The data that we have on them gives a less clear picture than the data on children over age three. For these younger children, it is not even clear what effects should be measured and how seriously to take the differences that are found.

Jay Belsky contests the claim by Clarke-Stewart in the same volume that a considerable proportion of the out-of-home care that children get in the United States is of a quality comparable to that which was observed to produce reasonably good results. He also rates the aggressiveness of children in day care, as well as the evidence that day care children are less attached to their parents, as more serious problems than she does. His conclusion, however, is not that we should reduce the use of day care but that we should devote to it far greater resources than we are currently doing, so that quality may be radically improved.[23]

We might in this connection ponder the results of all-mother care for one large group of children—those whose mothers are welfare recipients throughout their preschool years. Even allowing for the negative effects of their poverty and the concentration of poor, disorganized people in their neighborhoods, the outcomes for these children are not such as to testify to the positive effects of exclusively mother care. In fact, the Head Start program is an attempt to repair the deficiencies that plague a high proportion of these mother-raised children. One might argue that, whatever the benefits exclusively mother care has or has not for middle-class children, better outcomes for poor children require out-of-home care.

Not all opposition to day care stems from concern for children's well-being. Barbara T. Bowman points to another source of opposition to day care—the unhappiness in some quarters with the change in women's roles. She speaks of "the need in many Americans to hold more tightly to past cultural forms, even though these may be idealized. The stay-at-home mother, the biologically related two-parent family, and 'natural maternal drives' have come into head-on confrontation with women's achievement, personal happiness, and male nurturance."[24]

As a measure of the longing among some segments of the population for women to return to lifelong dependency, we may cite the evolution of the anti-day care movement into the antischool movement. Home schooling is usually presented by its proponents as a way of saving children from the corrupting influence of other children and of religion-free schools. Whatever its effect on the children, it is certainly a way of keeping mothers out of a job and dependent on the father until the youngest child is eighteen.

Even among those who express favorable views on the use of non-mother care, all but the bravest tend to assume tacitly, with Leach, that children's interests should be put first—that we should ask what is best for them and then do it—without regard to the interests of adult women. This implies that we should approve of mothers' leaving their children in others' hands and taking jobs only if it can be demonstrated that nonmother care is every bit as good as mother care. However, there is a positive value to women's freedom to pursue occupations other than child care provider, a freedom we do not question for men. Nonmother care is necessary to such freedom, and therefore desirable, even if it turns out to be somewhat inferior.[25] As Harriet B. Presser remarks, "In juggling work and family roles, there are many tradeoffs that have to be made between one's own interests and those of one's child and spouse. . . . As opportunities for rewarding activities outside the family have increased, women have become less willing to sacrifice their own interests for those of others (although they are still more willing than most men). Moreover, with the increase in marital instability, women's definitions of what is in their own interests, and those of their children, have changed."[26]

The issue of the *New York Times Book Review* that carried a generally admiring review of Leach's book also contained a review of *Next Time She'll Be Dead: Battering and How to Stop It*, a book documenting the high incidence of male violence toward wives and other sexual partners.[27] There is clearly a dissonance here that the "children first" proponents have not dealt with: women who devote themselves entirely to child nurture are the most vulnerable to their partners' violence (toward their children as well as themselves), because they have no independent resources they can mobilize in order to leave and because they may be socially isolated within the home.

Concerns about Government Efficiency and Intrusiveness

Another roadblock to government provision of child care for all but the poorest is the idea that government should interfere as little as possible with the operation of the marketplace. These free-market proponents hold that, at least for the nonpoor, government should not adopt policies that favor the use by families of any commodity over any other and that out-of-home child care is certainly no exception, even assuming it is not positively harmful to children.[28] They would argue that the appropriate government policy toward child care and the appropriate policy toward a commodity such as broccoli are identical. Some people enjoy consuming broccoli and others do not, and people should be free to follow their preferences in whether to buy it or not. But the taxpayers at large should not be forced to supply broccoli at no charge or at reduced charge to those who want to consume it. Nor is there a valid reason for the government to engage in broccoli farming—that is better left to private enterprise.

There are a number of responses that can be made to this line of reasoning. The validity of the theory that suggests that things are best when all buying, pricing, and producing are in the hands of nongovernment entities depends on all of the agents' being competent to look after their own interests and all the rules of the game being fair. But children suffer when parents are unlucky, lazy, stupid, unfeeling, or discriminated against, and no valid economic theory forbids government to rescue them. If obligatory child rearing for women is an unfair rule of the game, then subsidizing women's freedom from it is a legitimate activity for government and not in a class with subsidizing broccoli.

In France, where virtually all children older than three attend high-quality government-supplied nursery schools that are free to the parents, they believe that a vital educational purpose is being served and that both the children and the nation of which they are the future citizens benefit. There, the rationale for public schools has been extended further down the age scale for all income groups. Some public provision of care for the under threes is also done there, with the aim of keeping parents off welfare and in jobs and ensuring that the care is of high quality.[29]

The faction hostile to government provision or subsidy is also hostile to government involvement in setting compulsory quality standards for private enterprise. They point out that quality standards tend to raise costs and reduce the amount supplied. They feel the interplay of market forces, not the government, should determine what varieties of the product are available and at what cost.

This "let the buyer beware" attitude of the free-marketeers is inappropriate for child care, where those on the receiving end—the children—are not in a position to judge what is dangerous or neglectful and to desert subpar facilities on their own initiative. The cost issue is a serious one. Any proposed standards should have to pass a cost-benefit test. We do not require parents to buy a Volvo or a Mercedes to transport their children in the safest possible vehicle, but do require that they buy and use child seats. Similarly, the solution we come to on day care quality requirements has to balance considerations of quality and cost.

One difficulty in persuading the public to mount a large-scale child care program is the widespread doubt that American governmental entities would be capable of delivering excellent services to children, as European governments manage to do.[30] As already noted, American public schools have done a notoriously bad job with poor children. In this country, however, vouchers acceptable by nongovernmental providers would probably have to play a major part.

Concerns about the Federal Budget

A crucial roadblock in the way of large-scale government provision of child care is the idea that, given the current budgetary situation, the United States cannot afford to spend more on social welfare programs, even those like child care that would be of high value. What the phrase "cannot afford" might actually mean in practice is worthy of particularly close study by students of social policy. "Cannot afford" has two quite different meanings, and by mixing them up American politicians manage to avoid admitting to an unprincipled position.

This is best understood by considering our use of the phrase in everyday life. If I were to say that I "cannot afford" to buy a large house in the best neighborhood for $2.5 million, I would be using the phrase to convey that it would either be impossible or extremely financially imprudent for me to buy it. This is the primary meaning of the phrase. However, when I say I cannot afford a certain pair of $70 shoes, the phrase has a different meaning. Buying the shoes would be entirely possible with my current income and would not put me in any financial danger. I would merely have to eliminate some other expense or increase my borrowing modestly. I use the phrase "cannot afford" to mean that I do not desire the shoes sufficiently to rearrange my budget so as to buy them. With a larger income I might reconsider, but at present the shoes have a lower priority than the things I am already buying.

If a politician were to say we cannot afford to provide a high-quality no-fee day care program for lower- and middle-income families (to say nothing of treatment for drug addicts and alcoholics who desire to kick their habit, medical insurance for all, repairs for crumbling bridges, and libraries open evenings and weekends), in what sense would he or she be using the phrase? Given that such a program could be financed by a modest rearrangement of the budget, the objective situation is one of insufficient desire, as with the $70 shoes, not financial impossibility or extreme financial imprudence, as with the $2.5 million house.

When the politicians are saying (and the citizens are echoing) that we cannot afford to spend more on programs that would reduce child poverty, they are playing a word game—pretending to use the phrase in its extreme imprudence sense, rather than in its insufficient desire sense. No politician wants to say that we have better things to do with our resources than mobilizing them to improve child welfare in this country (through higher taxes or reducing other expenditures or borrowing) and that these better things include the B-2 bomber, farm subsidies, and spending for still more luxuries by the upper-income groups. That would not sound good or responsible. But saying that we cannot afford the programs sounds good, and the mixup in meanings allows us to relieve our conscience of the sin of neglecting large numbers of our children when it would be well within our power to do otherwise.

The $150 billion to $500 billion savings and loan crisis has illuminated the lack of seriousness of the "cannot afford" argument against child-welfare programs. The public money to make the S & L depositors whole was forthcoming with no debate at all, because it was feasible and desirable. Farm subsidies and high defense expenditures and large budgets for the Central Intelligence Agency will continue to be considered affordable. But until we change our notions of how desirable adequate child-welfare programs are, the public purse, which opens so easily and lavishly for other purposes, will not be available for them.

Parents currently buying child care also use the "cannot afford" phrase when they justify to themselves their behavior of buying less than the best-quality care. Like the politicians, they use this rhetoric to avoid saying, "I could buy high-quality care for my children, but choose not to so as to enable me to buy some things I value more." Whatever we think of such parents, the interests of the children would be served by public provision, which would limit the harm done to children by parents' choices. A merit good is one that we feel that citizens should have at their disposal, even if those who could buy it out of their private resources choose not to do so.

Those who use the "cannot afford" argument should consider the example of France. The French, who have a per capita income about 80 percent of ours, manage to afford to provide out of government funds places in nursery school that are free to the parents to all children out of diapers. They also provide a considerable number of highly subsidized places in public child care centers for infants and toddlers and provide subsidies to those parents who buy care on the private market. Their public spending on child care, income supplements for families with children, and various medical programs for children take up 10 percent of all the government spending they do, and 5 percent of their gross domestic product is devoted to such programs. As a result of all this spending, the rate of poverty among French children is about 6 percent, while that among children in our considerably more affluent country is 21 percent.[31]

Conclusion

A large-scale program of government subsidies or provision of child care is an essential ingredient in a welfare reform that would reduce child poverty in the United States. The program would benefit those now on welfare, the working poor, and those in the middle range of incomes. Providing or subsidizing child care is a way of delivering substantial help to lower-income parents. It would motivate and enable parents now on welfare to work. Since none of the benefit would be spendable by the parents for other goods, it is more likely to be perceived as a program benefiting innocent children rather than improvident adults.

Such a program would be in competition for funds for other programs that would help poor children: job training, public service jobs, drug and alcohol treatment programs for their parents, enhancement of elementary and secondary schools serving lower-income children, cash benefits not earmarked for child care, housing programs, programs to provide preventive medical care and sickness care. All of these are valuable; clearly we need a massive budget to deal with a massive set of dire and unmet needs of families with children. This is not the place to allocate that budget. Of all of these programs, however, it is worth remembering that child care is unique in giving parents the ability to help themselves and their children through paid work, thus achieving the status of contributors to society.[32]

An expensive program to fill the unmet needs of families with children is not now and for the medium term a likely political prospect. Such a program must await the time when we have a president more talented in framing and selling such an agenda and when the antigovernment rhetoric that now is so pervasive has been overcome by an even more obvious need for the action that only government can provide.

Notes

1. Philip K. Robins, "Child Care Policy and Research: An Economist's Perspective," in David M. Blau, ed., *The Economics of Child Care* (Russell Sage Foundation, 1991), pp. 11–49; James R. Walker, "Public Policy and the Supply of Child Care Services," in Blau, ed., *Economics of Child Care*, pp. 51–77; and Cheryl D. Hayes, John L. Palmer, and Martha J. Zaslow, eds., *Who Cares for America's Children? Child Care Policy for the 1990s* (Washington: National Academy Press, 1990).

2. Most simple theoretical models of markets assume that for each grade of whatever commodity is being traded there is one unique price charged to all buyers. Any shortage—the gap between supply and demand—is to be measured at that price. This is certainly an assumption that lacks realism in the child care market, and many others as well.

3. The interpretation that economists tend to give to proponents' claims of shortages and high prices makes these two claims inconsistent. If there really were a shortage of day care places in the sense that economists use the term shortage, that would signify that prices were too low to bring demand and supply into balance, not that prices were too high. However, as discussed below, the proponents mean something else entirely, so their claims are not inconsistent.

4. Barbara Willer and others, *The Demand and Supply of Child Care in 1990* (Washington: National Association for the Education of Young Children, 1991), p. 43.

5. It is common for proponents of government help with day care to argue that day care workers should be paid more than they are getting, which

amounts to saying that it would be beneficial if costs were higher than they actually are.

6. Agnar Sandmo, "Ex Post Welfare Economics and the Theory of Merit Goods," *Economica*, vol. 50 (February 1983), pp. 19–33.

7. Sandra L. Hofferth and others, *National Child Care Survey, 1990* (Urban Institute Press, 1991), p. 178.

8. Nancy Folbre, "Children as Public Goods," *American Economic Review*, vol. 84 (Papers and Proceedings, May 1994), pp. 86–90.

9. For a description of the Basic Needs Budget method, see Trudi J. Renwick and Barbara R. Bergmann, "A Budget-Based Definition of Poverty, with an Application to Single-Parent Families," *Journal of Human Resources*, vol. 28 (Winter 1993), pp. 1–24. The BNB includes specific allowances for minimally decent food, shelter, clothing, medical care, transportation, and child care that are tailored to the ages of the children and the work behavior of the parents. In computing the incidence of poverty using the BNB definition, the likelihood that a family would obtain medical insurance from an employer and free day care from relatives was taken into account.

10. Charles A. Murray, *Losing Ground: American Social Policy, 1950–1980*, (Basic Books, 1984).

11. *Statistical Abstract of the United States: 1993*, p. 64.

12. Irwin Garfinkel, *Assuring Child Support: An Extension of Social Security* (Russell Sage Foundation, 1992).

13. Material in this section derives from Barbara R. Bergmann, *Fighting Child Poverty in the United States and France* (Russell Sage Foundation, forthcoming). Some out-of-pocket medical expenses are allowed for in the adaptation of the BNB that is used here, but nothing for health insurance, assuming that all single parents will in future have that provided.

14. Harriet B. Presser, "Some Economic Complexities of Child Care Provided by Grandmothers," *Journal of Marriage and the Family*, vol. 51 (August 1989), pp. 581–91.

15. Sheila B. Kamerman and Alfred J. Kahn, eds., *Family Policy: Government and Families in Fourteen Countries* (Columbia University Press, 1978); Kamerman and Kahn, eds., *Child Care, Parental Leave, and the Under 3s: Policy Innovation in Europe* (Auburn House, 1991); "Child Care in OECD Countries," *OECD Employment Outlook* (July 1990), pp. 123–51; Jonathan Bradshaw and others, *Support for Children: A Comparison of Arrangements in Fifteen Countries* (London: HMSO, 1993); and Bergmann, *Fighting Child Poverty*.

16. Irene Powell and others, "Cost and Characteristics of High-Quality Early Childhood Education Programs," *Child & Youth Care Forum*, vol. 23 (April 1994), pp. 103–18.

17. About 23 percent of four-year-olds and 74 percent of five-year-olds are already enrolled in public nursery schools and kindergartens. Of four- and five-year-olds enrolled in public or private programs, 32 and 42 percent, respectively, go full time, according to the 1993 edition of the *Digest of Educational Statistics*. A fine-grained cost estimate of the additional cost of public

provision would have to encompass these facts. The attempt here, however, is to achieve a broad-brush estimate.

18. The 1994 study by the Family and Work Institute was reported in Barbara Vobejda, "Family Day Care 'Barely Adequate,'" *Washington Post*, April 8, 1994, pp. A1, A17.

19. Marcy Whitebrook, Carollee Howes, and Deborah Phillips, *The National Child Care Staffing Study* (Oakland, Calif.: Child Care Employee Project, 1989).

20. Penelope Leach, *Children First: What Our Society Must Do—and Is Not Doing—for Our Children Today* (Knopf, 1994).

21. Hayes, Palmer, and Zaslow, *Who Cares for America's Children?*, p. 135.

22. Alison Clarke-Stewart, "Consequences of Child Care for Children's Development," in Alan Booth, ed., *Child Care in the 1990s: Trends and Consequences* (Hillsdale, N.J.: Lawrence Erlbaum, 1992), p. 64. The two studies that showed adverse effects had "shockingly low" adult-child ratios and poor caregiver training. Clarke-Stewart goes on to remark that families that select day care for their children may be different from those that do not, and these differences may themselves produce differences in the children, making an attribution of the differences among children as deriving from effects of day care on them somewhat problematic (p. 66).

23. Jay Belsky, "Consequences of Child Care for Children's Development: A Deconstructionist View," in Booth, *Child Care in the 1990s*, pp. 83–94.

24. Barbara T. Bowman, "Child Development and Its Implications for Day Care," in Booth, *Child Care in the 1990s*, p. 98.

25. If out-of-home care turns out to be grossly inferior, both mothers and fathers can take turns at child care, as I have previously suggested; see Barbara R. Bergmann, *The Economic Emergence of Women* (Basic Books, 1986).

26. Harriet B. Presser, "Child Care and Parental Well-Being: A Needed Focus on Gender and Trade-Offs," in Booth, *Child Care in the 1990s*, p. 181.

27. The two reviews appear in Rickie Solinger, "Unsafe For Women," *New York Times*, March 20, 1994, sec. 7, p. 17; and Ann Hulbert, "All That Parents Can Do Isn't Enough," sec. 7, p. 3.

28. Gary S. Becker has argued in this vein. He would have government finance programs for poor children targeted to improve their human capital and health, but opposes child care subsidies for the better off. See "Sure, Spend More on Child Care, But Spend Wisely," *Business Week*, May 8, 1989, p. 24.

29. See Bergmann, "Can We Afford to Save Our Children?"

30. Ibid.

31. Ibid.

32. On what is and what should be considered "contributing" and "dependent," see Nancy Fraser and Linda Gordon, "'Dependency' Demystified: Inscriptions of Power in a Keyword of the Welfare State," *Social Politics: International Studies in Gender, State & Society*, vol. 1 (Spring 1994), pp. 4–31.

Chapter 5

Building Hope, Skills, and Careers: Creating a Youth Apprenticeship System

Robert I. Lerman

O N MAY 4, 1994, President Bill Clinton signed into law the School-to-Work Opportunities Act (STWOA). The goal of the law is to stimulate states and localities to create a new national system linking school-based and work-based training and ultimately upgrade the careers of young people not pursuing a four-year college degree. For President Clinton, the law is a first step in keeping his campaign promise to develop youth apprenticeships.

The president's remarks at the bill-signing ceremony dealt with some fundamental problems this legislation attempted to address: the rising inequality of earnings, especially the widening gaps between the college educated and those lacking a college education; the weak educational outcomes of U.S. students; and the nation's low productivity performance.

Meanwhile, several states, notably Oregon, Wisconsin, Maine, Pennsylvania, Indiana, and New Jersey, have already passed laws providing the framework for youth apprenticeships and related approaches to motivate students to do well in high school and to provide work-based training toward specific occupational competencies. While my main policy recommendation—youth apprenticeships and related work-based approaches—has already been enacted into law, there remain three roles for this chapter: to reexamine the problems facing adolescent children entering the job market, to present the case for youth apprenticeships in a way that directly confronts recent critiques of this idea, and to recommend a widening and deepening of the existing implementation strategy.

The basic argument is that a youth apprenticeship system can raise the incentives and motivation of high school students to learn, provide clear pathways and transitions from school to careers, expand the use of contextualized learning, increase the relevance of training, upgrade the quality of jobs, and encourage employers to upgrade jobs and to take a chance on young workers. While broad based and available to all young people, youth apprenticeships will do most to help the less advantaged and will achieve far more than largely unsuccessful, income-targeted programs.

Until now, shortcomings in policy have led to subpar job market outcomes for individuals and firms. The failure takes place mainly outside the market. Perhaps because schools lack direct incentives to maximize the job market success of students, they spend too little on information, counseling, and placement; provide training often unrelated to careers; and allow too little flexibility for work-based training. Without an infrastructure to set and verify occupational standards, to allow students to combine work-based training with a high school degree, and to create a social context for student involvement in youth apprenticeships, it will be too costly for employers and too risky for students. No mechanism exists for the market to create such an infrastructure, despite the resulting benefits to employers and students alike. It will take sustained effort to reorient public policy so as to build an effective school-to-work system.

The Disturbing Problems of Disadvantaged and Minority Youth

Until recently, concern over the transition from school to work emphasized problems of disadvantaged youth or the small group of long-term unemployed. In their edited 1982 collection *The Youth Labor Market*, Richard Freeman and David Wise summarize many of the results dealing with the period up to the late 1970s by noting, "In short, the data suggest that most teenagers do not have substantial employment difficulties, but that for a minority of young people, there are long periods without work that constitute severe problems."[1] Using 1985 data on twenty-one- to twenty-four-year-olds from the National Longitudinal Survey of Youth, I found similar patterns. The 20 percent with the most unemployment accounted for 87 percent of all unemployment of white young men and 80 percent of the unemployment of black young men.

While most young people were able to find jobs, blacks were encountering increasing job market problems. The unemployment rate of black eighteen- to nineteen-year-old men jumped from about 15 percent in 1954 to 35 percent in 1977; the proportion of black twenty- to twenty-four-year-old men holding jobs dropped from 78 percent in 1964 to 58 percent in 1981. Recent figures document the continuing problems of black young people. Even at the peak of the latest business cycle (1989), the unemployment rate of sixteen- to twenty-four-year-old black high school graduates was more than 20 percent. At age twenty-three, about one in four black men and women had no earnings at all.[2]

These impersonal job statistics mask much more serious social problems related to the poor career options of disadvantaged and minority young people. William J. Wilson sees the deteriorating job market for black young men as the underlying cause of the rising rates of mother-headed families and a growing underclass.[3] Between 1960 and 1989, the proportion of black children living with two parents dropped from about 67 percent to about 38 percent. To Elijah Anderson, the alienation associated with what he calls "endemic joblessness" has led to an oppositional street culture that can even engulf young people from "decent" homes.[4] Unable to gain self-respect through solid performance at school or on the job, street youth (especially young men) prove their manhood by showing their peers that they can conquer women sexually and become fathers and that they can steal something from another and flaunt it.[5] The tragic levels of street crime have made murder the leading cause of death of young black men.

Many suspects are implicated in this increasingly intractable problem. High rates of single parenthood generate high poverty rates and weak school performance. Poor school outcomes for some young people can ultimately bring down others, as peer pressure works against those trying to succeed. Among blacks, the normal pressure by nonachievers takes on a racial character as peers taunt their classmates who try to succeed or speak standard English as "acting white."[6] This forces many blacks to choose between their friends and trying to succeed. The declining wages of less-skilled men and even high school graduates further reduce the attraction of working hard to do well in high school, especially in a peer culture that takes a short-term view of life. Crime arises not only from direct economic incentives but also because violent behavior is often necessary to preserve self-respect.[7] Anderson notes that prison may enhance a young man's reputation after the toughening experience.[8]

These phenomena are widespread and have become worse among low-income black young people. John Bound and Richard Freeman calculate that 20 percent of black eighteen- to twenty-nine-year-old male dropouts were incarcerated in 1989, a rise of 12.7 percentage points since 1980.[9] By the mid-1980s, nearly one in three black young women had become an unwed mother by age twenty-one. The effects on schooling and jobs are disastrous. According to Bound and Freeman, the rising share of black dropouts with criminal records may have accounted for 70 percent of the decline in employment rates between 1979 and 1989. Moreover, the violence has extended to schools and has affected the innocent. By 1988 nearly one in five black eighth graders did not feel safe at school.

Although some studies show little impact on later employment from early joblessness (once we take account of personal characteristics), the same cannot be said for criminal records and unwed childbearing. Both clearly reduce long-term earnings and increase poverty among the young people and the generation they bring into the world.

The racial dimension complicates the problem by creating a vicious circle. The history of blatant racial discrimination and salient examples of continuing discrimination add to the bitterness of many inner-city young persons against the system and to their expectations that hard work in school will not pay off. Employers, sensing that a lack of basic skills and an unwillingness to work hard are common traits among lower-class blacks, discriminate by attributing their perceptions of average traits of blacks to individual black job applicants.[10] Even employers in the neighborhood are unlikely to take a chance on young applicants who lack a credible reference.[11] The evidence of continuing discrimination reinforces the rejection by ghetto black young people of the mainstream system and rationalizes their lack of effort in school.[12]

The nation has long confronted a jobs problem among economically disadvantaged and minority young people. But today the social consequences of the perpetuation of the problem are far more severe.

The Broad Problem of the Non-College Bound

In recent years, policy discussions of the school-to-work issue have shifted from a focus on the disadvantaged to an emphasis on the problems faced by the noncollege population, or about half of recent youth cohorts. The main elements of this problem are clear. Wages have been declining for male high school graduates and high school dropouts in absolute terms and relative to the wages of college graduates. The rising inequality within and between educational groups can be traced to the rising demand for skill and the slow growth in the skill and academic achievement levels of young people. But the limited academic capacities of young Americans are not inevitable; other countries have managed to raise the average skill levels of their young people well above U.S. levels.[13]

In part, noncollege youth perform poorly because they have little incentive to work hard in school. Although their long-term success is related to their abilities, their access to entry jobs or attractive careers looks unrelated to the ability to attain a B– instead of a C average.[14] Given that U.S. students are often bored in high school, have many satisfying uses of time other than studying, and are part of a peer culture often hostile to studying, it is not hard to see why clear monetary incentives are important.[15]

The circular flow can generate a low-level equilibrium. Partly because new high school graduates lack necessary skills, employers are reluctant to hire them for demanding jobs or to invest in training.[16] About 60 percent of all twenty-five-year-olds obtained no training after high school; the figures are even higher for noncollege youth.[17] Without the hope that their high school performance will lead directly to a rewarding career involving added training, too many students avoid the effort required to achieve high academic skills. Although there are other causes of the poor relative achievement of American students, today's weak connection between learning and postschool careers certainly contributes to the problem.

In the absence of close relationships between employers and high schools, the U.S. pattern of job shopping after high school is a productive and flexible response. Moreover, as James Heckman points out, the search and turnover processes of matching workers with jobs are productive. However, the results of this informal approach to school-to-work transition are often unsatisfactory. Paul Osterman reports that even by their early thirties, more than 35 percent of male high school graduates have failed to find stable employment.[18] The informal U.S. system performs worst for low-income and minority youth, since they lack the informal job contacts available to middle-class youth. Moreover, even among middle-class youth, Heckman does not compare the U.S. system with potentially better alternatives, nor does he dispute the notion that the U.S. system provides weak incentives for students to perform well in high school.

The rising demand for skill and the associated expanding wage premiums have a positive side. If employers willingly pay increasing premiums for educated workers, then creating better jobs mainly requires doing better in education and training. To reinforce this point, suppose we found—as scholars did find in the mid-1970s—that employers were reducing the premium they were willing to pay for skill. We would have to infer that employers have little use for extra skills, that adding educated workers might create academic unemployment or frustrations when their jobs end up requiring few of the capabilities they worked so hard to achieve. Fortunately, in today's world employers are increasingly demanding higher skills. If we can only raise education and skill levels, we will be able to turn the unskilled into well-educated workers.

While the mainstream youth problem looks tame compared to the problems facing the disadvantaged, the two problems are connected. If the career outlook for the typical high school graduate looks unrewarding, it will be difficult to make the disadvantaged enthusiastic about performing well in school and about avoiding crime and early childbearing.

The Policy Context: Limitations of Targeted Programs

Since the onset of the War on Poverty in 1965, federal employment and training policies have focused primarily on the disadvantaged youth component of the problem. Virtually all federal youth programs emanating out of the Department of Labor have targeted resources on low-income youth. Unfortunately, despite years of effort and a variety of approaches, targeted programs have failed to deal effectively with the underlying problem.

Recent and careful studies of diverse targeted youth training programs indicate that the programs achieved little to raise the long-term job success of disadvantaged youth participants. In an experimental design study of the primary Labor Department youth training program (Job Training Partnership Act, JTPA), analysts found that neither classroom training nor the combination of training and job search led to any positive earnings effects for male or female out-of-school young people.[19] In fact, the overall impact of being in the JTPA group was to reduce the earnings of young adults. For young men, the negative earnings impact was statistically significant. The long-term effects were also disappointing for the summer training and education program (STEP), another jobs and education social experiment linked to the summer youth employment program.[20] This program combined the provision of part-time summer jobs with innovative instruction in math, reading, and life skills for fourteen- to fifteen-year-olds from poor families. Although STEP was able to raise grade equivalencies of treatment group members over a fifteen-month period, the program was unable to produce positive effects on the education, employment, and parenting outcomes of treatment group members.

The one apparent success story of targeted youth training is the Job Corps. However, the positive evaluation evidence comes from the mid-1970s with young workers entering the job market of the late 1970s, and the study relied on a comparison group methodology, rather than the more persuasive experimental, random-assignment approach. Caveats aside, the findings of the Job Corps evaluation indicated gains for young men and women with no children. Three years after leaving the program, male Job Corps participants worked 63 percent of the year, 9 percentage points higher than the employment rate of the nonparticipant comparison group.

Unfortunately, attempts to build on the apparent Job Corps success have proved unsuccessful. Beginning in 1985, the Department of Labor and a number of foundations sponsored a new demonstration, JOB-START, which attempted to emulate the Job Corps strategy of basic education, occupational training, job placement assistance, and support services, but without moving participants to a group residential setting. Although JOBSTART succeeded in increasing the educational levels of participants, the program failed to exert any statistically significant impact on the earnings of young men or young women. With the present value of costs to taxpayers averaging about $4,600 and with participants gaining at most about $250 over four years, few are likely to become advocates for the JOBSTART approach.[21]

Finally, even a major demonstration project that provided opportunities to all disadvantaged young people in an area could not significantly alter their futures. In the late 1970s, the Congress mandated the youth incentive entitlement pilot projects (YIEPP), which guaranteed jobs to poor teenagers who stayed in school or returned to school. Although the return-to-school rate rose by 55 percent in 1978 and by 10 percent in 1979, YIEPP was unable to stimulate these dropouts to stay long enough to graduate from high school. In the three YIEPP sites that fully implemented the program, only 47 percent of black nineteen- to twenty-year-olds had graduated from high school as of fall 1981. The evaluators of YIEPP did estimate a postprogram gain in earnings of about $10 a week. But well after YIEPP the unemployment rates of YIEPP eligibles (most of whom participated) remained extremely high, reaching an incredible 60 percent among black young adults.[22]

Policymakers are beginning to see the limits of targeted approaches, especially in the context of a mainstream system that leaves large segments of a youth cohort without good career prospects. Targeted programs will never reach the appropriate scale to deal with such a problem. Moreover, if the median noncollege young worker cannot find a good job, why should a targeted program be expected to raise the skills of the disadvantaged enough to do so? Finally, targeted programs tend to become stigmatizing. Even when a broad-based program becomes highly targeted (as in the case of the Employment Service), the program may end up less effective for the very disadvantaged it was intended to help most.[23]

A Youth Apprenticeship School-to-Work System

Serious concerns pervade the U.S. system of education, training, and work transition for more than half the cohort not bound for a four-year college degree. But changing the system requires more than an add-on program and must relate to the complexities of a highly decentralized system with many sets of actors. Several proposals for fundamental change are school-based reforms, such as school vouchers to force competition; new compensatory education programs; and national standards for students and teachers. These approaches have merit, but they do not provide meaningful incentives to learn, nor do they improve the linkages between training and careers.

One method for ensuring that pupils and teachers see how performance leads to good jobs is the Japanese approach. Japanese employers typically offer jobs to high schools in a way that provides better jobs to the highly ranked high schools. In the senior year, schools nominate students for specific jobs, based partly on student performance and student interest. Employers hire only those nominated by the school staff. Students cannot apply unless they have the school's nomination.[24]

This screening process gives employers confidence in their potential workers. That, in turn, encourages many employers to engage in extensive on-the-job training. The system greatly increases the incentive for high school students to perform well. Grades play a major role in determining the nominations and thus the important first jobs of many Japanese youth.

While Japan's system does provide incentives and improved matches between workers and employers, it is unappealing in the United States because of its overwhelming emphasis on grades, school performance, and recommendations by teachers, as well as the absence of a work-based learning component. Moreover, it places a country's entire emphasis on one type of merit.[25]

Instead, I propose building a youth apprenticeship system modeled on the approach practiced in Germany, Denmark, Switzerland, and Austria. Such a system would and (in some places already does) embody a contractual arrangement between employers, workers, and schools whereby a seventeen- to eighteen-year-old (high school junior or senior) combines work-based and school-based learning over a two- to three-year period to achieve a certified competency in a career field along with a high school degree. The U.S. system would require an infrastructure to specify and test occupational competencies, to develop work-based and related school-based curriculums, to provide occupational information to students at least by junior high school, to train workplace trainers, to provide extensive counseling to students and parents, and to monitor the quality of the learning experiences.

As a mode of learning defined by Lauren Resnick, an apprenticeship involves "coached practice in actual tasks of production, with decreasing degrees of support from the master or more advanced colleagues. This practice takes place in the context of preparing a product that is socially valued."[26]

The *Economist* enthusiastically described the German apprenticeship system:

> Adolescents who were bored by school find their enthusiasm reignited, partly because they are treated more like adults and partly because they start to see the links between learning facts and earning a living. The cost of training is divided between the *Länder*, which provide the vocational schools, the employers, who pump 2% of their payroll costs into training, and apprentices themselves, who work for only a nominal salary. The transition between school and work, so traumatic elsewhere, is rendered almost painless. Above all, the system reinforces a culture in which training is cherished and skilled workers revered.[27]

Such a system in the United States would:

—Raise incomes of noncollege youth by increasing productivity. Comparative studies on German versus British and German versus French factories show clear productivity advantages for Germany, largely resulting from its high-quality apprenticeship system.[28] U.S. employers should be able to reap the high productivity associated with the larger supply of skilled workers. At the same time, the increased supply of skilled workers and reduced supply of unskilled should reduce earnings gaps.

—Provide clear pathways and incentives for youth. Young people would gain access to a wide range of career streams by late high school. By junior high, they would learn of the entry requirements and performance standards for each type of apprentice. The clear and immediate incentive to do well in school would be access to a desired apprenticeship;[29] the payoff during apprenticeship would be a long-term job with the firm, or at least a recommendation that other employers would trust.

—Use learning in context extensively. Cognitive researchers have been documenting the important advantages of contextualized learning. Many people learn best by doing, a fact not lost on teachers of medicine and law. Apprenticeships would emphasize active, not passive, learning; whole projects instead of fragmented knowledge; and skills taught in context instead of material unimportant to the learners.[30] Students would begin to see the direct relevance of what they are studying and gain self-confidence from their developing capability. Early experimental evidence from New York City's career magnet schools indicates that programs that give students a career focus improve their achievement in general subjects, including reading and math.[31]

—Improve the linkage between training and careers. Because employers are unlikely to offer apprenticeships in areas where there are few jobs, mismatches are less likely. Reliance on actual employer demands is more likely to lead to good matches than are occupational projections or the number of slots in a high school program. Hilary Steedman argues that the information flow between employers and trainees does indeed lessen the mismatch between training choices and employer positions.[32] Second, students are more likely to learn current practice rather than old approaches, since competitive employers specify the competencies. Steedman sees employer-based training as overcoming the usual information loss between firms and workers concerning the content of training. Certification can reduce the uncertainty concerning the skills a worker obtains and thus increases the portability and the market value of the training.

—Channel youth work into constructive settings. High school students often take jobs as unskilled service workers to earn spending money. Youth apprenticeship channels this impulse by attempting to make workplaces into learning environments and linking work with training toward an attractive career.

—Influence the structure of employer demand as well as the quality of labor. Most education and training programs simply try to change the worker. The development of apprenticeships causes employers to rethink their use of skill, to upgrade jobs by raising their skill levels, and to find ways to increase the use of noncollege youth with skills. Youth apprenticeships are one way for firms to develop well-trained and responsible line workers. The associated benefits can be a lean management structure and an improved ability to implement new technologies. In the context of a youth apprenticeship program, employers may become more willing to hire young people as trial employees.

Although youth apprenticeship is a universal strategy, its main benefits would flow to the very noncollege workers who have suffered wage reductions over the last fifteen years. For inner-city and minority youth, apprenticeships are especially promising.

A FORMAL PLACEMENT SYSTEM EQUALIZES ACCESS TO JOBS. Inner-city youth lack knowledge of the middle range of jobs and lack access through informal channels. Often, even when plants are located within inner-city poor areas, employers are unwilling to hire local residents because they do not trust them. Many firms hire by word of mouth or through other informal channels. Those with the fewest connections to jobs—without a working father or uncle or aunt—are at a serious disadvantage. Apprenticeships provide a formal mechanism in which employers can have confidence and can try out marginal workers.

APPRENTICESHIP EXPOSES YOUNG PEOPLE TO CONSTRUCTIVE ADULT PEER GROUPS. The peer pressure to become involved in crime and drugs and to have children outside marriage can be intense. When the child has only one parent present and is poor, overcoming these influences is extremely difficult. An apprenticeship can lead to a natural mentoring process in which the mentor/trainer has a stake in the success of the apprentice not only at the work site but in academic studies as well.

AN EARLY START IS CRITICAL TO IMPROVE INCENTIVES AND TO AVERT SERIOUS TROUBLE. Postponing adult job responsibilities until after two years of higher education might not create serious obstacles for the middle class but could prove disastrous for inner-city young people. By that time, too many will have become involved in crime or unwed parenthood. Given their poverty, few disadvantaged young people are willing to accept delay for uncertain returns years into the future.

APPRENTICESHIP ALLOWS EMPLOYERS TO WATCH YOUNG PEOPLE AS THEY LEARN CRITICAL SKILLS. Minorities and disadvantaged youth are most likely to suffer from group labels suggesting a lack of motivation, basic skills, and questionable integrity. An apprenticeship gives the young minority worker a chance to demonstrate his or her individual strengths during a probationary period, after which employers can make their long-term hiring decision. Indeed, employers may find school-to-work programs an especially appealing source of qualified minority workers.[33]

The youth apprenticeship model is not an untested idea, but rather a successful and effective system operating in advanced economies, including Austria, Denmark, Germany, and Switzerland. In Germany, as of 1991, about two-thirds of seventeen-year-olds were about to start apprenticeships; by age twenty-four, two-thirds of the cohort had passed their apprenticeships and received certification, and only about 10 percent of the cohort did not obtain any postsecondary certification.[34]

There are variations in the German system and across countries in the median year of entry, the extent and nature of school-based postsecondary education, and the breadth of the occupational qualifications. However, under the basic model, most seventeen- to nineteen-year-olds begin structured, two- to four-year programs of school-based and employer-based training culminating in a recognized occupational certification. On a largely voluntary basis, employers have generally provided enough apprenticeship places for all young people who wish to participate.[35] Patriotic and social concerns cannot be the primary motivator for employers since despite the abundance of places, only about one in four German employers actually offers any apprenticeships. At the same time, German multinationals find the apprenticeship approach so useful that they often set up programs in other countries, where patriotic concerns are irrelevant.

Apprenticeship systems in other countries operate alongside other institutions, including extensive occupational information programs for students, school-employer-labor partnerships in developing standards, and the use of apprenticeship certification as a requirement for entry into certain fields. Although it will take time to develop the full institutional setting in this country, we are already beginning to see small but serious youth apprenticeship programs operating in Wisconsin, New York, Pennsylvania, and Maine.

A good example of early efforts in the United States is the finance youth apprenticeship in Wisconsin. With a combination of school-based and work site training, apprentices move from teller-related functions to handling new accounts, lending, customer support, and accounting. At school, students take courses on the principles of depository institutions, marketing for depository institutions, business law, and operations. The state government, community colleges, and bankers collaborated to develop this impressive set of skill requirements. Wisconsin has already developed competency standards for twelve separate industries and has more than seven hundred students in apprentice slots. To illustrate the interest of some employers, the Wisconsin auto dealers association petitioned to have their industry included in the youth apprenticeship program. As discussed below, the new STWOA law will provide seed money to help states undertake similar activities and build broad-based systems.

Preliminary indications suggest that pilot youth apprenticeship and similar school-to-career programs yield positive effects. In a study of ten school-to-career programs, Jobs for the Future reported that the programs are expanding, changing the way students think about themselves, and strengthening linkages between employers and schools. In the organization's survey of 226 participants, students reported that work placements were "encouraging good work habits" (92 percent), were "more enjoyable than school" (65 percent), were "preparing me to advance to a better paying job" (83 percent), and had enhanced their motivation at school (56 percent); that classes were "more interesting" (56 percent) compared to those taken by friends not in the program and that participants had better relationships with teachers than nonparticipating students (51 percent). More than 75 percent of students said the program fostered interpersonal relationships with adults.[36]

Critique of the Apprenticeship Concept

For many U.S. policymakers, the issue is no longer one of desirability, but of implementation. However, the apparent consensus for building a youth apprenticeship system has come under attack from important critics.

Economists have long taken a dim view of traditional U.S. apprenticeships, mainly because they create barriers to entry and have discriminated against women and minorities. However, they have generally ignored the high quality of the training and increased productivity arising out of traditional apprenticeships.[37] Indeed, one reason minorities and women have fought so hard against discrimination in apprenticeships is that the positions provide excellent training that is highly valued in the marketplace. As in other areas, it is important for any youth apprenticeship system to take special care to avoid gender or racial discrimination. Even in the traditional programs, progress is evident for minorities, though less so for women.[38]

The fundamental issue here is the role of standards or programs that restrict entry into a given occupation. Since youth apprentice-ships will be employer driven, will not be subject to limitations on numbers, and will not demand rules preventing employers from hiring workers without an apprenticeship certification, legally binding exclusions will be unusual. A good indicator of the inability of trade unions to control youth apprenticeships as an entry barrier is their lobbying against legislation that emphasized such programs. Still, if the apprenticeship certifications become recognized creden-tials denoting skills valued by employers, they will raise natural bar-riers against those lacking credentials. Young people who enter ap-prenticeships at age seventeen and complete their training will have a clear advantage over those who shift from one field to another and decide on an occupation in their late twenties. But this result is the in-evitable outcome of building more skill into middle-level occupa-tions. So long as the barriers to entry are the market-driven result of the demand for genuine and documented skills, we should be no more concerned than we are with legal requirements placed on en-tering doctors, lawyers, and accountants.

Skill standards can convey valuable information to consumers and employers. When these values express themselves in the market-place, students have an incentive to increase their skills enough to meet the standards. Once specified, standards have a tendency to change slowly and to create artificial rigidities. However, so long as they do not have the force of law, employers can simply respond to artificial standards by paying a smaller or zero premium for certifica-tions or by choosing to hire uncertified workers.

The key question, then, is whether we can generally expect in a mature system that certifications denote occupationally relevant skills or signify little more than hard work. In his critique of the German system, Heckman argues that completion of apprenticeships "conveys more information about the tenacity of the trainee and his or her ability to finish a task than it does about the quality of the skill learned." He sees German exams as failing to certify specific skills rel-evant to firms. Since Heckman presents no quantitative standard for judging his proposition, it is difficult to confirm or refute this posi-tion. Steedman presents evidence that counters the notion that ap-prentice standards are artificial. Of the trainees in their first job, 78 percent employed in the firm providing the training (about 50 to 60 percent of graduates) reported that they used "a lot" of what they learned in training on their current job. Even among those trainees in different firms but in the same occupation, 67 percent said they used a lot of what they learned. Indirect evidence for the relevance of the training, especially among large firms, is the fact that firms are willing to invest heavily in the training. Even multinationals head-quartered in other countries are major sponsors of training.[39] Presumably, there are cheaper alternatives to documenting the persistence of workers.

If apprenticeship training did not convey genuine skills and were unresponsive to market needs, we would expect to observe high and rising wage premiums for the college educated just as we have in other advanced economies. In fact, for male workers the college wage premiums are much lower in Germany than in the United States; moreover, while the premiums of U.S. college-educated over high school-educated men jumped in the 1980s, the college-apprenticeship premium remained constant in Germany.[40] On the other hand, for women, the relative wages of apprentices to college graduates are no higher in Germany than the relative wages of high school to college graduates in the United States. Although it is not yet clear what accounts for the gender differential in the relative gains from apprenticeship, the evidence indicates that young German women do not enter the more financially rewarding apprenticeships.

To Heckman, the desirable features of apprenticeship are the added flexibility of firms in paying wages (about one-third of adult wages) and of students in selecting an educational place. Although the United States already has considerable wage flexibility, youth apprenticeships could contribute to freer choice by students among a large number of suppliers of training.

The major concern about a large-scale youth apprenticeship system is the expected reluctance of employers to commit themselves to formal positions involving in-depth work-based training.[41] Pessimistic authors draw on past or current U.S. experience, all of which has taken place in the absence of any large effort to establish the infrastructure for a broad-based youth apprenticeship system. Curiously, these analyses use employer reluctance to become involved in failed programs to demonstrate employer disinterest in an alternative approach. But it is the very failure of current systems—the placement of youth in high-turnover positions and the weak connections between schools and employers—that has motivated the movement to build a youth apprenticeship system.

The only examples of places with large-scale youth apprentice-ships are other countries. Since these modern economies are able to generate adequate numbers of slots for well over 50 percent of their youth cohorts (with only 25 percent of employers), why should the United States be unable to do so for at least 20–25 percent of our youth? Little is said about the success of other countries except for Germany. The German ability to create slots is said to have little rele-vance since rigidly high wages and restrictive layoff rules for adult workers make training apprentices more attractive both because of their relatively low wages and the long-term impact of new hires on the employer's work force. There is truth to these claims, but they should not be overstated. German employers can hire workers on fixed-term contracts of up to eighteen months (up to six months before 1986).[42] Moreover, U.S. employers have other economic incen-tives to participate that are less important in Germany—the high and rising premium they must pay for skilled workers and the high private costs of sending their potential workers to college.

Some worry that firms lack incentives to train workers in general skills because competing firms not providing training will hire the trained workers once the training is completed. Standard human capital theory posits that firms will be unwilling to pay for general training because of this mobility problem. However, Michael Feuer and Henry Glick point out that firms have an incentive to offer general training when they are providing specific training and that such firms are less subject to poaching of trained workers by other firms.[43] They argue that the provision of general training serves as a sensible way to insure workers against the risk of losses from their specific training investment due to actions by firms resulting from their stronger bargaining position. Further, they present empirical ev-idence that firms are willing to invest in the general training of scien-tists and engineers and that turnover rates do not rise as a result of firm-sponsored general training.[44] Additional empirical evidence showing employer willingness to finance general and company train-ing comes from Jonathan Veum's recent study of the impact of train-ing on the wages of twenty-seven- to thirty-two-year-old workers. Veum finds that off-site training financed by employers is portable and that workers do not pay for company training through a lower starting wage.[45]

Firms may voluntarily invest in general training because of the high relative costs of recruiting skilled workers, the cost savings from the joint acquisition of specific and general training, and the information advantage of training firms (over other firms) about the value of a trained worker.[46] To the extent concerns about poaching are important barriers to participation, we can adopt David Finegold's suggestion to liberalize regulations dealing with employment contracts so that individuals would have to be willing to remain with the employer for a specified period or compensate the employer for part of the training costs.[47]

Certainly, the willingness of employers to offer positions is the biggest question mark about the desirability and feasibility of a broad-based youth apprenticeship system. At this moment, no one can be confident that enough positions will emerge in the United States to achieve a large-scale system. In part, the numbers will depend on the costs and benefits from the perspective of several groups of actors.

Costs and Benefits from Alternative Perspectives

The first step is to list the costs and benefits from the perspective of various actors in society (the sum of these components is the social costs and benefits). Table 5-1 presents an illustrative list by apprentice, training employer, schools, and others. Two methods for developing informed guesses on the individual costs and benefits are to examine the experience of other countries with mature youth apprenticeship systems or to draw on small U.S. demonstrations with youth apprenticeships and related programs. In either case, figures must be treated with considerable caution.

Perspective of Employers Providing Apprenticeship Slots

Cooperation from employers is critical: what will they receive, at what price? Despite extensive analyses of costs and benefits to employers in Germany, there is considerable controversy about the magnitudes involved. As Steedman points out, about one-third of apprentices are in small craft firms where net costs are low relative to net costs in the remaining two-thirds, which are in medium or large firms. Soskice and Steedman argue that small firms are able to recoup nearly all of their training costs by paying trainees less than the value of their production.[48] But Harhoof and Kane estimate that craft firms

TABLE 5-1. *Costs (–) and Benefits (+) Expected from Youth Apprenticeship by Students, Employers, Schools, and Others in Society*

Components of costs and benefits	Students	Employers	Schools[a]	Others in Society
Trainee wages	+	–		
Trainer wages for time not spent on production		–		
Formal training costs of trainers		–		–
Costs of space and equipment used for training		–		
Reduced costs of recruitment of skilled workers		+		
Efficiency gains from restructured work force		+		
Option value of an excess of skilled workers		+		
Value of production of apprentice		+		
Reduced wage costs for firm-specific skills		+		
Reduced wage costs for general skills		+		+
Increased future wages of trainees	+			
Wages in alternative job	–			
Enhanced self-image and responsibility of trainees	+			+
Improved academic learning by trainees			+	+
Reduced transfer payments, increased taxes	–			+
Reduced criminal activity and time in prison	+			+
Added occupational information and counseling			–	–
Technical assistance and information sharing				–
Retraining of teachers			–	–
Development of curricula, standards	–		–	–
Reduced school hours during work site training			+	+
Special services to help disadvantaged youth				–

Source: Author's calculation.

a. The positive effect from the reduction in school costs may go partly to other school activities and partly to reduce taxpayer costs (or slow increases in school costs).

experience a net cost of nearly $6,000 a year (the $11,000 in gross costs (in 1990 dollars) to craft firms is offset by only $5,000 in worker productivity).[49] As they admit, this figure may overstate the supervisory costs (of $4,515), since the trainers (master craftsmen) can use their flexibility in scheduling training to correspond to periods of slack demand. The Harhoof-Kane estimates for the net costs of training in other sectors range from a low of $2,746 in agriculture to $9,381 in industry and trade firms to a high of $15,041 in public service.

The costs to U.S. employers are likely to differ from those in Germany. Harhoof and Kane cite average net cost figures for German firms in the context of a system providing slots for about 67 percent of a cohort. Assuming a distribution of costs in which the low-cost employers take advantage of the system first, a U.S. system offering slots to only about 25 percent may involve lower net costs to the average employer. On the other hand, at start-up the costs will be higher since supervisory workers will require training in how to train and mentor apprentices, though the government might bear some of these costs. So far, the wage costs of apprentices in U.S. demonstrations have been somewhat lower (about $3,500 in the first year and $5,200 in the second year), probably since U.S. apprentices appear to work fewer hours. It is difficult to know whether U.S. firms can save on nonwage costs. Osterman cites a surprisingly low figure of about $5,700 for nonwage costs in a presumably high-skill program in a Boston hospital.[50] Still, given the infancy of apprenticeship-type programs in the United States, it makes sense to assume employer costs no less than those experienced in Germany.

The long-term gains to employers are subject to controversy. In one sense, the gains must be enough to offset the costs since employers in Austria, Denmark, Germany, and Switzerland voluntarily provide enough slots for at least 50 to 67 percent of a cohort. The pattern of worker retention indicates economic logic in that firms with the highest net costs of training also retain the highest percentage of trainees. Harhoof and Kane explain that employers can recoup at least some of the productivity gains from providing general training because enough workers are immobile (face high moving costs) to be paid less than their post-training productivity. Still, large, capital-intensive companies probably bear a net cost that is not recouped. Soskice sees German companies as nevertheless engaging in training to ensure that they can recruit and retain enough highly skilled workers to stay in high value-added production. Competing firms that do not undertake apprenticeships might hire workers trained in other firms, but they face the risk of ending up with the less effective of those trained. They could pay a higher premium but they would still lack information about which of the trained workers will be best for their firm. Even if they could lay off less desirable workers poached from other firms, the poaching strategy will be costly because of the wasted costs of the firm-specific training and lower productivity.

Other benefits to employers involve reduced recruitment, hiring, and screening costs. In the Boston ProTech demonstration, even after a first-year experience involving considerable start-up costs, the human resource representatives of five of six participating hospitals saw ProTech as cost effective in meeting labor needs. Potential savings in recruitment costs were an important part of the benefits.[51] A representative of a hospital participating in Binghamton, New York, made similar comments about the high costs of recruiting skilled technicians. In addition to advertising expenses, the costs could easily mount to $2,000 per worker hired. Placement firms receive up to 15 percent of the annual salary of a technician, legal secretary, or similar-level employee. Firms will save much of this initial cost and achieve subsequent savings if apprentices stay longer with the firm than do other new hires.[52] To the extent that the program involves minorities, employers can achieve additional savings in meeting equal opportunity objectives, recruiting, hiring, providing specific training, and screening to ensure the candidate is qualified.

Another potential benefit to employers is the option value of having an excess of skilled workers. It is not simply a matter of using apprentices instead of regular workers to adjust the firm's total employment level to changing demands for the firm's production.[53] Rather, the ability to draw on extra skilled workers is akin to buying an option. In a world of certainty, firms would not pay a premium for having more skilled workers than skilled positions. However, demand may increase unexpectedly or a larger-than-expected number of skilled workers may leave or be temporarily absent, and skilled workers from the outside may be difficult to hire and to give necessary firm-specific training fast enough to deal with a short-run shortfall. In these instances, employers may indeed be willing to pay something for the option of having an excess of skilled workers available.

TABLE 5-2. *Sample Annual Costs and Benefits to Employers Where Present Value of Annual Benefits Equals Annual Costs*

Dollars

Types of costs and benefits	Costs and benefits[a]
Annual trainee wages	−5,000
Annual trainer wages for time not spent on production	−5,000
Formal training costs per year of trainers	−500
Costs per year of space and equipment used for training	−1,000
Annual value of production of apprentice	4,000
Present value of reduced costs of screening and recruitment of skilled workers	1,500
Present value per year of the firm-specific skills used by apprentice	4,000
Present value per year of reduced wage costs for general skills	1,500
Option value per year for excess of skilled workers	500
Total net costs	0

Source: Author's calculation.

a. Figures are presented in terms of the present value of the impact on costs and benefits of a year of apprenticeship.

One gain that is particularly hard to measure is the potential increase in efficiency from the firm's carefully examining its skill structure, expanding on a high-skill strategy, and making decisions about how best to structure its work force. Some see the adoption of apprenticeships and other training initiatives as a step in becoming farsighted enough to create "high performance work organizations."[54] In the absence of evidence for this view, I will not attribute benefits to such possibilities.

Finally, the employers providing the training will share in the benefits of a larger, lower-cost pool of skilled workers in the market as a whole. Of course, if training employers hire only a small proportion of trained workers, this benefit might be small. However, if 25 percent of employers provide training and the cost of skilled workers in their market falls by say, $4,000 an employee, then this benefit could amount to $1,000 an employee in annual savings for training firms.

Given this discussion, the guesses in table 5-2 represent how average costs and benefits can work out so as to make the investment by the marginal training employer worth the costs.

Perspective of Students

The purely economic impact on students is simple to determine in principle. The only direct cost is the forgone earnings the trainee might have experienced by earning less on the apprenticeship than he or she would have earned on a competing job. The primary benefit is the present value of the earnings gains resulting from taking the apprenticeship. The forgone earnings component is likely to be small or even negative. This is because some of the time spent and paid at the work site will be at the expense of time spent in the classroom. For example, if eight of the twenty hours spent at each week's work site displaced time in the classroom, the student could afford a trainee wage 40 percent below the wage paid at the alternative job.[55] Since sixteen- to eighteen-year-olds earn on average about $4.90 an hour, students are unlikely to bear an economic cost from participating. With such low economic costs, net benefits to students are likely to be high. If the program raised potential earnings by only $1,000 a year for thirty years, the present value of these benefits would be $20,000 (at a 3 percent real discount rate). This is a highly conservative estimate since earnings premiums for associate degree graduates over high school graduates are much higher than $1,000 a year.

Beyond the economic gains is the improvement, sometimes dramatic, in the attitude of students about learning, about realistic opportunities, and about their own competence. Although no systematic studies are available, scores of students in U.S. demonstration projects have testified about how apprenticeships pulled them away from a boring, dead-end high school experience toward a desire to learn and a satisfaction with their capacities to accomplish real and important tasks. A C student who enters a hospital apprenticeship program in Binghamton, New York, returns to school with his colleagues to request more science. For his senior project presented to other students, he takes pride in preparing all the tests required in an autopsy. A high school dropout in Boston returns to a school finance apprenticeship and suddenly becomes highly motivated to learn. Participants often report raising their grades and their aspirations enough to pursue a college career. Parents consistently are happy with the positive changes in their child's attitudes and performance.[56] More than half of student participants in school-to-career programs surveyed by Jobs for the Future reported that their involvement increased their motivation in high school and improved their relationships with teachers.[57]

To the extent that apprenticeship programs can succeed in reducing the boredom and frustration of young people, in raising their self-esteem through actual accomplishment, in giving them the realistic prospect for a rewarding career, additional social benefits could well emerge. Reductions in crime could yield the most significant benefits—to apprentices, to other students, to potential victims, and to taxpayers. In the cost-benefit analysis of the Job Corps, the social benefits from reduced crime were among the most significant in making the program look cost effective. Although participants in the Job Corps come from a much more at-risk group than prospective apprentices, positive effects of apprenticeship could well spread beyond the apprentices themselves and exert a positive effect on school peers and ultimately on the atmosphere at inner-city high schools.

Given these economic and social benefits accruing to students, it is no wonder that even start-up apprenticeship programs in the United States have generally attracted many more student applicants than places.

Perspective of Schools and Taxpayers

In examining costs and benefits to the school system and taxpayers, it is important to distinguish between short-term start-up costs (including operations well below the optimal scale) and the costs of a mature system. I shall focus on the mature system. One cost will be payments to intermediaries (either in the public or private sector) who make the program operate smoothly. These people solicit employers to become involved and offer slots, bring employers and the school system together, assure that the training is of high quality, oversee the contractual arrangements between employers and students, make participants aware of the occupational standards in other areas, provide technical assistance to employers and schools, and explain the program to parents and the broader public.

Other tasks that might be undertaken in the schools themselves include the use of occupational awareness curriculums, the organization of work shadowing, additional counseling oriented toward the workplace and apprenticeship training, curriculum development, and reorganizations that reduce class size. Unfortunately, few good data are available at this point as to the cost of these tasks in a mature program of adequate scale. In her review of the early stage of Boston's ProTech program, Susan Goldberger reports annual per student costs of about $3,500. However, she points to several reforms that might lower costs significantly.[58]

Schools should certainly achieve savings from a mature program. After all, if 20 percent of a school's students require only 50 to 60 percent of the usual number of classes, teacher and classroom requirements should decline significantly. Assuming school system savings on the basis of a proportion of average costs, the reductions would amount to about $4,000 a student. Even if the actual cost savings at the margin are below a proportion of total average costs, I still project a savings of $3,000 a student a year. While schools might object to any cut in their budget, the changes can occur over time, either though reducing increases in their budgets or allowing some of the counseling and curriculum development funds to flow through the school system.

Thus savings for schools in a mature system should come close to offsetting additional costs. However, at start-up, the per student costs are likely to exceed the per student benefits. Developing curriculums, attracting employers, and familiarizing students and parents with a new system are more difficult tasks at the beginning of the enterprise. Costs are higher, and they must be spread over a small number of apprentices.

A well-functioning system will require additional functions best undertaken beyond the local level. These include the development of occupational and industry standards, technical assistance, information sharing, and research. Again, the average costs of these activities will depend on the number of participants. The federal government is already providing limited support to pay for skill standards and some technical assistance. Certain states and local areas have already proved capable of creating skill standards in tens of industries at costs well under $100,000 per standard.[59] Since there are complementary sets of skills across industries and occupations, the costs should decline further with the expansion to two hundred standards. While these costs will only have to be incurred intermittently, financing technical assistance, dissemination, and research will be an ongoing task. The recently passed Goals 2000 legislation has already created a National Skill Standards Board to carry out these functions not only with regard to youth apprenticeships, but with regard to ways of attaining skills in other ways as well.

Finally, a set of special services will be required to assure broad participation from inner-city and minority students. As Ronald B. Mincy and Hillard Pouncy show, achieving success with these young people is difficult because of low entry skills, high dropout rates, and location mismatches between the students, their schools, and the jobs.[60] Mincy and Pouncy suggest several ideas to deal with these problems, including preapprenticeship activities for inner-city students well before eleventh grade, mentor-advocates outside the work site, counseling to employers, and transportation services. I have no good estimate for the per pupil cost of these activities, but state governments are already proposing to reorganize other activities to include these types of services.

Another suggestion for widening access to inner-city young people comes from the Children's Home Society of New Jersey and their proposed expansion of KIKS/Workforce 2000. This program begins by providing small groups of fourth to eighth graders with enhanced services to promote academic and social development, self-esteem, and life coping skills. From this group, the program develops peer leaders to enter apprenticeships and, at the same time, to serve in helping young children deal with issues of alcohol and drug use, sexual activity, and functioning in an often violent society.

So far, the evidence is that women and minorities are entering school-to-career programs at least in proportion to their local shares of the student population. Concerns about participation by poor and minority youth led the Congress to mandate funding under the School-to-Work Opportunities Act for special funding to local sites with high concentrations of poor children. As I argue below, large-scale big-city demonstrations are desirable partly because they would provide an indirect method of targeting toward disadvantaged students in areas where improving school-to-career options is most crucial.

Overall, the benefits appear high in comparison to the costs. With employers and schools coming close to breaking even, a modest earnings gain by participants would be enough to justify the program on economic grounds. Of course, if the noneconomic and external benefits materialize, the returns to the program will be outstanding to students and to the general public. However, the figures at this point are too limited to convince skeptics. A detailed analysis of ongoing programs in Wisconsin, Maine, New Jersey, and local sites should provide useful information on this issue.

Relationship to Other Approaches

This section examines two of the many possible competing approaches to solving school-to-work transition problems. One is an education strategy, which aims to raise the educational performance of youth by increasing spending on schools at the secondary and post-secondary level. The second is a mixed school-to-work strategy, involving a wide range of options linking young people to employment. This is the strategy that various states appear to be pursuing in response to the STWOA.

Nothing in my proposal should be taken as denigrating effective methods to improve the way schools educate students. For many, improved academic skills will be necessary in order to enter an apprenticeship. However, as noted above, the pure education strategy has several weaknesses. First, it ignores a major aspect of student motivation, especially for high school students: clear evidence that what they learn will pay off in terms of good jobs and careers. Even school-based systems aimed at the job market have problems in this area, partly because only about 30 percent of vocational education students report working in education-related jobs. Second, it does little to deal with the fact that young people have different learning styles. Perhaps because educational planners enjoyed and succeeded in school-based learning for sixteen-plus years of school, they cannot understand why every student should not do so. Those proposing a purely school-based approach discount the accumulating evidence of the effectiveness of contextualized learning. Third, high school students attach a very high priority to earning spending money. Under a purely school-based system they are likely to work in jobs that involve little training or linkage with their education. Fourth, a school-based system keeps youth in a purely youth peer culture that prolongs adolescence.

A mixed STWOA strategy is a more appealing competitor to youth apprenticeships. Under this approach, which has been largely adopted in the Clinton administration's STWOA, states and localities would use expanded cooperative education, tech-prep programs, and career academies. Space does not permit separate assessments of each alternative, but some of these approaches have positive elements similar to those in youth apprenticeships.

Career academies are usually schools operating within regular public schools, organized around a particular occupational field, such as health care, finance, or travel.[61] These programs do increase the relevance of education and can provide closer linkages between schools and employers. In addition, the programs provide continuity and a family atmosphere, partly because students remain with the same teachers and other students for their last three years of high school. In several occupational fields, the programs appear to be achieving considerable success in motivating students to learn, encouraging teachers to link the curriculum closely to related occupational or industry fields, providing rewarding internships, and offering mentoring. The career academy model is generating interest across the country and becoming an important part of the overall educational system in Oakland, California, and Philadelphia. Patricia Clark, the director of the Oakland Health and Bioscience Academy, reports that all students, including marginal students, thrive educationally, rarely drop out of school, take and pass more difficult courses, learn a great deal about occupations in a major industry, and become more mature and directed in the atmosphere of the academy.[62] Evaluations using non-experimental methods indicate that academies in California and Philadelphia have reduced dropout rates.[63]

Cooperative education programs could evolve into well-structured and more effective youth apprenticeship programs, but only if they embodied more in-depth and sustained training and if they did more to link work-based and school-based training with the aim of having students achieve recognized occupational standards.[64] Still, even in the absence of adequate supervision and placement efforts by schools, cooperative education is able to attract large numbers of employers, many of whom retain interns after the program ends. The fact that a less serious program with limited administrative support is able to attract employers is a hopeful sign for youth apprenticeship efforts.

Tech-prep programs also offer some hope for achieving many of the same goals of youth apprenticeship so long as they do not delay a youth's serious involvement with the individual employers and the realities of the workplace. Unless these elements are present, the programs will not provide nearly as much in the way of confidence-building, contextualized learning, constructive adult peer groups, and strengthened incentives to perform well in school. Young people may see these other approaches as simply an alternative major, not a serious and sustained effort to gain the competencies necessary for a particular field. From the employer viewpoint, the alternative programs do not combine all of the functions of screening, tryout employment, production by the apprentice, and firm-specific, work site training. Neither tech-prep nor the academy programs will able to tailor their mix of slots in response to the demands of employers as smoothly as apprenticeship programs can.

Additional Steps Necessary for Large-Scale Implementation

The idea of building a youth apprenticeship system has moved from the world of policy analysts to small demonstrations and subsequently to federal and state legislation. Yet there is a long way to go before achieving large-scale implementation.

The federal implementation strategy underlying the STWOA is simple: let states choose what they want to do, within very broad mandates. This approach has important advantages, especially at this stage of development. Because youth apprenticeships have not proved their effectiveness in the United States, it would be difficult to impose this model on a national basis. On the other hand, the inclusion of every type of school-to-work program weakens the effort to develop a coherent and comprehensive system. If a new system is to act as an additional route (other than a college degree) to successful careers, parents and employers will have to be able to recognize the meaning of a new certification. The differences among industries and occupations will already make this difficult. Having a multitude of STWOA models will complicate matters much further.

A second problem with the STWOA strategy is the inability to take advantage of important scale economies. Currently each state must develop its own industry and occupational competency standards, curriculums, and method of assessment and monitoring. Alternatively, it can conduct its own research on existing standards, curriculums, and assessment methods. There is little federal guidance. The dispersal of efforts under the STWOA will never allow for a large-scale test of the effectiveness of youth apprenticeships. For this reason, I agree with the National Academy of Sciences panel on postsecondary education for the workplace that the United States should stage a large-scale demonstration in a few cities.[65] The report points out that a citywide demonstration involving 20 to 25 percent of a cohort might affect not only apprentices but others, by improving the milieu of the school so that student peers no longer discourage academic achievement and by changing the expectations of eighth- and ninth-grade students. Employers, students, parents, and teachers would come to know the system and be more willing to participate. The natural mentoring of large numbers of inner-city youth could have other positive social effects. Scale within individual programs is also important for judging the costs of the program and the ability of the system to create special courses relevant to apprentices.

If the demonstrations reached a large scale, they would provide an important test of the new system. Should the demonstration cities succeed in motivating students, raising their academic achievement and graduation rates, training apprentices to achieve high levels of competence in particular occupations, increasing earnings, and re- ducing crime, citizens in other cities would demand that their schools and governments emulate these successes. To the extent the demon- strations did not succeed, serious research and analysis would be available to describe which components performed well and which poorly. It will be much more difficult to learn from the current highly dispersed approach.

Finally, federal, state, and local government officials could recog- nize their roles as employers to develop youth apprenticeships, espe- cially in occupations with counterparts in the private sector. Currently the government is one of the least-active employers of young workers in responsible positions. Instead of simply preaching to private employers to become involved, the government should lead by example through the development of apprenticeships in the public sector. In doing so it would confront directly the issues faced by schools, private employers, and students.

A good place to start, where jobs are plentiful and the skills of ex- isting workers are often limited, is in the secretarial or administrative assistant field. The current approach involves little training, a short probation period, and stringent restrictions on firings. Instead, the federal government could enter into apprenticeship arrangements with students for a two- to three-year period. During that period, as- piring workers would have to demonstrate their capabilities in a whole range of skills, from technical skills (mastering word-process- ing and spreadsheet programs) to organizational skills and social skills. After the apprenticeship certification, the government could choose whether to hire the person for a permanent job.

Conclusion

A large-scale youth apprenticeship system has the potential for dealing effectively with the nation's two youth problems: the low skills, motivation, and career options of non-college-bound youth and the more intractable economic and social problems of inner-city youth. Already, in all the initial serious youth apprenticeship programs, the response from students is overwhelmingly positive. Early skepticism about the desirability of a noncollege option has given way to enthusiasm from parents, students, and usually teachers as well. The attraction of a skilled career paying good wages is enough to make weak, formerly bored students into productive people who see a real future for themselves.

To me, the real question is not whether we can develop effective youth apprenticeships, but at what scale. Although legislation enabling the development of a system became law only in the spring of 1994, continued support for youth apprenticeships will depend on achieving quick results, on moving beyond a few hundred apprentices to a few hundred thousand or a million within the next few years. Making progress will require that federal, state, and local officials provide resources, leadership, and a team spirit among employers, parents, students, teachers, and school administrators to build this new system.

Success can mean hope for millions of American youth that by working hard and staying out of trouble, they can enter a financially rewarding and satisfying career. An effective youth apprenticeship system is one of the public policies that can play a major preventive role in reducing our nation's devastating levels of crime, illegitimacy, and poverty.

Notes

1. Richard B. Freeman and David A. Wise, eds., *The Youth Labor Market Problem: Its Nature, Causes, and Consequences* (University of Chicago Press, 1982), p. 6.

2. Richard H. de Leone, "School-to-Work Transition: Failings, Dilemmas, and Policy Options," in *Dilemmas in Youth Employment Programming: Findings from the Youth Research and Technical Assistance Project*, vol. 1 (Employment and Training Administration, Department of Labor, 1992), pp. 223–91.

3. William Julius Wilson, *The Truly Disadvantaged: The Inner City, the Underclass, and Public Policy* (University of Chicago Press, 1987).

4. Elijah Anderson, "The Code of the Streets," *Atlantic Monthly*, May 1994, pp. 80–94.

5. Elijah Anderson, "Sex Codes in the Inner City," in Robert I. Lerman and Theodora Ooms, eds., *Young Unwed Fathers: Changing Norms and Emerging Policies* (Temple University Press, 1993).

6. Newspaper accounts from a number of cities cite this phenomenon. See, for example, Ron Suskind, "In Rough City School, Top Students Struggle to Learn—and Escape," *Wall Street Journal*, May 26, 1994, pp. A1, A8; and Janita Poe, "A Black-on-Black Educational Barrier: Achievers Told Success Is a Sellout," *Chicago Tribune*, January 1, 1994, p. 1. Also see John U. Ogbu, "Minority Status and Literacy in Comparative Perspective," *Daedalus*, vol. 119 (1990), pp. 141–68.

7. W. Kip Viscusi, "Market Incentives for Criminal Behavior," in Richard B. Freeman and Harry J. Holzer, eds., *The Black Youth Employment Crisis* (University of Chicago Press, 1986), pp. 301–52.

8. Anderson, "Code of the Streets."

9. John Bound and Richard B. Freeman, "What Went Wrong? The Erosion of Relative Earnings and Employment among Young Black Men in the 1980s," Working Paper 3778 (Cambridge, Mass.: National Bureau of Economic Research, July 1991), p. 23.

10. See the discussion in Harry J. Holzer, "Youth and the Labor Market in the Nineties," in *Dilemmas in Youth Employment Programming: Findings from the Youth Research and Technical Assistance Project* (Employment and Training Administration, Department of Labor, 1992). Holzer draws on studies by Kirschenman and Neckerman on attitudes of employers in Chicago, as well as the Urban Institute studies of matched pairs of white and black applicants.

11. In his study of the Red Hook neighborhood of Brooklyn, Philip Kasinitz found that employers discriminated against local residents because they associated them with crime and poor work attitudes. The discrimination was not entirely racial since members of other racial groups in the area were also cast as undesirable and since employers did hire black West Indian immigrants. Employers relied on referrals from existing workers to allow them to determine which workers would be reliable and honest. See "The Real Jobs Problem," *Wall Street Journal*, November 26, 1993, p. A8.

12. Based on his research on blacks and Mexican Americans in Stockton, California, John Ogbu, "Minority Status," points out that while parents encourage children to get a good education, their low-level jobs, unemployment, and problems with "the system" convey a different message. "The result, inevitably, is that such children become increasingly disillusioned about their ability to succeed in adult life through the mainstream strategy of schooling" (p. 158).

13. See the evidence of the weak performance of U.S. high school students in Martin Neil Baily, Gary Burtless, and Robert E. Litan, *Growth with Equity: Economic Policymaking for the Next Century* (Brookings, 1993), pp. 112–21. For an opposing view that argues U.S. students are performing well academically, see David C. Berliner, "Educational Reform in an Era of Disinformation,"

paper presented at the meeting of the American Association of Colleges for Teacher Education, San Antonio, Texas, February 1992.

14. John Bishop, "Why the Apathy in American High Schools?" *Educational Researcher*, vol. 18 (January–February 1989), pp. 6–10, and "Why U.S. Students Need Incentives to Learn," *Educational Leadership*, vol. 49 (March 1992), pp. 15–18. See also Albert Shanker, "Give Students a Reason to Work Hard," *Wall Street Journal*, July 15, 1991, p. A10.

15. Young people report their dislike of school is the largest reason they drop out of high school. See Melissa R. Roderick, *The Path to Dropping Out: Evidence for Intervention* (Auburn House, 1993), pp. 26–27.

16. As one example of the dissatisfaction with the capacities of workers, about half the small manufacturers responding to a National Association of Manufacturers survey reported that a lack of skilled labor and lack of basic education skills are two major problems. See Office of Technology Assessment, *Worker Training: Competing in the New International Economy* (1990), p. 166.

17. Lisa M. Lynch, "The Economics of Youth Training in the United States," *Economic Journal*, vol. 103 (September 1993), pp. 1292–1302, especially p. 1296.

18. Paul Osterman, "Is There a Problem with the Youth Labor Market and If So, How Should We Fix It?" in Katherine McFate, Roger Lawson, and William Julius Wilson, eds., *Poverty, Inequality, and the Future of Social Policy: Western States in the New World Order* (Russell Sage, 1995), pp. 387–414.

19. Larry L. Orr and others, *The National JTPA Study: Impacts, Benefits, and Costs of Title II-A* (Bethesda, Md.: Abt Associates, March 1994).

20. Gary Walker and Frances Vilella-Velez, *Anatomy of a Demonstration* (Philadelphia: Public/Private Ventures, 1992).

21. George Cave and others, *JOBSTART: Final Report on a Program for School Dropouts* (New York: Manpower Demonstration Research Corp., 1993), pp. xviii, 214, 221.

22. George Farkas and others, *Post-Program Impacts of the Youth Incentive Entitlement Pilot Projects* (New York: Manpower Demonstration Research Corp., 1984), p. 112.

23. John Bishop, "Improving Job Matches in the U.S. Labor Market," *Brookings Papers on Economic Activity*, 1:1993, pp. 335–90.

24. James E. Rosenbaum and Takehiko Kariya, "From High School to Work: Market and Institutional Mechanisms in Japan," *American Journal of Sociology*, vol. 94 (May 1989), pp. 1334–65. They report that the Japanese use of grades as a visible selection device creates strong incentives for high school achievement. "Schools must select students who satisfy employers to keep on receiving their job allocations in the future, and employers try to continue hiring a school's graduates to preserve a stable source of employees of dependable quality" (pp. 1343–44).

25. To quote the OECD report, "As long as there is a single pecking order in education or employment, status differences are inevitable, and are not going to be altered by merely cosmetic changes in labels and titles. However,

when there are multiple status hierarchies (i.e. several kinds of pecking order) involving different kinds of criteria, courses are more likely to be seen as 'different' rather than 'unequal'." The inclusion of all forms of postcompulsory education and training in a single institutional, administrative, and certificatory framework may reinforce the single hierarchy, if such a hierarchy ultimately embodies a single set of values. In the education system, such values tend to reflect the dominant values of higher education, as the apex of the system; hence the emphasis is placed on theory, abstraction, and cognitive-intellectual ability. Within such a single hierarchy, vocational education cannot easily raise its status, because it tends to rate low on such measures. However, where postcompulsory education has developed multiple institutional forms, there may be a greater diversity of values, and a plurality of hierarchies." See Organization for Economic Cooperation and Development, *Pathways for Learning: Education and Training from 16 to 19* (Paris, 1989), p. 87.

26. Lauren B. Resnick, "Literacy in School and Out," *Daedalus*, vol. 119 (Spring 1990), p. 171.

27. *Economist*, "Education: Coming Top," November 21, 1992, p. 11.

28. See, for example, S. J. Prais, "Vocational Qualifications of the Labour Force in Britain and Germany," *National Institute Economic Review*, no. 98 (November 1981), pp. 47–59; and Hilary Steedman and Karin Wagner, "A Second Look at Productivity, Machinery and Skills in Britain and Germany," *National Institute Economic Review*, no. 122 (November 1987), pp. 84–96. Also see the summary of their studies and additional references in Office of Technology Assessment, *Worker Training*.

29. Wolfgang Lempert and Stephen F. Hamilton report that school performance is highly significant in the allocation of students to specific apprenticeships. See "The Impact of Apprenticeship on Adolescents: A Prospective Analysis," *Journal of Research on Adolescence* (forthcoming).

30. As Lauren B. Resnick pointed out, today's schools use different learning methods from those used at work and elsewhere. Schools employ individual approaches in which students manipulate symbols and abstract thoughts; elsewhere people work in groups and use tools to deal with specific situations. See "Learning in School and Out," *Educational Researcher*, vol. 16 (December 1987), pp. 13–20.

31. Robert L. Crain, Amy Heebner, and Yiu-Pong Si, *The Effectiveness of New York City's Career Magnet Schools: An Evaluation of Ninth Grade Performance Using an Experimental Design* (Berkeley, Calif.: National Center for Research in Vocational Education, 1992).

32. Hilary Steedman, "The Economics of Youth Training in Germany," *Economic Journal*, vol. 103 (September 1993), pp. 1279–91.

33. Osterman, "Is There a Problem with the Youth Labor Market?"

34. Steedman, "Economics of Youth Training."

35. Germany did experience a shortfall of places from 1982 to 1986, but this was an exceptional period that combined a serious recession with a peak level of seventeen-year-olds. See Steedman, "Economics of Youth Training," pp. 1279–91.

36. American Youth Policy Forum and Jobs For the Future, *Promising Practices: A Study of Ten School-to-Career Programs* (Boston, 1995), pp.13–15.

37. Steven G. Allen, "Further Evidence on Union Efficiency in Construction," *Industrial Relations*, vol. 27 (Spring 1988), pp. 232–40.

38. General Accounting Office, *Apprenticeship Training: Administration, Use, and Equal Opportunity: Report to Congressional Requesters* (1992), pp. 21–25.

39. Heckman, "Is Job Training Oversold?" p. 108; and Steedman, "Economics of Youth Training," pp. 1286–87. Edwin Artzt, chairman of Proctor and Gamble, stated at President-elect Clinton's economic conference in December 1992 that their only source of new manufacturing hires for their eight manufacturing plants in Germany comes through the apprenticeship program. He went on to say that while P&G has plants all over the world, their most efficient plants are in Germany.

40. Robert I. Lerman and Julia I. Lane, "Earnings Inequality and Educational Stratification in Germany and the U.S.," American University, Department of Economics, 1993.

41. See Alan M. Hershey and Marsha K. Silverberg, "Employer Involvement in School-to-Work Transition Programs: What Can We Really Expect?", paper presented at Association for Public Policy and Management Conference, Washington, October 29, 1993; Osterman, "Is There a Problem with the Youth Labor Market?"

42. Dietmar Harhoof and Thomas J. Kane, "Financing Apprenticeship Training: Evidence from Germany," Working Paper 4557 (Cambridge, Mass.: National Bureau of Economic Research, December 1993).

43. Henry A. Glick and Michael J. Feuer, "Employer-Sponsored Training and the Governance of Specific Human Capital Investments," *Quarterly Review of Economics and Business*, vol. 24 (Summer 1984), pp. 91–103.

44. See M. Feuer, H. Glick, and A. Desai, "Is Firm-Sponsored Education Viable?", *Journal of Economic Behavior and Organization*, vol. 8 (March 1987), pp. 121–36.

45. Jonathan Veum, "Training, Wages, and the Human Capital Model," Working Paper 262 (Department of Labor, Bureau of Labor Statistics, January 1995).

46. Margaret Stevens summarizes these arguments in "An Investment Model for the Supply of Training by Employers," *Economic Journal*, vol. 104 (May 1994), pp. 556–70.

47. David Finegold, "Making Apprenticeships Work," *RAND Issue Paper*, no. 1 (March 1993).

48. Steedman, "Economics of Youth Training," p. 1286; and David Soskice, "Reconciling Markets and Institutions: The German Apprenticeship System," in Lisa M. Lynch, ed., *Training and the Private Sector: International Comparisons* (University of Chicago Press, 1994).

49. See Harhoof and Kane, "Financing Apprenticeship Training," table 2.

50. Osterman, "Is There a Problem with the Youth Labor Market?"

51. Susan Goldberger reports that Boston area hospitals spend $350,000

per institution on advertising for employees. In addition, they typically employ ten to twenty full-time recruiters, search firms, and sign-on bonuses. See *Creating an American-Style Youth Apprenticeship Program: A Formative Evaluation of Project ProTech* (Boston: Jobs for the Future, February 1993), pp. 46, 50.

52. If firms hire three of every four apprentices and extra costs of recruiting skilled workers over the costs of recruiting apprentices amount to $2,000, the benefit per apprentice would be $1,500. The estimate in table 5-2 ignores the longer likely duration of apprentices (over typical new hires) with the training firm.

53. Katherine Abraham and Susan Houseman, cited in Harhoof and Kane, "Financing Apprenticeship Training," p. 17, point to high firing costs as a rationale for German employers' training more skilled workers than required on a current basis. But Harhoof and Kane argue that since 1986 restrictions on layoffs have been loosened and employers can use the option of hiring workers on an eighteen-month fixed contract to avoid high layoff costs.

54. See Commission on the Skills of the American Workforce, *America's Choice: High Skills or Low Wages!* (Washington: National Center on Education and the Economy, 1990). Also see Heckman's response.

55. This assumes that the utility from hours at the work site is no less than the marginal hours spent at school. If the loss of school time reduced the student's academic achievement, such losses might militate against the long-term earnings gains expected from apprenticeship. In fact the opposite appears to be the case from anecdotal comments by many student apprentices in the U.S. demonstrations.

56. Robert Van Dine, who helped initiate a Williamsport, Pennsylvania, youth apprenticeship in metal trades, remarked, "I haven't found one parent who hasn't seen a positive change in their child." See Edwin Kiester, Jr., "Germany Prepares Kids for Good Jobs; We Were Preparing Ours for Wendy's," *Smithsonian*, March 1993, pp. 44–57.

57. Jobs for the Future, *Promising Practices*, p. 14.

58. Goldberger, "Creating an American-Style Youth Apprenticeship Program."

59. New Jersey's school-to-work proposal estimates a figure of $25,000 per occupational competency for twenty occupations per year. See State of New Jersey, *From Learning to Earning: New Jersey's School-To-Work Opportunities Implementation Proposal* (Trenton, N.J., 1994), pt. 3, p. 2.

60. Hillard Pouncy and Ronald B. Mincy, "Out-of-Welfare Strategies for Welfare-Bound Youth," in Demetra Smith Nightengale and Robert H. Haveman, eds., *The Work Alternative: Welfare Reform and the Realities of the Job Market* (Urban Institute Press, 1995).

61. For a portrait of career academies, see David Stern, Marilyn Raby, and Charles Dayton, *Career Academies: Partnerships for Reconstructing American High Schools* (San Francisco: Jossey-Bass, 1992).

62. Presentation by Patricia Clark at the Fourth Annual National Leadership Forum on School-to-Work Transition, Boston, July 28, 1995.

63. Stern, *Career Academies*, pp. 56–70.

64. Irene Lynn and Joan Wills report that employers of cooperative education students apparently provide very little formal training. See *School Lessons, Work Lessons: Recruiting and Sustaining Employer Involvement in School-to-Work Programs* (Washington: Institute for Educational Leadership, 1994).

65. Janet S. Hansen, ed., *Preparing for the Workplace: Charting a Course for Federal Postsecondary Training Policy* (Washington: National Academy Press, 1994).

Chapter 6

Health Care Goes to School: An Untidy Strategy to Improve the Well-Being of School-Age Children

Julia Graham Lear

Two CONTENDING forces in the field of public policy have created a difficult terrain on which to build social policies that support poor children. On the one hand, there is widespread concern that any new government program, even those targeted on the youngest and most vulnerable members of society, will increase the federal debt or press states beyond their fiscal capacity. On the other, despite concerns about public spending and persistent antigovernment rhetoric, there has been sustained political willingness to consider the needs of poor children. These needs, documented in recent years by nearly a dozen reports sponsored by various bipartisan or independent bodies, appear to reinforce a national interest in "doing" something for poor children, particularly if the "doing" can be cost contained and targeted on those most in need.[1]

One intervention on behalf of poor children that meets the criteria of targeted and limited spending is the school health center.[2] Over the past twenty years, these centers have demonstrated potential for responding to the persistent health problems and limited access to care affecting low-income students. School health centers, usually sited in communities where child and adolescent health professionals are few and needs are great, have increased availability of physical and mental health services for school-age children. While the future of all children's health care has been clouded by the failure to achieve universal health insurance, recent experience suggests that broad replication of these centers can help children and their families overcome barriers to needed health services.

Recapping the Need

While most children are in excellent health and receive adequate care, too many children in the United States neither see a physician at recommended intervals nor receive treatment for episodic or chronic problems.[3] The difficulties confronting these mostly low-income children are compounded by the higher rates of health problems associated with poverty and the greater barriers poor children experience in securing care.

Health Problems of School-Age Children

The most common complaints of school-age children include injuries, chronic conditions, and mental health problems. Injuries kill more than eight thousand children age fifteen and younger annually. Chronic conditions limit the routine activity of between 2 and 6 million children ages eighteen and younger.[4] Mental health problems affect even larger numbers. The National Institute of Mental Health estimates that 7.5 million young people (12 percent of our children) have at least one diagnosable disorder. Half of these children are said to have seriously handicapping conditions.[5] Problems affecting adolescents, including violent death, pregnancy, and substance abuse, have stirred continuing worries about behaviors that compromise individual and societal well-being.[6]

Poverty in the United States increases the number of health problems affecting children. Poor children, reported in 1993 to number 15.7 million (22.7 percent of the total under-eighteen population), have a frequency rate for many medical problems that is double to triple the norm. Child deaths due to disease are triple to quadruple those of other children and deaths due to accidents are double to triple those of other children.[7]

Barriers to Health Services

The primary reason children are unable to secure timely and appropriate care for their health problems is financial. In 1991, more than eight million children under age eighteen had no health insurance. These children were less likely to receive preventive or early intervention care.[8] Eliminating financial barriers by guaranteeing universal health insurance coverage remains the most essential step toward ensuring health care for low-income children.

Health insurance alone, however, will not solve all problems. Unequal distribution of physicians and other health professionals across the United States, inadequate transportation services, cultural barriers, and institutional practices all impede access to care. In Chicago, for example, the child-to-pediatrician ratio in poor neighborhoods is 5,887:1, in contrast to a national average of about 1,000:1.[9] Even when physicians are present in a community, they may refuse to see medicaid-enrolled children. In some instances, medicaid rules get in the way of service. For example, nearly half the state medicaid programs do not reimburse for mental health services provided by psychologists or clinical social workers, even when they are supervised by psychiatrists.[10]

Adolescents face additional barriers to care. Adolescents are more likely than other age groups to be uninsured. About 15 percent have no health insurance.[11] Many, despite legal protections, are also unable to secure confidential services related to sexuality, substance abuse, or emotional problems. And all adolescents confront a shortage of physicians or other health professionals trained in adolescent health care.

If poor children do not receive adequate health care, does it make a difference? Health economist Victor Fuchs has written that in rich nations health services do not ensure better health for any age group: genetics, income, and behavior are more important in determining health status.[12] Most who have studied the matter agree, while emphasizing that health care plays a variable role, depending on patient age, health problem, and other factors. Barbara Bergmann suggests elsewhere in this volume that in the United States as in other wealthy countries, quite apart from questions of efficacy, health care is considered a "merit good"; that is, most people believe that a decent society makes health care available to everyone, regardless of other factors. While the congressional impasse on health care reform suggests something less than a national consensus on universal access to care, support for children's health services appears to continue in the face of federal and state budget cutting.[13]

Launching a School Health Center Initiative

Building on continued public support for programs directed toward children's well-being, this chapter proposes meeting the health care needs of a large number of unserved and underserved school-age children by establishing comprehensive school health centers in up to 7,500 elementary and secondary schools across the United States. The centers would provide a broad range of physical and mental health services as well as preventive care and health-promoting activities. The eligible schools would be elementary and secondary schools with student populations exceeding 500 and in which 50 percent or more of the students are entitled to participate in the free or reduced-price lunch program. The centers would link existing efforts in primary care, public health, school health, and health education with emerging systems of managed health care to ensure that the health care requirements of the neediest children are met.

HOW MANY CENTERS? While poor children can be found in nearly every public school, those in greatest need and with the fewest resources are most frequently found in schools with the highest concentrations of poverty. The Department of Education estimates that approximately 20,000 elementary schools and 5,000 secondary schools have enrollments in which more than 50 percent of the students are poor. However, many elementary schools have enrollments too small to sustain a full-time school-based health center. There are 8,300 elementary schools in which 50 percent of students are from poor families and which also have enrollments in excess of 500.[14] Those schools, plus an estimated 2,000 very poor secondary schools, would be eligible for school health centers.

It is unlikely that all 10,300 schools would be interested in participating in the program. First, while poor communities are most likely to have large numbers of children with significant untreated health problems, this is not always the case. Therefore, a few low-income schools would not have students with compelling unmet health care needs.[15] In other communities, space limitations within the school; labor market constraints; opposition from community members, school faculty, administration, or school board; competing priorities (for example, establishing recreation programs or family resource centers); or an absence of a sponsoring medical organization may also deter a school or a school district from participating in a health center initiative. A reasonable guess might be that 7,500 of the eligible schools would ultimately seek to establish centers if they were financially viable.

HOW MUCH WOULD IT COST? If 7,500 public elementary and secondary schools were supported to establish and operate comprehensive school health centers, the total cost would be $1.5 billion annually (at an average cost per center of $200,000).[16]

WHO SHOULD PAY? The answer to this question is everyone, and hence this strategy is untidy. There would be no single source of dollars, no czar or czarina for school-based health care. Some central standard setting would exist because health care, especially health care for the poor, is homogenized to some degree by the role of the federal government in medicaid and, potentially, by the role of the federal government in health care reform. But schools are a matter of local and state control, and health care itself is organized and staffed in quite different ways across the country. A patchwork of funding sources and participating partners seems appropriate to the health and education systems that would be involved in the new strategy.

The degree to which various levels of government and private agencies would contribute would depend, in part, on whether the federal or state governments expand health insurance coverage for all children and on the degree to which school health centers are included in the changing structures of health care financing. Specific measures at the federal and state level would be essential to assist school health centers either to receive adequate grant support to sustain the centers or to recover a significant portion of their operating costs through payment for patient services. Currently most school health centers are paid little for patient care due to the large number of uninsured students they care for, the poor coverage for primary and preventive care offered by many private health insurance plans, and a variety of regulations that limit medicaid participation.

The Federal Role

The collapse of health care reform in 1994 and election of a Congress that is not eager to resume the health care debate create a challenge to crafting a federal role to support school health centers. Despite bipartisan approval of funding for school health services during the health reform discussions, current anti-Washington rhetoric and Republican presidential politics likely preclude the possibility of a major federal initiative as was envisioned in the Clinton proposal.[17]

The new Republican-led Congress, however, creates both opportunity and necessity for rethinking the federal role in improving health care for poor children in a period of retrenchment. Two useful possibilities present themselves: providing vision and leadership on the continued importance of child health services and offering a small, well-constructed grant initiative that models the delivery of effective health services.

VISION AND LEADERSHIP. In the midst of post–health care reform angst, political leaders and federal officials urgently need to remind the nation of its obligation to continue to build the network of services for children. Creating a vision of a health care system that serves all children and defining the role of school health centers within that system is particularly beneficial when the health care system is changing radically. Poor children face uncertain treatment in the emerging health care systems that are dominated by integrated service networks, complex managed care programs, and Wall Street–oriented financing plans.

THE GRANT INITIATIVE. A federal grant program could build on recent work by the Department of Health and Human Services and link with state-led initiatives to develop school health centers as part of a multifaceted effort to improve health care for unserved and underserved school-age children.

At present direct federal support for school health centers is small indeed. Despite support within the Clinton administration, less than $6 million is designated for school health centers by the Department of Health and Human Services.[18] An expanded but politically viable federal initiative might underwrite the establishment of 350 school health centers, a number slightly less than 5 percent of the target 7,500 but large enough to increase significantly the number of poor children served and the number of viable models in every interested state. A reasonable schedule for development of 350 excellent, stan-

TABLE 6-1. *Funding Required to Support New School-Based Health Centers, Fiscal Years 1996–99*

Millions of dollars

Fiscal year	Number of new sites	Start-up funds	Continuation support	Total
1996	50	7.5	—	7.5
1997	75	11.3	5.0	16.3
1998	100	15.0	10.0	25.0
1999	125	18.6	12.5	31.1

Source: Author's calculations.

dard-setting centers might be 50 in fiscal year (FY)96, 75 in FY97, 100 in FY98, and 125 in FY99. The numbers in table 6-1 demonstrate how this strategy might work.

The average cost per center would be $200,000, and the federal government would provide 75 percent of that cost in the start-up year and 50 percent in succeeding years. Determining factors in selecting sites would be willingness of health care organizations and school systems to redeploy some of their personnel and redirect some of their funding to support the centers. For example, a city mayor might choose to use some Office of Substance Abuse Prevention funds to support the mental health professionals at the center. The state mental health system might also encourage community mental health centers to place staff within the health centers. Schools might choose to use chapter 1 education funds or funding for health-related services for special education students to contribute to the functioning of the center. Schools with pupil-support personnel, such as social workers, counselors, nurses, or psychologists, could link their staff with the new centers.

Continuation support would not exceed 50 percent of the average cost of the center because the centers would increasingly be woven into the mechanisms that fund clinical care. Schools with a mostly insured population might eventually secure up to 50 percent of the operating cost of the centers. Schools with large numbers of uninsured students would face a greater challenge to survive.

To set a school health center initiative in motion, the Congress and the executive branch need to appropriate funds to finance the start-up of new school-based health centers and set aside additional dollars to support the nonreimbursable services and activities provided by the school health centers. Federal agencies that might participate in a school health center initiative include the Bureau of Maternal and Child Health, the Bureau of Primary Health Care, the Center for Mental Health Services, and the Center for Substance Abuse Prevention.

The State Role

One significant result of the collapse of national health care reform is that state governments are assuming major responsibility for nurturing and sustaining service initiatives such as school health centers. Many states are already investing heavily in the centers. In 1994 thirty-two states reported allocating an estimated $38.8 million to local governments or health institutions to provide comprehensive primary care services in schools. California, Delaware, and Massachusetts are all supporting more than 20 centers; Connecticut has made grants to 50; and New York State is supporting nearly 150.[19]

There is growing awareness, however, that the shrinking public health dollar and the emergence of managed care require a thoughtful and intentional state policy to encourage the participation of both private and public funds to support the health centers if established centers are to survive and if new centers are to open.

The first step states must take to facilitate the development of school-based health centers is to identify the barriers to school health centers and construct public policies that remove or reduce them. The primary barrier to the creation of school health centers is financial. The fundamental question is how to fund additional primary care for poor children while public grants are not expanding and threatening to shrink. Paradoxically, the rapid expansion in managed care—particularly medicaid managed care—creates an opportunity for states to move aggressively to develop school health centers.

Managed care has grown dramatically in the past few years, and medicaid managed care has grown even more dramatically. Between 1991 and 1993, the number of medicaid beneficiaries enrolled in managed care plans increased from 8.1 million to 33.6 million. Since 1993 seven waiver applications have been approved by the federal Health Care Financing Administration that will allow states to bring all medicaid enrollees under a state-funded managed care initiative, the medicaid Section 1115 demonstration waivers. Applications from eight more states are under review in Washington, while at least ten additional states are in the process of developing applications.[20]

One characteristic of the waiver request—and the aspect that creates the most opportunity for school-based health centers—is that although the initial impetus for the waiver has been to contain health care costs, waivers are also used as vehicles to expand insurance for the uninsured, coordinate care for the enrollees, and ensure that quality standards are met. Thus the 1115 waiver application process creates a powerful opportunity to reassess the health care needs of poor children, rethink the adequacy of primary care services, and adopt strategies that support the development of additional primary care delivery sites. And these sites might include school-based health centers.[21]

Within the 1115 waiver, there are three primary strategies a state can pursue to make sure that the new medicaid managed care system makes a school-based health center strategy viable: a regulatory approach, a market model, or a pooled funding approach. Each has some strengths and weaknesses; none is likely to be adopted in its purest form. All have the advantage of helping state officials think about what is required to establish a financing system for a new health care delivery mechanism.[22]

REGULATORY APPROACH. Under this approach, the state medicaid office—either in its 1115 waiver application or in its contract with the managed care plans—specifies that the plans must contract with and reimburse school health centers for care provided to their enrollees. The state might designate cost-based reimbursement or it might require that the plans reimburse the centers at the market rate, with the state providing additional dollars for the uncompensated health education and classroom services frequently provided by school health centers. While this approach provides certainty of participation in the managed care network for the centers, it burdens the managed care plans by insisting they contract with school health centers that might not meet a plan's standard of care. It also burdens the school health centers, which would likely be required to negotiate contracts and undertake complex billing and accounting procedures with a large number of managed care plans.

MARKET-BASED MODEL. In a privatized approach the state might determine that managed care plans should reimburse for school-based health services of a specified type. Regulations would define the services and conditions under which certain health care services should be provided at a school. For example, regulations might state that if 20 percent or more of a school's population belonged to a plan, then the plan must offer certain services at schools with specific characteristics. How the plans would organize to deliver those services would be left to the market. If a health center were located in a school, then plans might choose to contract with the center. The plans also might choose to contract with school nurses or other health personnel. As with the regulatory approach, this strategy places a heavy administrative burden on the school health center staff and may be difficult to implement in health markets with a large number of plans enrolling medicaid children.

POOLED FUNDING APPROACH. Under this strategy, the state defines the eligible populations to be served and the services to be funded with state dollars. The state may then inform the managed care plans that if they want to participate in the state's 1115 waiver program, the plans pay a tax to the state, perhaps a set amount per adolescent per month, which would then be placed in a state pool that could include MCH block grant funds, chapter 1 funds, juvenile justice funds, and other categorical funds. The state funds could then be used to draw down the federal match under medicaid and enlarge the pool further. The state would then have an expanded pool of funds to support local school health centers. The benefit of this approach is that it relieves individual school health centers from a billing and accounting burden. The disadvantage is that at the clinic level it reduces the connection between service volume and revenues and, at the state level, increases the state agency's obligation to monitor and tend to productivity as well as other standards.

A New Approach to Children's Health Care

The first school health centers were established about twenty-five years ago. The twin themes of increasing access to care for adolescents and reducing teen pregnancy appear early in discussions of the centers. Their expansion, however, has been fueled primarily by concern that adolescents in general have not been well served by the traditional health care delivery system and a desire in particular to increase health care for low-income students. The first health centers were established primarily in high schools, but increasingly state initiatives and community programs have developed centers in elementary and middle schools.

In the past ten years, the number of school health centers increased from about fifty to more than six hundred. This expansion was fueled primarily by state support. In 1994, states allocated $12 million of their Title V (maternal and child health) block grant funds and $22.3 million in general funds to support the centers.[23]

The school health centers blend medical care with preventive and psychosocial services; they also organize broader school-based and community-based health promotion efforts. How this is done varies from school to school, community to community, but is suggested by the four examples below.

New York City

At Far Rockaway High School, located on the isolated Far Rockaway peninsula in Queens, almost one-third of the 2,000 students had no regular source of health care before the school clinic opened. Finding health care was a particular challenge for these students because one-quarter had recently immigrated to the United States and one-half were foreign born. Only one-quarter were living with both parents, and one-third were enrolled in special programs for academically at-risk students or had repeated a grade.[24]

In 1987, the Adolescent Division of North Shore University Hospital and the Far Rockaway High School staff organized a school health center, to be open year-round, five days a week, 8:00 A.M.–4:00 P.M., with weekend coverage by the nearby St. John's Episcopal Hospital emergency department. The center is staffed by two nurse practitioners, a clinical social worker, part-time physicians, and trainees in the fields of medicine, nursing, and psychology. During the 1992–93 school year, 1,015 (of 1,600) students made 4,722 visits to the health center. Twenty-five percent of visits were for acute medical problems; 21 percent were for mental health issues; 14 percent were for job, sports, or routine physical examination; 13 percent were for gynecological problems; 12 percent were immunizations; and 6 percent were for chronic conditions.

Although the visit categories sound routine, the time devoted to these visits suggests the intensity of need. Only 19 percent of visits lasted less than ten minutes; 38 percent lasted from ten to twenty minutes and 43 percent lasted longer than twenty minutes. In addition to clinical services, the health center staff organized educational sessions and special events for students, faculty, parents, and the community.[25]

Denver

Denver's first three school-based health centers have acquired a slightly different focus. While the clinics at Lincoln, East, and Manual high schools also enroll about 70 percent of the school population and provide a similar set of physical and mental health services, the school population is more diverse, including more Asian and white students as well as students from families above the poverty line but below the median community income. These students are also more likely to have community-based health providers. Despite their better access to community resources, the students keep the Denver clinics busy: 1,480 students made a total of 7,598 visits during the 1992–93 school year. The medical director thinks that students use the clinic because they believe the services are more likely to be confidential than those provided by private physicians or HMOs.

The health centers also deliver a high volume of mental health and alcohol and drug treatment services. Mental health and substance abuse services constitute about half the total, with medical services about 45 percent and a special violence prevention program 3 percent. Close links to school staff promote the use of these services. Under agreement with the school system, students caught using drugs or alcohol are given the option of staying in school if they agree to attend a prescribed number of sessions with the substance abuse counselors. Similarly students involved in violence or abusive relationships are referred by school administrators as well as the courts to the clinics' specialized violence prevention and intervention counseling services.[26]

Bridgeport, Connecticut

At Blackham Elementary and Middle School in Bridgeport, Connecticut, the health center serves an ethnically diverse mix of the very poor, not so poor, and the simply poorly insured. At Blackham, the health team is joined by a dentist. The volume of dental work in the city's four school-based dental suites is such that a full-time dentist stays busy spending one day a week at each school health center and allocating the fifth day to the school with the longest waiting list.

When asked to compare her elementary school and high school health centers, the clinic director notes that for about 75 percent of the care, the content—acute care, chronic care, and mental health—is relatively similar. But at the elementary school an outreach worker has been hired to make home visits and to assist families to secure social services.

The health center serves as a base on which to build a variety of support and social services for students and their families. For example, a large number of boys from the sixth, seventh, and eighth grades have been referred to the male outreach worker due to concerns about gang involvement, truancy, and school performance. The outreach worker has formed a "men's group" to create a network of support for young boys headed for trouble.[27]

Portland, Oregon

For the Multnomah County Health Department, school health centers are an intervention to address the problem of teen pregnancy. When the health department opened its first center at Roosevelt High School in 1986, the site was selected not only because a large number of students had no health insurance, but also because the school's neighborhood had a high teen pregnancy rate.[28] The seven Multnomah County school health centers provide comprehensive physical and mental health services; they also offer a full range of family planning services, including dispensing condoms and prescribing other contraceptives. Family planning represented 40 percent of the care provided during the 1992–93 school year.

In 1992 the state of Oregon adopted its Benchmarks process to guide funding decisions. Reducing teen pregnancy and teen drug abuse were established as two urgent benchmarks. Based on the results of a study comparing student behaviors at schools with health centers and schools without health centers over a two-year period, the state has expanded its funding for the health centers. The Oregon

Health Department has noted the positive impact the health centers had on targeted behaviors: students in clinic schools were more likely to see a health provider in the previous year than students in non-clinic schools; students in clinic schools were less likely to report having sex in the month before the survey than students in nonclinic schools; and students in clinic schools reported less binge drinking than students in nonclinic schools. According to the Oregon Health Department, "In each of these selected survey questions, the students in the Clinic Schools demonstrated improvements in health related behaviors compared to Control Schools."[29]

Arguments in Support of a School Health Center Strategy

Despite the failure of Clinton health care reform, the potential for expanded health insurance coverage for children and adolescents continues as states use managed care initiatives to insure a greater number of poor and near-poor children.[30] Therefore, the question remains, How do we make this potential access to care a reality? School health centers, which represent a dollar-limited, population-specific strategy involving both the federal and state governments, are a realistic approach in the current fiscal and political environment.

SCHOOL HEALTH CENTERS INCREASE ACCESS TO CARE. The fundamental reason to support a school health center strategy is that these centers will increase access to health care for low-income, school-age children. Data from a large number of school-based health centers, summarized in table 6-2, confirm the potential of health centers for increasing access to care.[31]

Students use the health centers frequently, as demonstrated by the number of enrollees, total visits, the number of visits per user, and the ratio of repeat to new visits. Analysis of a particularly busy health center indicated that the most frequent clinic users were students with more high-risk behaviors, lower grade point averages, and a greater self-identified need for mental health services than the average users.[32]

In a study of twenty-four school-based health centers, the centers were found to provide care to a large number of students who had not had care recently, did not report a regular source of care, and did not have health insurance. Twenty-four percent of the new students

TABLE 6-2. *Frequency of Diagnostic Categories in Selected School-Based Health Centers with Comprehensive Capacity*

Percent unless otherwise specified

Item	Connecticut elementary school	New York middle school	New York high school	Colorado high schools (2)	Oregon high schools (7)
Grade level	K–8	6–8	9–12	9–12	9–12
Students in school	1,200	1,700	1,700	3,926	8,858
Enrollees in SBHC	968	668	1,000	2,595	4,336
SBHC visits per year	1,927	2,942	5,214	7,590	18,600
Diagnoses per year	2,253	2,942	5,942	7,590	23,343
Diagnostic categories					
Well child/adolescent	8	15	19	14	12
Gynecology/sexually related	4	4	24	9	42
Mental health/social work	33	26	16	42	16
Injury/orthopedic	5	6	6	6	5
Neuro/ophthalmology	10	8	3	2	<1
Cardio/respiratory	8	4	4	2	3
Dermatology	6	3	3	3	4
Hematology	<1	2	3	<1	1
Gastroenterology	3	4	5	1	1
Dental	9	15	8	<1	<1
Ear/nose/throat	9	3	3	2	5
Infections	3	6	6	6	4
Drug and alcohol services	—	—	—	14	1
Other[a]	<1	<6	<3	<3	<5
Total	100	100	100	100	100

Source: Columbia University School Health Policy Initiative, "National Work Groups Define School-Based Health Center Services," ACCESS to Comprehensive School-Based Health Services for Children (Columbia University School of Public Health, 1994), p. 3.

a. Includes endocrine/obesity, urologic, allergic, and unspecified services.

who enrolled in the health centers during the 1992–93 school year stated they had not received medical care in more than two years, 35 percent said they did not have a regular source of care, and 47 percent stated they did not have health insurance.

SCHOOL HEALTH CENTERS FIT WITHIN A STATE-DRIVEN HEALTH POLICY ENVIRONMENT. While consensus on health care reform currently eludes Congress, health care policy continues to be high on state legislative agendas. School health centers are congruent with the purposes of health care reform, whether that reform is driven by the federal or state governments.

States are essential partners in a school health center initiative. They make the laws regulating health professionals, write the medicaid rules regarding which providers shall be reimbursed, fund public health measures, and allocate a variety of federal block grant funds. Reallocation of federal dollars in the health and education arenas frequently requires the participation of state governments. States also support the training programs that affect the supply and quality of health professionals available to the centers. As noted previously, with many states moving medicaid recipients into managed care plans, the main engine for financing school-based health centers will become medicaid managed care.[33]

Many states are attempting to shift emphasis and spending from specialty care to primary care by expanding medicaid benefits to more low-income residents. If the school-based health centers can persuade state governments or the organizers of health services that they offer cost-effective ways to increase access to primary care for underserved young people, states with larger numbers of poor and uninsured children may take the lead in establishing more school health centers.

SCHOOL HEALTH CENTERS FOCUS PUBLIC FUNDING ON THE "DESERVING POOR." A children-focused policy may have particular political appeal in a climate hostile to providing services and income to poor adults. An initiative that benefits children directly and adults only indirectly sidesteps opposition generated by programs that are perceived as benefiting the "undeserving" poor. The continued expansions of medicaid coverage for children during the Reagan years and the willingness of states to implement some of the more generous federal options suggest that, even in a harsh political climate, there remains support for policies that respond directly to children's needs.

SCHOOL HEALTH CENTER STRATEGY BUILDS ON RECENT WORK. A fairly solid base for reform has been laid not only by the stream of reports over the past ten years but also by small-scale demonstrations of school-based health centers in a number of cities and states. As noted at the beginning of this discussion, foundation studies, federal agency papers, commissions staffed by Democrats and Republicans, calls for action issued by corporate leadership, and state governments have all affirmed the need to alter the conditions and opportunities for children. Local and state initiatives supporting school health care have created a cadre of seasoned clinicians, political leaders, parents, students, and community advocates who can both demonstrate how to make such an initiative work and testify to the impact of the centers.

Arguments against a School Health Center Intervention

As school-based health centers have become increasingly popular, policy analysts have begun to look more carefully at this new primary care delivery mechanism and have raised at least four substantive objections.

SCHOOL HEALTH CENTERS WILL BE DUPLICATIVE AND UNNECESSARY. Perhaps the most powerful argument against a national strategy to expand school health centers is that they are redundant in a system that provides all poor families with medical care. This argument maintains that when families have financial access to services through health care reform, they will seek care from office-based physicians along with middle- and upper-income Americans. School health centers will then constitute an expensive duplicative effort. A corollary to this argument is that programs for poor people provide poor care. Since school health centers are mostly located in poor communities, school health centers, like other institutional providers—outpatient departments, emergency rooms, and community health centers—are likely to provide inferior-quality care.

Running counter to this argument is widespread agreement that we not only need to squeeze dollars from the overdeveloped acute care component of our health care system, but we need to direct those dollars into capacity expansion at the primary care level. The experience of the past decade is that a laissez-faire approach is unlikely to increase primary care capacity in poor urban neighborhoods or remote rural areas. As noted, the number of children's physicians increased sharply over the past ten years, but these physicians did not locate in the poorest neighborhoods. Issues such as race and class bias further constrain the operation of supply and demand forces. The medical marketplace is unlikely to allocate the needed share of health care resources to the poor.

Two additional factors argue against the proposition that universal health insurance will suffice to secure access to primary care for all school-age children. These are the shortage of personnel trained in adolescent health care and the social and economic changes that make it difficult for even more affluent parents to use the current primary care system for their children. Personnel shortages decrease the likelihood that even well-insured students, ages ten to seventeen, will find health care that is attuned to their needs. More broadly, a recent study found that employees of a large company whose health benefits included immunization for their children had not immunized their children according to recommended schedules and that substantial numbers of children were unnecessarily vulnerable to preventable diseases. Nearly all parents said they had a physician or clinic where they could take their children for sick and well child care, but difficulties in getting off work, long waiting times to see a physician, and concerns about out-of-pocket costs, inconvenient office hours, and difficulty in securing appointments deterred them from making timely appointments for their children.[34]

SCHOOL HEALTH CENTERS HAVE NOT ALLEVIATED ADOLESCENTS' PROBLEMS. One of the great confusions surrounding school health centers is the notion that a health center established in a school constitutes an intervention that can, by its existence, alter health-compromising and socially destructive behaviors. In many cases this confusion has been encouraged by health center advocates, who have maintained that school health centers are a panacea for teen pregnancy, alcohol abuse, dropping out of school, and violence. For those who anticipated this cascade of benefits, there has been great disappointment.[35]

The disappointment is misplaced. School health centers are beneficial because they increase access to care for that part of the population that has been least served. They have overcome traditional barriers to medical care and they have expanded access to mental health services by bringing these services into a multidisciplinary model. Moreover, because they are organized and staffed in ways that make health professional training programs possible, the school health centers have the potential to expand the supply of health care professionals trained to care for school-age children.

This is not to say that school health centers cannot assist in intervening in problematic behaviors. By expanding the care system for children and adolescents and, in particular, by creating a health service in which adolescents feel comfortable and trusting, the opportunity is created for interventions that can affect a large number of young people.[36]

SCHOOL HEALTH CENTERS SERVE THE WRONG POPULATIONS. School health centers, this argument contends, are not the most important thing we can do to improve child health. Other measures would improve child health more: implementing universal health insurance, immunizing more children, attracting more women into earlier prenatal care, initiating aggressive community programs to reduce childhood injuries, increasing training programs for child and adolescent mental health professionals, and expanding preventive and primary care services for high-risk, underserved populations. While there is consensus that universal insurance is essential to overcome the highest barriers to health care, there is no consensus regarding priorities among these other needs. Children's health also would benefit from a long list of interventions, most of which have little to do directly with health care: for example, reducing the rate of child poverty or raising the taxes on beer and cigarettes. School health centers make sense in a time of fiscal constraint because they can be targeted to needy communities; they provide a range of services that respond to the unmet needs of a particular population, and they link children to the continuum of care offered by the health care system.

Critics also point out, correctly, that school health centers will not care for children who are not enrolled in school. While school health centers in elementary schools may serve family members or community residents as part of their outreach efforts, high school centers especially are unlikely to serve young people not enrolled in school. Principals in poor communities are security conscious and do not allow strangers in their buildings. Only clinics that have separate entrances to their facilities are likely to receive permission to serve outsiders, and that permission may be granted only after the school administration has come to trust the staff.

To reach out-of-school and incarcerated young people and others who are at highest risk, there must be multiple sites committed to treating patients the health care system has been least anxious to serve.

Barriers to Implementation

While sustained concern about children's well-being and rapid changes in state financing of health services for children create opportunities to increase access to health care through school health centers, political, legal, and technical obstacles must be overcome.

Political Opposition

In some communities, two religious groups—the Christian Coalition and members of the Roman Catholic Church hierarchy—have organized substantial opposition to school health centers. Opponents of school health centers maintain that the centers encourage teen sex and, by permitting patient confidentiality, come between parents and their children. In response, parents and students, the most compelling proponents of the centers, argue that the centers fill an unmet need and are supported by families who use the local schools. Supporters also point out that parental consent requirements give parents the final say in whether their children use the health centers.

The willingness of conservative church groups to influence the school health center debate at the national level is unclear. Conservative Protestant groups have made outcomes-based education and sex education their priority issues at the local level, and nationally their political agenda has focused on abortion. Not all diocesan leaders within the American Catholic Church oppose the health centers or are willing to stop others from establishing them. Throughout congressional consideration of health care reform there was no evidence of a concerted effort to strip the proposed legislation of its language supporting school-related health services. Indeed, in the last congressional vote on the school health services portion of health care reform legislation, the Senate Labor and Human Resources Committee voted 17–0 to support the section of the bill allocating funding for school-related health services. However, the important role of the Christian Coalition in the Republican victory in the 1994 congressional elections suggests that the GOP may be drawn to a more conservative position than it took during the earlier health care discussions.

Caps on Federal Discretionary Spending

In addition to potential political opposition, a federal initiative to support school health centers must clear barriers posed by the Budget Enforcement Act of 1990 (BEA). The BEA requires that increased discretionary funding in one area must be offset by reductions in other programs. Given the structure of the congressional appropriations committees, this requirement means, in practice, that an increase in one discretionary health program requires a reduction in another health program. This effectively sets one discretionary program against another and weakens the ability of school health centers to secure support from organizations whose own line items may be threatened by the creation of a school-based health center category.

While budget caps make it inevitable that a federal grant program may support only a fraction of the centers needed, there are opportunities in current federal programs to fund additional school health centers. For example, in FY1995 the Department of Health and Human Services budgeted $65 million for substance abuse prevention demonstrations for high-risk youth and $22.5 million for substance abuse prevention demonstrations for pregnant women and infants. Moreover, traditional providers of some services to poor children were scheduled to receive substantial funds: community health centers ($616 million) and maternal and child health block grant programs ($684 million). In the Department of Education, four programs might support health-related services: compensatory (chapter 1) education—$6.7 billion, Individuals with Disabilities Act special education grants to states (IDEA, part B)—$2.3 billion, Drug-Free and Safe Schools programs—$466 million, and Goals 2000, a new federal initiative to support school reform—$372 million. Funds from these programs could be teamed with a school health center initiative to reduce the need for new money.[37]

A Difficult Fit

Negotiating the fit between the health centers and medicaid (or medicaid managed care) requires resolving issues that have limited medicaid support for school health centers in the past.

One barrier to arranging for medicaid reimbursement of services provided in schools has been a statutory prohibition against medicaid reimbursement for services provided free to nonmedicaid patients. Historically, school health centers have chosen to increase access to care by not billing patients or their families. Medicaid officials have frequently been unwilling to be the sole payer for care. The "no free care" prohibition, however, does not apply to services given under the Individuals with Disabilities Act or to Title V grantees and providers. With Title V providing funds to many sponsors of school health centers, the Title V exclusion will make it possible for a number of school health centers to participate in medicaid.[38]

Medicaid officials have also argued that they will not pay twice for care. That is, if care is already paid for by other sources, such as state or federal grants, then medicaid will not reimburse for services. In the past, medicaid programs have refused to pay for care to medicaid-enrolled students at school health centers on the grounds that state or other grant support has already paid for their care. Documenting the health centers' total operating costs and demonstrating that grants are not paying the full cost of care is a partial response to these concerns.

Medicaid managed care programs have been confronted with similar concerns regarding duplication of payment. Capitation payments to managed care plans are based on an estimate of what the state would pay for an actuarially equivalent group of people under a fee-for-service arrangement for a given time period, usually a year. Thus, capitation payments are calculated to cover the cost of all identified care. School health centers, which may not be included in a student's managed care network, may seek to bill medicaid separately for services rendered. One solution to this problem may involve "carving out" funds for services provided by the school-based health centers from the medicaid managed care monies and continuing to pay fee for service to school health centers (similar to arrangements in Maryland and New York for family-planning services). Alternatively, medicaid may mandate that managed care plans include school health centers in their provider networks and reimburse the centers for care out of the plan's capitation payment.

Finally, some managed care plans have been reluctant to establish relationships with school health centers due to uncertainty about the quality of their care. A precondition to negotiating a contract between a school health center and a managed care organization is ensuring that the medical director of the managed care organization is comfortable with the care provided by the school health center. In the limited number of contracts negotiated between school health centers and managed care plans, this goal has required health centers to host site visits, share clinical data, permit review of medical records, and respond to questions concerning operating procedures, productivity and provider training. Health Start, a nonprofit corporation in St. Paul, Minnesota, which operates six school-based health centers as well as several community clinics, successfully undertook all these steps to reach a contract with RamseyCare, the largest medicaid managed care provider in Ramsey County. With 75 percent of Health Start's patients estimated to be enrolled in managed care by the end of 1994, successful negotiations were essential to survival of its health centers.[39]

Standardizing the Package

Product standardization is an essential component of quality control and linkage of school health centers to managed care systems. At present twenty-two states either mandate or recommend a specific model of services and staffing for school health centers.[40] However, the drive toward standards creates tensions with one of the strengths of school health centers—community control. A long-standing tenet of school health centers is that they are overseen by a community advisory committee and that key policies and program direction are defined at the local level. Accommodating the need for localities to have flexibility in the development of school health centers while recognizing the importance of defining a set of core services is one of the key challenges of the next several years.

Preserving the Integrity of the Model

Assuming that federal and state support for school health centers can be secured, an equally challenging task is ensuring that the funds are used as intended. Recent experiences both within the federal health reform discussions and state initiatives in school health care suggest substantial ambivalence regarding the importance of a comprehensive school health center model. The two most common objections are that a comprehensive school health center model is too prescriptive and cannot be adapted to local needs and that rural areas may have difficulty recruiting a multidisciplinary staff and should not be penalized because of the geographical maldistribution of health professionals.

These arguments bring to mind a passage from Lisbeth Schorr's book, *Within Our Reach*, in which she discusses why so many health and social service demonstration programs have failed when they "went to scale."[41] Chief among the culprits has been the tendency to dilute the model. Sometimes dilution occurs because politicians want more sites than available monies permit and the model cannot be sustained at half the original cost. But just as likely to diminish the program are actions that dilute and modify the model. The enthusiasm for school health centers has come from their demonstrated effectiveness in bringing a range of medical and mental health services to children in need. Although one can sympathize with the desire to respond to local priorities or not penalize communities that suffer from health professional shortages, as Schorr reminds us, not replicating the model leads to disappointing results. Moreover, not tending to the model will make it unlikely that the centers will be incorporated into the evolving managed care health system. Negotiating contracts between school health centers and managed care plans and planning state-level support for the centers requires knowing precisely what core services will be provided. Without assurance of a core service package, policymakers at the state level are less likely to feel compelled to assure the centers' participation in the service network for low-income children.

The Future for a School-Based Health Center Initiative

The time is right for a school health center initiative. Concern about the declining well-being of poor children has created an impetus for change. The experience of the past twenty years has developed a model of health care delivery responsive to the needs of school-age children and an appropriate vehicle through which the nation can increase its investment in poor children. A school health center initiative has the potential to draw on the strengths of our multiple layers of government and their diverse sources of funding and leadership.

But those who remember the promise of health care reform in the 1970s, who have been encouraged by the popular support for Head Start, or who dare to hope that the relentless decline in the well-being of poor children may trigger a renewed commitment to their care will remain cautious. Cultural conservatives worry deeply about what programs should be permitted in schools. "Natural" allies of school health centers strategize to make sure that a new initiative does not undercut funding for already established health programs in schools. And the strongest supporters of school health centers have operated most effectively at the community level, frequently within the friendly confines of public health departments. It remains to be seen whether this new vehicle for comprehensive care for low-income children, lacking established friends in medicaid or well-organized lobbyists in the state legislatures, can survive the tumultuous change in the health care economy and negotiate the rough politics of redividing a shrinking public pie.

Notes

1. Committee for Economic Development, *Children in Need: Investment Strategies for the Educationally Disadvantaged: A Statement* (New York and Washington, 1987); William T. Grant Foundation Commission on Work, Family and Citizenship, *The Forgotten Half: Pathways to Success for America's Youth and Young Families* (Washington, 1988); Carnegie Council on Adolescent Development, *Turning Points: Preparing American Youth for the 21st Century* (New York: Carnegie Corp., 1989); U.S. Department of Health and Human Services, *Healthy People 2000* (1991); Office of Technology Assessment, *Adolescent Health*, 3 vols. (1991); Advisory Council Commission on Social Security, *Commitment to Change: Foundation for Reform* (1991); National Commission on Children (U.S.), *Beyond Rhetoric: A New American Agenda for Children and Families: Final Report of the National Commission on Children* (1991); Annie E. Casey Foundation, *Kids Count Data Book: State Profiles of Child Well-Being* (Baltimore, Md.: annual, 1990–95); and David A. Hamburg, *Today's Children: Creating a Future for a Generation in Crisis* (Random House, 1992).

2. School health centers are variously known as school-based health centers, school-based clinics, and school-linked clinics. This chapter uses the term *school health centers* to refer to integrated health services located on a

school campus, which provide primary medical and mental health care and are sponsored by mainstream medical organizations.

3. Barbara Starfield, "Child and Adolescent Health Status Measures," *The Future of Children: U.S. Health Care for Children*, vol. 2 (Winter 1992), pp. 25–39.

4. Children's Safety Network, *A Data Book of Child and Adolescent Injury* (Washington: National Center for Education in Maternal and Child Health, 1991), pp. 9–11. Paul Newacheck and William Taylor, "Childhood Chronic Illness: Prevalence, Severity, and Impact," *American Journal of Public Health*, vol. 82 (March 1992), p. 369. In analyzing a special questionnaire on chronic illness that was included in the National Health Information Survey for children in 1988, the authors estimate that 31 percent of children under eighteen, or almost 20 million children, have one or more chronic conditions. In this study chronic conditions did not include cancers or mental health problems that did not have a physical manifestation.

5. National Institute of Mental Health, *National Plan for Research on Child and Adolescent Mental Disorders, a Report Requested by the U.S. Congress*, submitted by the National Advisory Mental Health Council (Department of Health and Human Services, 1990). Estimates of children experiencing mental health problems overlap to an uncertain degree with estimates of children suffering from chronic conditions.

6. Phyllis Ellickson and others, *Forgotten Ages, Forgotten Problems: Adolescents' Health* (Santa Monica, Calif.: RAND, 1993). See also Alan Guttmacher Institute, *Sex and America's Teenagers* (New York and Washington, 1994).

7. Bureau of the Census, "Income, Poverty, and Valuation of Non-Cash Benefits," Current Population Reports, Series P-60, no. 188 (Department of Commerce, 1992), p. 22, table 8; and Starfield, "Child and Adolescent Health Status Measures," p. 33. See also Paul W. Newacheck and Barbara Starfield, "Morbidity and Use of Ambulatory Care Services among Poor and Nonpoor Children," *American Journal of Public Health*, vol. 78 (August 1988), pp. 927–33.

8. Robert F. St. Peter, Paul W. Newacheck, and Neal Halfon, "Access to Care for Poor Children: Separate and Unequal?" *Journal of the American Medical Association*, vol. 267, no. 20 (May 27, 1992), p. 2760.

9. Janet D. Perloff, "Health Care Resources for Children and Pregnant Women," *The Future of Children: U.S. Health Care for Children*, vol. 2 (Winter 1992), p. 84.

10. Ellickson and others, *Forgotten Ages, Forgotten Problems*, p. 21.

11. Paul W. Newacheck, Margaret A. McManus, and Joann Gephart, "Health Insurance Coverage of Adolescents: A Current Profile and Assessment of Trend," *Pediatrics*, vol. 90 (October 1992), p. 589. While medicaid expansions are increasing the number of insured adolescents, the federal mandatory phase-in of adolescents living in families with incomes up to 100 percent of the federal poverty line will not be complete until 2001. For those privately insured, exclusions for preventive and primary care as well as substantial deductibles curtail adolescents' access to care.

12. Victor Fuchs, *Who Shall Live? Health, Economics, and Social Choice* (Basic

Books, 1974); and Victor Fuchs, "National Health Insurance Revisited," *Health Affairs*, vol. 10, no. 4 (Winter 1991), p. 13.

13. Eugene M. Lewit and others, David and Lucile Packard Foundation, "Analysis," *The Future of Children: U.S. Health Care for Children*, vol. 2 (Winter 1992), pp. 7–24. While political fallout from November 1994 is still evolving, to date, budget-trimming proposals at the state and federal level have not directly targeted children's programs. In New York State, for example, Governor George Pataki's proposed budget sharply cut state-funded health services for adults while preserving funding for most children's programs, including school health centers.

14. Personal communication with Judy Wertzel, special assistant to the assistant secretary for elementary and secondary education, Department of Education, April 28, 1994.

15. Documenting need for new services requires careful data collection and analysis. In addition to asking if families have regular sources of care for their children, it is necessary to ask where the children received care during their last several episodes of illness or who provided a physical examination and how recently.

16. Since personnel costs account for approximately 80 to 85 percent of the health center budgets, the total cost is a function of staff size. Staff size, in turn, should depend on the number of students enrolled at the host school and the level of their health care needs.

The average cost of seven school health centers in Multnomah County (Portland), Oregon, was $185,000 in 1991–92. Diane Ruminski and Howard Klink, "School-Based Health Centers: A Model for Delivery of Adolescent Health Care in Portland, Oregon," *Journal of Ambulatory Care Management*, vol. 16 (January 1993), pp. 29–41. The average cost of three full-time centers in Baltimore County during their start-up year, 1992–93, was $225,000. Personal communication with Judi Wallace, Baltimore County Third Party Payment Project, jointly sponsored by Baltimore County schools and health department.

17. Rosenberg and Associates, "Financing Adolescent School-Related Health Centers under the Proposed National Health Security Act," January 1994. Available from Making the Grade, George Washington University, 1350 Connecticut Avenue, N.W., Suite 505, Washington, D.C. 20036. Title III (Subtitle G, Part 5) of the administration's Health Security Act called for investment of $100 million in FY1996 in school-related health services, growing to $400 million in FY1999 and FY2000, with support totaling $1.5 billion over five years. The Education and Labor Committee of the House of Representatives reported out its version of health care reform with a similar level of support for school health services. In its version of Title III, the Senate Labor and Human Resources Committee increased support for school-related health services to $2.35 billion over six years. The Senate committee unanimously approved this section of health care reform legislation.

18. See *Federal Register*, vol. 59, no. 89 (May 10, 1994), pp. 24171–74.

19. John J. Schlitt and others, "State Initiatives to Support School-Based

Health Centers: A National Survey," *Journal of Adolescent Health*, vol. 17, no. 2 (August 1995), pp. 68–76.

20. "Where They Stand, Part II: 1115 Waivers Dot the Landscape," *State Health Notes*, vol. 16, January 23, 1995, p. 1.

21. Because the federal ERISA statute exempts employer-based self-insured programs from state regulation, states cannot mandate private plan participation in school health centers. The private market can be tapped to contribute to school health centers only through a voluntary approach.

22. Rosenberg and Associates, "State-Sponsored School-Based Health Center Programs: Issues for Long-Term Financing." Available from Making the Grade, George Washington University, 1350 Connecticut Avenue, N.W., Suite 505, Washington, D.C. 20036.

23. Schlitt and others, "State Initiatives to Support School-Based Health Centers."

24. Martin Fisher and others, "School-Based Adolescent Health Care: Review of a Clinical Service," *American Journal of the Diseases of Children*, vol. 146 (May 1992), pp. 615–21.

25. Martin Fisher and Linda Juszczak, "Final Report for the Far Rockaway High School Clinic," to the Robert Wood Johnson Foundation, August 13, 1993.

26. Bruce Guernsey, "The Denver School-Based Clinics: Annual Report for the 1992–93 School Year." See also David Hill, "The Doctor Is In," *Teacher Magazine* (February 1994), pp. 18–25.

27. Personal communication with Kristine Hazzard, MSW, supervisor, School-Based Health Centers, Department of Health, Bridgeport, Conn., July 15, 1994.

28. Ruminski and Klink, "School-Based Health Centers," p. 31.

29. Oregon Department of Human Resources—Health Division, "School-Based Clinics Helping Keep Oregon's Teens Healthy," February 1993.

30. During 1993 and 1994, states appeared to be anticipating health care reform by covering more children under medicaid. In North Carolina, for example, the state legislature approved expanding medicaid coverage to all adolescents age nineteen or younger who are below the federal poverty line. This measure took effect October 1, 1994. The impact of the proposed Medigrant program is not certain but threatens expanded coverage for low-income Americans.

31. Columbia University School Health Policy Initiative, "National Work Groups Define School-Based Health Center Services," *ACCESS to Comprehensive School-Based Health Services for Children* (Summer 1994), p. 3. See also Fisher and others, "School-Based Adolescent Health Care," pp. 615–21; and Ellen L. Marks and Carolyn H. Marzke, *Healthy Caring: A Process Evaluation of the Robert Wood Johnson Foundation's School-Based Adolescent Health Care Program* (Princeton, N.J.: MathTech Inc., 1993).

32. Larry I. Wolk and David W. Kaplan, "Frequent School-Based Clinic Utilization: A Comparative Profile of Problems and Service Needs," *Journal of Adolescent Health*, vol. 14, no. 6 (September 1993), pp. 458–63.

33. Harriette B. Fox and Lori B. Wicks, *Background Report on Adolescents and Medicaid Managed Care*. Available from National Academy for State Health Policy, 50 Monument Square, Suite 502, Portland, Maine 04101.

34. Jonathan E. Fielding, William G. Cumberland, and Lynn Petitt, "Immunization Status of Children of Employees in a Large Corporation," *Journal of the American Medical Association*, vol. 271, no. 7 (February 16, 1994), pp. 525–30.

35. A troubling aspect of the disappointment in school health centers is an unstated suggestion that it is not sufficient for health centers to assure adolescents access to health care. Rather, the argument seems to be that only if the health centers reduce poor children's bad behaviors and their health consequences should we concern ourselves with whether those children and youth receive help for their multiple, untreated problems.

36. The absence of a provider network in which adolescents trust creates difficulties in initiating programs designed to combine service delivery with behavior-changing interventions. The first requirement for launching an intervention is that the target population be willing to come to a particular location. Persuading young people to attend community-based services or programs is difficult. See Julia G. Lear, Henry W. Foster Jr., and Jennifer A. Baratz, "The High-Risk Young People's Program: A Summing Up, "*The Journal of Adolescent Health Care*, vol. 10, no. 3 (May 1989) pp. 224–30.

37. Personal communication, Committee on Appropriations, House of Representatives, July 18, 1995.

38. Memorandum from Linda Sizelove, HCFA Medicaid Bureau, to Camden Yards Work Group on School Health, March 10, 1994.

39. Donna J. Zimmerman and Christopher J. Reif, "School-Based Health Centers and Managed Care Health Plans: Partners in Primary Care," *Journal of Public Health Management Practice*, vol. 1, no. 1 (January 1995), pp. 33–39; and Office of Inspector General, School-Based Health Centers and Managed Care: Examples of Coordination (Department of Health and Human Services, 1993), p. 6.

40. Schlitt and others, "State Initiatives to Support School-Based Health Centers."

41. Lisbeth B. Schorr, *Within Our Reach: Breaking the Cycle of Disadvantage* (Doubleday, 1988).

Chapter 7

Saving the Children: Crime and Social Policy

John J. DiIulio Jr.

IF WHITE SUBURBANITES were victimized in disproportionate numbers by convicted criminals out on probation or parole, then there would be little policy debate about keeping violent and repeat criminals locked up. Witness the tragic murder of Polly Klaas, a suburban white child, at the hands of a released career criminal, which triggered a political rush toward tougher criminal sanctions. But in the 1980s all the murders of inner-city black children at the hands of plea-bargain–gorged violent predators and drug dealers elicited no such political response.

America does not have a crime problem; inner-city America does. The poverty gap between blacks and whites in this country may be shrinking, but the crime gap between them has been growing. No group of Americans suffers more when violent and repeat criminals are permitted to prey on decent, struggling, law-abiding inner-city citizens and their children than what Hugh Pearson, writing in the *New York Times*, called "black America's silent majority."[1] As Harvard law professor Randall Kennedy has keenly observed in the *Wall Street Journal*:

> What is really at stake in many controversies with racial overtones is not simply an interracial dispute but an actual or incipient intraracial conflict. Although blacks subject to draconian punishment for crack possession are burdened by it, their black law-abiding neighbors are presumably helped by it. . . . Although black youngsters who wish to stay out late are burdened by a curfew, blacks who feel more secure because of the curfew are benefited. Although black members of violent gangs are burdened by police crackdowns, blacks terrorized by these gangs

are aided. . . . Too little attention has been given to the complexity of black communities and to the varied, and often conflicting, ways in which government policies will affect different sectors of such communities.[2]

Likewise, in his November 1993 speech to black pastors, President Bill Clinton imagined that if Dr. Martin Luther King Jr. could return to the pulpit today, he might say, "I fought to stop white people from being so filled with hate that they would wreak violence on black people. I did not fight for the right of black people to murder other black people with reckless abandon."[3]

For whatever reasons, the federal government has never responded sensibly to the realities of inner-city crime and related social problems. For example, the federal anticrime bill that was enacted in the summer of 1994 contained a rhetorically satisfying but practically useless mix of "punishment" and "prevention" programs. Likewise, the string of anticrime measures approved by the Republican-controlled House of Representatives in February 1995 contained not a single provision targeted on the disorder and violent crime problem of America's most distressed inner-city communities. In conjunction, H.R. 4, the block grant–based "welfare overhaul" bill passed by the House on March 23, 1995, attempted to deter out-of-wedlock child-bearing by denying additional benefits for children born to certain categories of mothers on welfare. Whatever the positive social consequences of such a measure, it would virtually guarantee that more inner-city women would have abortions and that any children who were born to them out of wedlock and remained in poverty would be even less well parented, less well fed, and more at risk of being abused, neglected, and forced to find their own way on drug- and crime-ravaged streets.

Whether it comes from the left or the right, whether its sponsors are Democrats or Republicans, whether the preferred policy equation equals "three strikes and you're out plus two years and you're off" or "midnight basketball plus more Head Start," there is a surreal quality to most contemporary federal anticrime proposals and social policies for children.

There are, however, at least five measures that, taken together, might help to save inner-city children and close the country's morally repugnant and socially devastating black crime gap: (1) take basic remedial measures to secure inner-city neighborhoods, (2) put more police on inner-city streets, (3) reduce the concentration of liquor outlets in poor urban neighborhoods, (4) lock up violent and repeat inner-city criminals, and (5) remove severely neglected and abused children from inner-city homes.

Measuring the Gap

Studies by the Bureau of Justice Statistics show that by 1992, blacks and whites had virtually identical personal theft (purse snatching, pocket picking, larceny without contact) victimization rates. The household crimes (burglary, larceny, motor vehicle theft) rate for blacks remained about 33 percent higher than the rate for whites. Still, from 1973 to 1992, victimization rates for both blacks and whites declined rather steadily for personal theft and household crimes. But in 1992 the violent crime victimization rate for blacks was the highest ever recorded. For teenage black males (age twelve to nineteen), the violent crime victimization rate was 113 per 1,000. This compared to 94 for teenage black females, 90 for teenage white males, and 55 for teenage white females. The rate was 80 for young adult black males (age twenty to thirty-four) compared to 52 for young adult white males. And the rate was 35 for adult black males (age thirty-five to sixty-four) versus 18 for adult white males. At the interracial extremes, the chances that a black male teenager would be victimized by violent crime were 6.3 times that of a white adult male, 7.5 times that of a white adult female, 18.8 times that of an elderly white male (age sixty-five and older), and 37.7 times that of an elderly white female.[4]

It has long been true, as pointed out in 1969 by the National Commission on the Causes and Prevention of Violence, that crime in America is "chiefly a problem of the cities of the nation, and there violent crimes are committed mainly" by and against "the young, poor, male inhabitants of the ghetto slum."[5] But never before has violent crime been so concentrated among teenage and young adult male inner-city blacks. For example, FBI data show that Philadelphia's total crime rate in 1990 was about twice that of the four surrounding suburban Pennsylvania counties, and its violent crime rate was more than three times that of those counties. Forty-two percent of Pennsylvania's violent crimes occurred in Philadelphia, which contained only 14 percent of the population, and most of Philadelphia's violent crime was concentrated among young males in several predominantly black neighborhoods of north and west Philadelphia.[6]

Likewise, Milwaukee experienced some sharp declines in reported crimes in the late 1980s. For example, reported assaults dropped city-wide by 44 percent from 1986 to 1990. But the incidence of violent crime in Milwaukee's inner city remained very high. For example, in 1991 violent crime rates in the city's low-income, predominantly black districts were dozens of times higher than in its middle- and upper-income, predominantly white districts. At the extremes, citizens who resided in the poor districts had more than thirty times as much chance of being murdered, assaulted, or robbed as citizens who resided in the wealthier districts.[7]

National data tell much the same tale. Between 1987 and 1989 the average annual rate of violent victimization among city residents was 92 percent higher than among rural residents and 56 percent higher than among suburban residents.[8] Most black Americans reside in metropolitan central cities. In 1992, 54 percent of black males versus 27 percent of white males age twelve and older lived in metropolitan central cities. In 1992, the rate at which black males in metropolitan central cities experienced violent crimes was 2.6 times the rate at which nonmetropolitan white males experienced them. Even within metropolitan central city populations, the rate at which black males experienced violent crimes was 1.5 times higher than the rate for white males (up from 31 percent higher in 1989).[9]

In 1988 blacks in the nation's seventy-five most populous urban counties were 20 percent of the general population but 54 percent of all murder victims and 62 percent of all defendants; most murder victims were male, black, and between the ages of fifteen and forty-five.[10] In Washington, D.C., America's "murder capital," from 1985 to 1988 about three-quarters of all homicides were committed by young black males against other young black males residing in Southeast and other depressed, predominantly black sections of the city.[11]

In 1991 black youth were arrested for weapons law violations at a rate three times that of white youth, and the violent crime arrest rate for young blacks was five times higher than that of young whites (1,456 versus 283 per 100,000). Between 1976 and 1991 the homicide victimization rate among white youth was stable at 2 to 3 per 100,000.

Between 1976 and 1986 the murder rate for black youth fluctuated between around 7 and 10, then rose steadily to about 14 in 1988, 18 in 1990, and 20 in 1991.[12]

Indeed, between 1973 and 1992, while most Americans became less likely to be victimized by most types of violent crime, the violent crime victimization rate for young black males increased by about 25 percent. And between 1985 and 1992, the homicide rate among young black males increased by about 300 percent (versus 50 percent for comparable young white males).[13]

These facts and figures justify inner-city black Americans' fears. Between 1985 and 1991 the number of Americans who saw crime as a major problem in their neighborhood rose from about 5 percent to 7 percent, and crime was not the number-one neighborhood problem identified by citizens nationwide. But over the same period the fraction of black Americans living in central cities who identified crime as a major problem in their neighborhood rose from 12 percent to nearly 25 percent, and crime was identified as the number-one neighborhood problem by black central-city citizens.[14] More than one-fifth of black children in these neighborhoods fear being attacked going to and from school. Nationally, 54 percent of black children worry a lot or some of the time about becoming a crime victim, and 27 percent of black children versus 5 percent of white children think it is likely that they will be shot.[15]

Likewise, a survey released in May 1994 by the Children's Defense Fund and the Black Community Crusade for Children showed that 46 percent of black adults say their greatest fear is violence against their children and children they know. Such fears are especially ripe among the residents of cities that have experienced a surge of black youth crimes, including homicides. For example, a poll conducted in May 1994 for the mayor of New Orleans found that 86 percent of those surveyed listed crime as the city's biggest problem.[16]

Color-Blind Justice?

Crime in America is predominantly intraracial, not interracial. About 84 percent of single-offender violent crimes committed against blacks are committed by blacks, and 73 percent of violent crimes committed against whites are committed by whites. Likewise, nearly 90 percent of multiple-offender violent crimes committed against blacks are committed by blacks, while about half of multiple-offender crimes committed against whites are committed by whites.[17]

As a National Academy of Sciences study concluded, "Few criminologists would argue that the current gap between black and white levels of imprisonment is mainly due to discrimination in sentencing or in any of the other decisionmaking processes in the criminal justice system."[18] Once one controls for such characteristics as the offender's criminal history or whether an eyewitness to the crime was present, racial disparities melt away. To cite a typical example, a 1991 RAND Corporation study of adult robbery and burglary defendants in fourteen large urban jurisdictions across the country found that a defendant's race or ethnic group bore almost no relation to conviction rates, disposition times, or other key outcome measures.[19]

In 1980, 46.6 percent of state prisoners and 34.4 percent of federal prisoners were black. As the prison population increased during the 1980s, the percentage of it that consisted of blacks changed little. By 1990, 48.9 percent of state prisoners and 31.4 percent of federal prisoners were black. Compared to white prisoners of the same age, black prisoners are more likely to have committed crimes of violence. In 1988 the median time served in confinement by black violent offenders was 25 months, versus 24 months for white violent offenders. For crimes of violence, the mean sentence length for whites was 110 months versus 116 months for blacks, while the mean time served in confinement differed by only 4 months (33 months for whites versus 37 months for blacks).[20]

At the federal level, a 1993 study showed that the imposition between 1986 and 1990 of stiffer penalties for drug offenders, especially crack cocaine traffickers, did not result in racially disparate sentences. The amount of the drug sold, the seriousness of the offenders' prior criminal records, whether or not weapons were involved, and other characteristics of offenses and offenders that federal law and sentencing guidelines establish as valid considerations in sentencing decisions accounted for all of the observed variations in imprisonment sentences.[21]

Similarly, a recent analysis of data representing 42,500 defendants in the nation's seventy-five largest counties finds "no evidence that, in the places where blacks in the United States have most of their contacts with the justice system, the system treats them more harshly than whites." The same species of conclusion holds firmly for the death penalty. As a recent review of the scientific literature demonstrated beyond a reasonable doubt, once one controls for all relevant legal and other variables, there is simply no systematic evidence of racial disparities in post-1972 capital sentencing.[22]

In short, the best available research indicates that race is not a significant variable in determining whether a convicted adult offender is sentenced to probation or prison, the length of the term imposed, or how prisoners are disciplined.[23]

Of course, American justice is not purely color blind. For example, there is some evidence that minority juvenile offenders in certain jurisdictions are more likely to be placed in secure institutions (as opposed to community-based programs) than comparable white minority juvenile offenders.

But it is easy to exaggerate the extent of racial disparities in the juvenile justice system. For example, there are hundreds of post-1969 studies of minorities in the justice system, barely two dozen of which find any overall pattern of racial discrimination. Yet a 1993 research summary published by the Office of Juvenile Justice and Delinquency Prevention (OJJDP) asserted that there was "substantial" evidence of racial discrimination against minority juveniles in the justice system. The OJJDP study was drafted in October 1989, outside reviewers' comments were available in February 1991, and the report itself was released in December 1993. But the report's postscript states that because of "time pressures" and "numerous requests" for the report, the OJJDP decided to publish it essentially as drafted.[24]

Even if one takes it as an article of faith that America remains a highly racist society, and, in turn, that the juvenile justice system remains a racially motivated and biased system, it would strain credulity to maintain that profound and systemic racial biases in the policing, adjudication, and correctional treatment of juveniles somehow vanish once offenders reach the ostensibly no less racist adult system in the same purportedly racist country.

Moreover, to focus on small and speculative differences in how certain types of black and white juveniles are handled in certain jurisdictions is to obscure the fact that both white and black predatory juveniles are getting a free ride from the system in most places. In the late 1970s and early 1980s the deinstitutionalization of juvenile offenders begot horror stories about convicted juvenile murderers, rapists, and robbers who spent little or no time behind bars.

Champions of keeping dangerous juvenile criminals on the streets continued to make the same old case, but the data simply did not support it. Many states toughened the laws governing juvenile offenders, and some states that had handled juvenile predators via low- or no-penalty family courts placed them under the jurisdiction of criminal courts with stronger sentencing authority. For example, in the late 1970s the national publicity surrounding the case of a hardened fifteen-year-old criminal who murdered two men on a subway and received the maximum family court sentence of five years led New York State to change its juvenile penal code so that such offenders could in the future be handled by the state supreme court and be subjected to a maximum penalty of nine years to life.[25]

But in New York State and elsewhere, these laws simply have not been duly enforced, with the result that in many states chronic juvenile criminals of every race, creed, and color continue to commit violent crimes with virtual impunity. That is why 93 percent of judges in the juvenile justice system say juveniles should be fingerprinted, 85 percent believe juvenile criminal records should be made available to adult authorities, and 40 percent think the minimum age for facing murder charges should be fourteen or fifteen.[26]

Beyond the statistical arguments for color-blind justice are even more compelling moral and jurisprudential ones. The Anglo-American criminal law tradition is predicated on individual rights and responsibilities. In our system of justice, a defendant is obliged to muster evidence of discrimination within the four corners of a particular case, not automatically escape a date with the executioner or get out of jail free because a judge is able to squint at aggregate data, swallow spurious correlations, and surmise that a "pattern" of discrimination exists.

In every major opinion survey on crime, clear majorities of both blacks and whites say they favor the death penalty for persons convicted of murder, doubt that most criminals who commit violent crimes can be rehabilitated, demand that juveniles who commit violent crimes be treated the same as adults, favor virtually every type of gun control measure save an outright ban on gun ownership, oppose the legalization of marijuana and other illicit drugs, believe that there is too much violence on television and that it contributes to crime, strongly favor making parole more difficult, and know there aren't enough police on the streets and are willing to pay more in taxes to get more.[27] The list goes on and on.

There are, however, two major and persistent differences between blacks and whites on crime. First, in every year since 1973, a majority of blacks (versus a minority of whites) have answered "yes" when asked whether they would be afraid to walk alone at night in their own neighborhoods.[28] The criminal victimization data, as reported above, reveal that this split in black-white opinion is rational, not hysterical or reactionary.

Second, about 75 percent of blacks (versus 35 percent of whites) believe that blacks are treated more harshly than whites by the criminal justice system.[29] Clearly blacks are more ambivalent than whites about locking up predatory street criminals, because they believe that the system is racist. Boston University's Glenn Loury calls this ambivalence "a fact of deep political significance," and so it is.[30] The appropriate response, however, is to reveal this "fact" as the polarizing but persistent myth that it is. Those intellectual and political elites, black or white, who insist on reinforcing and perpetuating what William Willbanks has aptly described as "the myth of a racist justice system" must not be allowed to prevail or go unanswered. The black crime gap is real, not rhetorical or racist, and average black Americans' fear of crime at a time of declining crime rates nationwide must be addressed.

Target-Hardening the Inner City

The black crime gap results largely from differences between the private spending decisions and danger-avoidance capacities of inner-city black Americans versus more affluent Americans and from the degree to which each group is directly affected by the consistency with which the criminal justice system—courts, cops, and corrections—detects, detains, prosecutes, and punishes violent and repeat street criminals.

Over the last two decades most Americans who could afford to have done things to make the environments in which they and their families live, work, go to school, and recreate relatively impervious to crime. They have moved away from places where street crime and disorder are rife. They have installed burglar alarms and bought anti-auto-theft devices. They have formed neighborhood watch groups in racially homogeneous, low-density neighborhoods where strangers are easy to spot. They have avoided shopping in or even driving through bad neighborhoods.

Likewise, businesses that could manage to do so have relocated from the central cities to the metropolitan periphery, refrained from investing or reinvesting in the places they left behind, and equipped their buildings or corporate campuses with security systems. Retail stores in suburban malls, corporate headquarters in redeveloped downtown areas, upscale apartment complexes, urban special services districts, private urban universities, and gated, private suburban communities have responded by hiring small armies of private security guards.

However, for at least three basic reasons, inner-city Americans have not been able to secure their environments in this way. First, they are too poor to move. They must walk the streets that the rest of us can avoid; they must cope with the dangers that the rest of us can minimize or avoid entirely. In its report on adolescents in high-risk settings, the National Research Council noted correctly that merely living in high-crime areas may increase the risk of victimization.[31] For crime-plagued inner-city public housing tenants, the only alternative to the projects is homelessness.

Second, most inner-city Americans are simply too poor to invest in home security systems and the like. To my knowledge, none of the private foundations that spend millions and millions of dollars to analyze and alleviate inner-city problems have ever spent a penny on such mundane things as deadbolt locks for public housing residents or private security for public housing complexes.[32]

Third, efforts to secure inner-city neighborhoods by erecting gates at public streets, automatically evicting drug dealers from public housing, and installing metal detectors in public schools often meet with stiff legal challenges or require political or financial resources that the community either does not possess or cannot easily sustain.[33]

The Incredibly Thin Blue Line

Unlike the rest of us, therefore, inner-city blacks must rely almost exclusively on the justice system for protection against criminals. At every level this system has failed them.

For starters, inner-city residents complain that there is hardly ever a police officer around when they need one. Through 1983, the American Housing Survey (AHS) asked respondents in sixty thousand households whether their neighborhood had adequate police protection. Black central-city residents were almost twice as likely as whites to say that it did not, and six times as likely to report that they had considered moving because of a lack of police presence in their neighborhood. (Unfortunately, the AHS stopped asking this question after 1983.)[34]

Most big-city police departments are stretched too thin, and police are not allocated among neighborhoods strictly or even mainly according to the levels of crime and disorder that their residents actually face. The solutions are to (1) redirect existing police personnel to high-crime neighborhoods, add new police manpower, and focus it on the same neighborhoods; (2) empower police to work with law-abiding residents and community leaders to aggressively check disorders that are associated with crime and citizens' fear of crime (graffiti, aggressive panhandling, vagrancy, public drunkenness, open drug use); and (3) arrest the bad guys and charge them for any crimes to the full extent of the law.

In the 1980s, as the inner-city drug and crime epidemic expanded, many big-city police forces contracted. Between 1977 and 1987 the number of officers per capita in fifty-nine big-city police departments decreased, and the total number of officers dropped in sixteen of the fifty largest cities.[35] Even if more cops were on the beat during the 1980s, it is not certain that they would have made a major and positive difference. Indeed, early in the decade James Q. Wilson and George L. Kelling concluded in their now-famous "broken windows" essay in the *Atlantic Monthly* that some inner-city neighborhoods had become "so demoralized and crime-ridden as to make foot patrol useless."[36]

The fact, however, is that while just about every other kind of experiment with big-city policing has been made, the effects of increasing greatly the number of officers on regular foot patrol in crime-ridden inner-city neighborhoods have not been tested. It has been shown that police crackdowns—brief, intensive deployments in targeted areas resulting in far higher than average arrests—rarely succeed in reducing crime, in part because criminals quickly move to other, often nearby, locations.[37] But we simply do not know what would happen if there were, in effect, no place left for the criminals to go save into the back of a police wagon.

More precisely, we do not know what, if any, effects routinized saturation community policing—quadrupling or quintupling the number of officers on regular duty (foot patrol and auto patrol) in and around drug-infested, crime-torn urban neighborhoods—would have either on crime rates or on citizens' fear of crime. Many criminologists doubt it would have positive and lasting effects. However, even in the heyday of studies that raised doubts about the relationship between the numbers of police and crime rates, none were heard demanding reductions in police protection for the places where they lived and worked. And several recent econometrically sophisticated studies of the relationship between numbers of police and rates of crime have found evidence that more police spells fewer crimes.[38]

Putting more police on inner-city streets is bound to be expensive because only a tiny fraction of all cops are ever actually on patrol. There are two ways to measure the number of big-city police officers per capita. The first is to compare the total number of officers on the payroll to the total population of the city. For example, in 1991 New York City had a population of about 7.2 million and a police force of about 28,000. Between 1987 and 1991 the number of officers per 1,000 residents in New York City fell from 3.78 to 3.65.[39]

The second measure is the average actual street enforcement strength per capita at any given time. David Bayley has found that in New York City the actual street enforcement strength was only 6.3 percent, meaning that in 1991 there were only about 1,750 cops on the city's streets—0.237 officers per 1,000 residents—at any given time.[40] There are many cities where the actual street enforcement strength is even lower than in New York City. For example, in 1991 San Francisco, a city of nearly 750,000, had a total police force of about 1,800, but only about 120 officers actually on the streets at any given time, or 0.162 officers per 1,000 residents.[41]

Even if the actual average street enforcement strength equaled 20 percent—and there is no big city that comes close—the numbers would not be comforting. For example, 20 percent enforcement strength would put about 5,300 officers on the streets of New York City, or 0.730 officers per 1,000 residents. Likewise, it would put about 370 officers on the streets of San Francisco, or 0.497 officers per 1,000 residents.[42]

The additional rub is that big-city police departments simply do not allocate the relatively tiny number of officers actually on the streets at any given time in accordance with the actual crime risks faced by citizens in various neighborhoods. For example, on any given night in Washington, D.C., which has more officers per capita than any other big city, there are too few officers to answer calls or conduct thorough, on-the-spot investigations in homicide-plagued minority neighborhoods, but plenty of cops to watch over public buildings, upscale restaurants, and college hangouts in the more affluent or tourist-rich sections of town.

In his seminal study of disorder, crime, and community breakdown, Wesley G. Skogan found a high degree of consensus across demographic categories as to what citizens mean when they say they want to live in a safe, orderly neighborhood. The short list includes streets free of drug dealers, no rowdy teenagers, no threatening derelicts, no soliciting prostitutes, no predatory criminals, buildings without graffiti, and no drive-by shootings. Likewise, there is a high degree of consensus that it would be good for police officers to interact more closely with community residents and leaders, solving problems rather than merely reacting to them, and inspiring public trust and confidence rather than stirring worries about intimidation and brutality.[43]

For saturation community policing in the inner cities to work, the increased manpower and enforcement emphasis would need to go hand in hand with administrative changes that give beat police the time and the professional incentives to engage the entire range of neighborhood problems, from working with school principals in dealing with truant teenagers to dispersing loitering teenagers in front of liquor stores, from walking kids to and from school to shutting down open-air drug markets within a glance of the school gates. Otherwise, the effects of putting more cops on inner-city streets could well be more perverse than positive—arresting and throwing the book at everyone, but helping and solving the problems of no one, and clogging the courts without cleaning up the streets.

To be doubly clear, the aim should be not only to increase substantially the number of visibly present officers on inner-city streets, but to ensure that they engage in community- or neighborhood-oriented patrols. To achieve that end, it would be wise to consider requiring that police live in the inner-city neighborhoods that they patrol. Some fear that police who live where they work would be more vulnerable to corruption and more prone to abuse their discretion or "play favorites." But such concerns need to be balanced against the probable benefits of better police-community relations and of fielding cops who possess an intimate knowledge of the places they police and feel a personal stake in the communities they patrol.

Undoubtedly, most of the police officers who would bid for such neighborhood-centered duty would be black or Latino. That prospect should be viewed as a great and positive opportunity, not a potential calamity or problem. Make no mistake: most police of whatever background strive to do a good and honest job of relating to the people and places they patrol. Racial tensions complicate police work in urban America, but the fact that these tensions are not far worse than they are is a tribute to police professionalism. Still, the unadorned fact is that most white suburbanites get white cops, while too many black inner-city citizens and their children do not see substantial numbers of officers of color on patrol or in charge. But if the inner-city beat becomes a priority assignment, then those minority officers who assume it will have a new, steady personnel ladder to climb up into the highest ranks of their departments. Everybody wins.

Unfortunately, federal policy has done nothing to advance the cause of enhancing police protection in inner-city neighborhoods. The $8.8 billion "100,000 cops" provision of the 1994 federal crime bill provides only a few years of seed money to grantee jurisdictions. The program is neither targeted on the inner cities (as of this writing, the latest round of grants went to sixty-six hundred small- and medium-size towns) nor strictly focused on stimulating community- or neighborhood-oriented patrol practices. Worse, the Republican alternative to this measure, which passed the House in February 1995, would roll some $10 billion into "police and prevention" block grants that would concentrate most of the available resources where the nation's crime problem is least severe.[44]

The Alcohol-Disorder-Crime Nexus

In only one area of relevance to the inner-city crime problem has the federal government consistently targeted anticrime law enforcement resources, namely, drug policy. In the 1980s, Congress passed bills containing new antidrug law enforcement measures every two years. The results of these policies have been mixed at best, and there is no consensus about how best to prosecute the nation's "war on drugs" in relation to its inner-city crime dilemma.[45]

One little-noticed casualty of the war on drugs has been attention to alcohol-related crime and other alcohol-induced social ills. Between 1976 and 1993, the number of Americans who favored an outright ban on alcohol rose from 13 percent to 21 percent; black support for prohibition runs close to 30 percent. More generally, there is growing public support for measures that restrict alcohol availability and consumption.[46]

Unfortunately, scientific research on alcohol-related crime and other social ills has been crowded out by studies of the social costs and consequences of drug abuse.[47] Still, a number of significant findings have emerged from the literature on the epidemiology of alcohol-related crime and other problems. Perhaps the single best summary of the evidence in relation to crime is this: "Alcohol use has been associated with assaultive and sex-related crimes, serious youth crime, family violence toward both spouses and children, being both a homicide victim and a perpetrator, and persistent aggression as an adult. Alcohol 'problems' occur disproportionately among both juveniles and adults who report violent behaviors."[48]

Of course, the fact remains that most crime is not related to drinking, and most drinking never results in crime. But some people are far more prone to crime and violence when they are drinking or drunk than when they are clean and sober. For example, "While under the influence of alcohol, a parent may strike a child, a college student may force a date to have sex, friends may escalate an argument into a fist fight, a robbery victim may attempt to resist an armed mugger, and soccer fans may turn disappointment over an unsatisfactory game into a riot."[49]

Still, all scientific studies of the subject stress that the complex relationships between excessive drinking, social disorders, and violent crimes are contingent on a wide variety of circumstances. As one study stressed, much of "the connection between drinking and violence is attributable to the fact that intoxication is often coincident with situations in which the probability of aggression would be elevated regardless of the presence of alcohol." Moreover, "conceptions of how drinking affects social behavior are largely a product of social learning, shaped more by powerful cultural, economic, and political forces than by scientific evidence regarding the direct effects of alcohol or tobacco."[50]

But exactly the same species of cautions can be made—indeed, have been made—in reference to the relationships between drug abuse, crime, and other social problems. The empirical evidence that

"drug abuse causes crime" is of the same kind and quality as the evidence that "alcohol abuse causes crime"—namely, plentiful but in-
ferential, generally persuasive but not scientifically precise.

What the literature suggests is that alcohol, like drugs, acts as a
multiplier of crime. Aggressive behavior or criminality often occurs
before involvement with drugs or alcohol, but the onset of use (especially but not exclusively in cases where use leads to abuse and addiction) results in higher levels of aggressive or criminal behavior. If
anything, the evidence that alcohol abuse drives crime and other
social problems is probably more weighty than the evidence that
drug abuse does so.

An estimated 10.5 million Americans are alcoholics, and 73 million
Americans have been directly affected by alcoholism in some form.
Each year the nation suffers some forty-five thousand alcohol-related
traffic fatalities. Cirrhosis of the liver ranks among the top ten leading
causes of death in America. Half of black men ages thirty to thirty-
nine drink heavily. Black males are at extremely high risk for acute
and chronic alcohol-related diseases, such as cirrhosis of the liver, hep-
atitis, heart disease, and cancers of the mouth, larynx, tongue, esoph-
agus, and lung.[51]

In short, no illicit drug on which there is scientific research, not
even crack cocaine during the 1980s, has ever produced negative
social consequences on the order that legal spirits have.[52] While
"heroin, cocaine, and marijuana have addictive qualities, none of them
approach the levels of use or addiction evident in socially tolerated
drugs such as alcohol or tobacco."[53] Indeed, the estimated per capita
death rate per 100,000 citizens is 150 for alcohol use, versus 4 for
cocaine use.[54] Both alcohol and drugs are indeed multipliers of crime
and other social problems. But it would seem that alcohol multiplies
these problems by one hundred, while drugs multiply them by ten.

Such comparisons between the harmful effects of alcohol (or
tobacco) versus drugs are normally paraded as a preface to arguments
in support of legalizing some or all illicit substances. Logically,
however, they serve just as well as a springboard for considering
whether it makes sense to restrict the availability of alcohol by prohibiting the proliferation of liquor outlets and taking related measures
to reduce consumption among those citizens who are most at risk.

Neighborhood disorder takes many forms—public drinking, prostitution, catcalling, aggressive panhandling, rowdy teenagers, bat-

tling spouses, graffiti, vandalism, abandoned buildings, trash-filled lots, alleys strewn with bottles and garbage. But no social disorder is at once so disruptive in its own right and so conducive to other disorders and crime as public drinking. In Skogan's study of community breakdown in American cities, public drinking was ranked first among the disorders identified by residents across forty neighborhoods.[55] In conjunction, there remains no doubt that "increased alcohol consumption is associated with increased violent crime" and little doubt that "interventions that reduce drinking may also reduce violent crime" and related disorders.[56]

Some of the solitary statistics that can be teased from the last few decades of research on liquor, disorder, and crime are simply striking.

—Sixty percent of convicted homicide offenders drank just before committing the offense.[57]

—Sixty-three percent of adult jail inmates incarcerated for homicide had been drinking before the offense, versus about 27 percent of juvenile corrections inmates incarcerated for homicide.[58]

—Sixty percent of prison inmates drank heavily just before committing the violent offense for which they were incarcerated, and 40 percent "of all persons convicted of rape, assault, or burglary had been heavy drinkers in the year before they went to prison."[59]

—Between 1973 and 1992, the rate of violent victimizations among young black males (ages twelve to twenty-four) increased by 25 percent, and between 1985 and 1992, the black male homicide rate increased by 300 percent.[60] Most of these violent crimes, including homicides, are committed by poor inner-city black males against other poor inner-city black males. Other things being equal, however, the relationship between poverty and homicide is stronger in neighborhoods with higher rates of alcohol consumption than it is in neighborhoods with average or below-average rates of alcohol consumption.[61]

—Numerous studies report a strong association between sexual violence and alcohol, finding that "anywhere between 30 and 90 percent of convicted rapists are drunk at the time of offense."[62]

—Numerous studies indicate that while aggressive and criminal behavior among young people begins well before the onset of alcohol use, juveniles (especially young males) who drink to the point of drunkenness are more likely than juveniles who do not drink to get into fights, get arrested, commit violent crimes, and become recidivists later in life.[63]

—Alcohol-dependent male factory workers are more than three times as likely to physically abuse their wives than are otherwise comparable, non-alcohol-dependent male factory workers.[64]

It is important, however, not to be swept away by the seemingly self-evident power or suggestiveness of such findings. For example, the high incidence of drinking among convicted criminals does not necessarily prove that drinking stimulates crime; it may be nearer to being evidence that criminals who drink are more likely to get caught and convicted than criminals who do not drink or do not drink a lot. The fact remains that alcohol consumption "has no uniform behavioral effects," and it is often difficult or "impossible to judge whether alcohol is a genuine or a spurious correlate of violence or under what circumstances alcohol may contribute to the occurrence of violence."[65] Overinterpreting disturbing aggregate statistics is a mistake that has plagued much of the applied research and policy-relevant commentary of the drugs-disorder-crime nexus; it ought not be repeated here.

It is equally important, however, not to discount or deny the probable—and in some cases patently obvious—connections between liquor, disorder, and crime. Where these connections are concerned, researchers will probably never be able to untie or cut through every last causal knot, at least not in ways that meet every last test of scientific validity. But common sense supposes that the connections are real and quite important. Some research may challenge or complexify the suppositions of common sense. Generally speaking, however, the more sophisticated the model and methods, the more it happens that research reinforces rather than rebuts the counsels of common sense.

So it is with the scientific literature on alcohol availability, alcohol consumption, and alcohol-related crime and social problems: other things being equal, easy availability increases consumption, and consumption increases the incidence of disorder, crime, and other problems.[66]

Regulating Spirits

The practical question is how best to cut disorder and crime by restricting (without prohibiting) alcohol availability and consumption among those citizens who are most at risk. The scientific research literature that addresses this question is in its infancy. Still, already a number of fascinating, well-documented, and important findings have emerged. The main finding is that both changes in the price of alcohol and changes in liquor law regulations can succeed in reducing alcohol availability, alcohol consumption, and alcohol-related problems, including violent crime, among at-risk youth and adults.

First, it is clear that alcohol price and alcohol consumption tend to vary inversely: the more it costs, the less people buy; the less they buy, the less they consume; the less they consume, the fewer the social problems that result. Alcohol taxes influence per capita alcohol consumption, and per capita alcohol consumption is closely linked to violent crime rates.[67]

—On average, a 10 percent increase in alcohol consumption can mean an estimated 9.13 percent increase in robberies, a 6.8 percent increase in rapes, a 5.8 percent increase in assaults, and a 0.87 percent increase in homicides. A 10 percent increase in a state beer tax can mean an estimated 0.48 percent reduction in per capita alcohol consumption and in turn a 1.32 percent drop in rapes, a 0.87 percent drop in robberies, a 0.32 percent drop in homicides, and a 0.26 percent drop in assaults.[68]

—A 10 percent increase in the price of alcohol can mean an estimated 3 percent reduction in beer consumption and a 10 percent reduction in wine consumption.[69]

One aspect of the drinking-disorder-violent crime nexus that must be considered is its apparently age-specific character. Most violent crime is committed by young males. Drinking in males normally begins around adolescence and rises until the late teens or mid-twenties. Longitudinal research suggests that the relationship between drinking and serious crime is strongest before young males reach age 31.[70] The "good news," however, is that young people (including the high fraction who drink only beer) tend to be highly price sensitive. As one of the most comprehensive studies concluded, increasing beer taxes to their real (inflation-adjusted) 1951 levels in 1990 "would have reduced the number of heavy drinkers among youth" by "almost 20 percent." Such a reduction in youth drinking would spell fewer adult alcoholics, fewer traffic fatalities, and fewer violent deaths.[71]

Figuring out precisely what types of taxing or other fiscal strategies work best in discouraging alcohol consumption can be extremely complicated (to put it mildly). Under the user fee conception of a socially optimal tax rate, the challenge is to set alcohol taxes "high enough so that the total revenues from these taxes are equal to the total external costs resulting from alcohol abuse."[72] But that is far easier said than done. Even as an exercise in advanced econometrics or public finance economics, things can get very difficult very quickly. For one thing, no one really has a reliable estimate of just what the annual total external costs of alcohol abuse are. One 1985 study, for example, estimated that the total economic costs of alcohol abuse were (in constant 1983 dollars) $116 billion in 1983 and $136 billion in 1990 and would rise to $150 billion by 1995. The same study estimated that about 60 percent of the costs of alcoholism consisted of lost employment and reduced economic productivity, while about 13 percent were due to health care and treatment. But various drug legalization advocates have come in with estimates many times that amount, and it is an inherently difficult task to estimate the total costs to society of so complicated a phenomenon as alcoholism or violent crime.[73]

There is no doubt that price changes can have some effect on alcohol consumption and alcohol-related problems. There is, however, a second approach—namely, laws and regulations that directly reduce the physical availability of alcohol. For "independent of the effects of beverage prices, and controlling for the endogeneity of sales and availability, the physical availability of alcohol" is "directly related to sales of spirits and wine."[74]

A number of first-rate studies have already found "statistically significant relationships between per capita outlet densities and consumption and alcohol problem rates." Policies that reduce the geographic density of liquor outlets have been found to work in a wide variety of settings. "Fewer outlets per square kilometer and/or lower per capita outlet densities would result in reductions in both consumption and problems."[75]

The fact, however, is that most states do not have strong liquor law regulations and procedures. Even states that do have strong liquor laws and regulations on the books tend to underfund the agencies that are responsible for enforcing them. Naturally anemic funding often leads to inadequate enforcement.[76] And whether related to funding levels or other variables, loose enforcement opens up the possibility of socially harmful concentrations of liquor outlets and other regulatory failures that can lead to a hornet's nest of alcohol-related social problems, including disorder and crime.

—Liquor outlet densities have been found to be related in important ways to alcohol problems and felony arrest rates.[77]

—A detailed study of forty-four alcohol beverage control (ABC) jurisdictions in the United States found that the strict enforcement of formal laws constraining access to alcoholic beverages, including laws that effectively regulate densities of alcohol outlets, can succeed in reducing alcohol consumption and alcohol-related problems. But in "the absence of increased enforcement, it is unlikely that any formal alcohol beverage control law would have any effect upon the distribution and sales" of alcohol.[78]

—A study of all twenty-five California ABC offices and 167 ABC investigators found that the state's liquor laws were loosely enforced. Community concerns and considerations of community welfare generally received short shrift in decisions governing the granting of retail liquor licenses. The ABC investigators were "less concerned with public health and welfare than with the rights of the applicants." The study concluded "that the selling of alcohol in California is treated more as a right than a privilege. This is a finding of some significance, because it underscores the relationship between outlet densities and consumption."[79]

Tightening Liquor Control Regimes

Few states devote many human and financial resources to the development and enforcement of rigorous liquor laws and regulations that might succeed in cutting the physical availability of alcohol, reducing the density of liquor stores in urban areas, and, in the bargain, cutting crime and other alcohol-related problems in poor, minority, high-crime, inner-city neighborhoods. America's liquor-control regime has remained fairly inert, structured without any apparent regard for the connection between alcohol availability, consumption, crime, and other social problems—and calculated to give the state almost zero capacity to regulate and directly enforce liquor laws. Not surprisingly, loose liquor control regimes permit high concentrations of liquor outlets in low-income urban neighborhoods, and, in turn, such concentrations are strongly correlated with crime.

A picture is worth a thousand words (and a few dozen regressions). Maps 7-1 and 7-2 show a definite relationship between liquor outlets and crime in Milwaukee. The city tracts are divided into five groups, with those in the top quintile having the highest crime rates and those in the bottom quintile the lowest. If one knew nothing

MAP 7-1. *Milwaukee Crime Rates and Liquor License Locations, 1993*

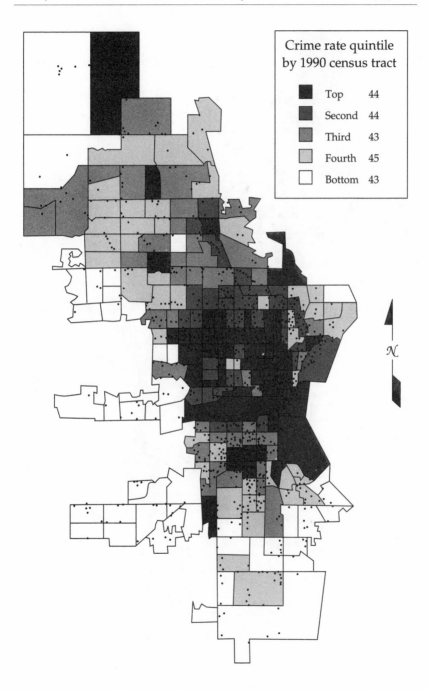

Crime rate quintile
by 1990 census tract

■ Top 44
■ Second 44
■ Third 43
□ Fourth 45
□ Bottom 43

N

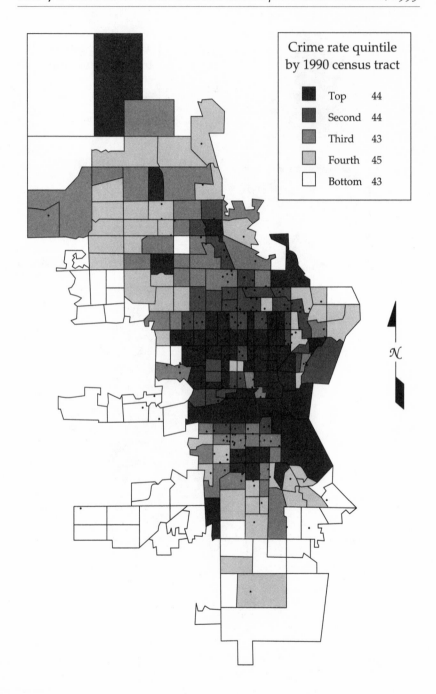

Crime rate quintile
by 1990 census tract

■	Top	44
■	Second	44
■	Third	43
■	Fourth	45
□	Bottom	43

about either the city or what the dots on the map represented and simply drew circles around the places where the dots are clustered, Milwaukee's poor, minority, high-crime, inner-city neighborhoods would be enclosed in those circles.

Apart from the sheer strength of the liquor-crime correlation, what is most striking about these findings is the role played by class A malt-only liquor licenses. These account for 15 percent of the licenses in the sample (245 license locations). The malt-only outlets are most thickly clustered in Milwaukee's inner-city neighborhoods. In fact, a descriptive analysis of the data revealed that the best way to predict where malt-only outlets were located was to identify tracts with less-than-average citywide annual family income and greater-than-city-wide-average proportional black population. Fully 81 percent of tracts with less-than-average income and greater-than-average black populations had malt-beer-to-go stores. There is virtually nowhere else in the city, and probably hardly anywhere else in the state, where so many liquor stores—let alone so many of a particular kind—are so heavily concentrated. Ongoing research indicates that the same is true for other inner-city communities all across the country.

Broken Bottles

But should one leap to the conclusion that if inner-city neighborhoods had fewer liquor outlets, they would also have less alcohol consumption and less crime? The answer is that while one should not leap to that conclusion, anyone who cares about reducing community breakdown and crime in the inner city should begin moving in the direction of policies that restrict alcohol availability and reduce the density of liquor stores.

Think about it. Middle-class Americans would not tolerate for one second laws that permitted any such concentration of liquor (let alone beer-to-go) stores in or around the places where they and their loved ones live, work, shop, go to school, or recreate. It makes no sense to insist that it is all merely a matter of free markets, as if liquor stores simply go where the people want what they sell and sell to whomever they want. As a nation, Americans have embraced laws that raise the drinking age to twenty-one, punish drunken drivers, and educate the young about the dangers of alcohol and drug use. At various times, California and other states have attempted to limit the density of liquor outlets around college campuses; indeed, California once had a statute that prohibited liquor stores and bars within a one-mile radius of a college campus.[80]

Nor, for that matter, can one hide behind a fog of empirical uncertainties about the connections between liquor, disorder, and crime. In the end, academic statistical exercises are no substitute for live ethnographic realities. Imagine what it is like for a typical inner-city child,

> let's call him John, to grow up near Florence and Normandie avenues, the flash point of the [Los Angeles] riot. To middle-class African-Americans and whites, liquor stores are generally a remote presence, located far from where adults pray and children play. But to John, Tom's Liquor is a short walk from his house, school and the storefront church in the same shopping strip. A slew of transactions take John to Tom's. He tags along with his mom when she goes to cash her welfare checks free of charge. With no supermarket nearby, John goes to Tom's when he wants a candy bar. Even when his mother takes him to the adjoining neighborhoods, John rarely sees a bank or supermarket. . . . Many neighborhood traits convey disorder but unchecked public drinking is a particularly potent affirmation that "no one cares." That is the message John gains by observing Tom's Liquor, where winos and crack addicts congregate at night in the parking lot. . . . In fact, eight times in the 14 months preceding the riot, LAPD dispatchers sent squad cars to the store to investigate robberies, assaults, and a shooting.[81]

One doubts that readers of this volume would want to live where John does or have their children switch places with him. As noted above, many analysts accept the "broken windows" thesis—when a broken window in a building goes unfixed, soon all of its windows are broken. The broken window is an invitation to incivility, disorder, and crime. "Where disorder problems are frequent and no one takes responsibility for unruly behavior in public places, the sense of 'territoriality' among residents shrinks to include only their own households; meanwhile, untended property is fair game for plunder or destruction . . . [and] a concentration of supposedly 'victimless' disorders can soon flood an area with serious, victimizing crime."[82]

But broken bottles have an even worse effect on community order and safety than broken windows. The fact that government itself licenses the entire mess by letting the liquor stores proliferate and the broken bottles pile up so high in poor, inner-city neighborhoods is the single most compelling symbol that nobody cares, the ultimate invitation to disorder and crime.

Without adopting either the most sinister or the most cynical perspective on the subject, it seems clear that the high concentration of liquor outlets in these urban neighborhoods reflects "the relative power of alcohol producers and wholesalers, who supply liquor outlets, banks who loan money to store owners, and state regulators whose activities are more oriented toward the interests of alcohol industry lobbying groups than the regulation of that industry, and the relative powerlessness of the poor and unemployed individuals and groups who live in greater concentration in these areas of high outlet density."[83]

Preserving Social Capital

The time has come for states and cities to experiment with policies aimed at cutting crime by cutting alcohol availability and consumption. The place to begin the experiment is in those poor, minority, high-crime neighborhoods where the density of liquor outlets exceeds citywide averages. The theory behind this policy experiment should be guided by the large and methodologically sophisticated body of research that documents that in inner-city neighborhoods, the relationship between poverty on the one side and crime and disorder on the other is mediated by community norms and the extent of citizens' attachments to traditional institutions like home, school, and church.[84]

As a rule, the stronger are community norms and traditional institutional attachments, the weaker is the link between poverty and crime and the lower are the chances that children growing up in disadvantaged settings will become deviant, delinquent, or predatory (assault, rape, rob, burglarize, deal deadly drugs, or murder). Studies have shown that religious affiliation fosters less drinking.[85] Indeed, one major study finds that even after controlling for all relevant individual characteristics (race, gender, education, parental education, family structure, religious involvement, and so on), young people whose neighbors attend church are more likely to find a job, less likely to use drugs, and less likely to be involved in criminal activities whether or not they themselves attend church or have other attachments to traditional institutions.[86]

But in poor neighborhoods where alcohol is readily available and liquor outlets dot every intersection, informal and indirect social controls on deviant, delinquent, and criminal behavior are diluted. Where broken bottles fill the gutters, social capital goes down the drain. In economic terms, high rates of alcohol consumption and high densities of liquor outlets create negative externalities that compete against, cancel out, or overwhelm the positive externalities associated with traditional institutions and behaviors like churchgoing. Whether or not they themselves drink to excess, hang out at bars, or engage directly in related behaviors, it is probable that poor, inner-city youths who grow up in places where drinking is common and liquor outlets are everywhere are more likely than otherwise comparable youths to have diminished life prospects that include joblessness, substance abuse, and serious trouble with the law. Indeed, as one recent study speculates, this is probably true even with respect to homicides: "Social bonds that tie individuals to each other and to larger social collectivities have played a key role in the understanding of how crime and violence come about. . . . [But social bonds] break down in the presence of high rates of alcohol consumption. . . . The basic form of this relationship may be one in which higher alcohol consumption reduces the effectiveness of attachment to institutions, thus leading to higher rates of homicide."[87]

There are at least two specific types of policy experiments that should be considered as means of deepening our understanding of the alcohol-disorder-crime nexus and confronting the apparent reality that "drinking does indeed cause violence: interventions that reduce drinking can also tend to reduce violent crime."[88] And there is one specific policy change that should be avoided at all costs—namely, lowering the drinking age.

CONDUCT SYSTEMATIC EMPIRICAL RESEARCH ON ALCOHOL AVAILABILITY AND CRIME. As a first step, it would be necessary to develop a rich database that includes detailed information about the precise degrees of spatial overlap between liquor outlets, the incidence of communal disorders (public fighting, child and spousal abuse, aggressive panhandling, rowdy teenagers), rates of criminal activity (assault, rape, robbery, homicide), and the frequency of police response (911 calls, arrests). To build such data sets would require the concerted efforts and cooperation of a number of different state and local agencies (police departments, social service agencies).

IMPOSE STRICTER ZONING ORDINANCES FOR LIQUOR STORES. There have been few systematic, scientifically rigorous studies of the relationship between alcohol ads on the one side and the incidence of excessive drinking, disorder, crime, and related social problems on the other. But it seems clear that the alcohol industry believes that these ads make a positive difference to their sales. Liquor manufacturers bombard urban neighborhoods with messages like this one, from a malt liquor commercial:

> Get a grip, take a sip,
> And you'll be picking up models
> And it ain't no puzzle my cousin
> 'Cause I'm more a man
> I'm downin' a forty [a forty-ounce bottle]
> Be a man and get a can of St. Ides [a high-alcohol malt beer].[89]

Indeed, the alcohol industry seems perfectly well aware of the relationship between alcohol, disorder, and crime—in some infamous cases, it has been quick to exploit it for commercial gain. In the early 1990s, for example, one of the billboard spokesmen for St. Ides malt liquor was Ice Cube, a "gangsta rapper" whose hits include the song "Black Korea." The song includes lyrics such as "Pay respect to the black fist or we'll burn your store right down to a crisp" and "Don't follow me up and down your market, or your little chop-suey ass will be a target." Ice Cube appeared in a poster holding a can of St. Ides flashing a gang sign and claimed in a televised ad, "I gotta 40 [ounce bottle] every 'hood that you see me in."[90] Only after a vigorous protest by Korean merchants did the company that produces St. Ides pull the ads.

In many big cities, "religious leaders in black communities have taken to the streets to whitewash old billboards, thereby ridding their communities of the destructive advertisements."[91] But city officials ought to take the lead in enforcing zoning limitations on billboard alcohol advertising, banning such ads from the horizons of schools, churches, and public housing centers.

DO NOT LOWER THE LEGAL DRINKING AGE. States should also refuse to enact other measures that would increase alcohol consumption, disorder, crime, and other social problems. There is a tremendous stock of research showing that lowering the legal drinking age increases alcohol-related traffic fatalities.[92] And unless one simply refuses to accept the overwhelming weight of the evidence on the relationship between drinking, disorder, and crime, then one must believe that reducing the minimum drinking age or any other measure that would increase, rather than further limit, the availability of alcohol would have socially undesirable, even disastrous, consequences—most especially in America's inner-city neighborhoods.

Locking the Revolving Door

Simultaneously putting more cops on the streets and clamping down on alcohol availability is one thing; keeping violent and repeat criminals behind bars is quite another. Inner-city blacks and their children face a disproportionate risk of criminal victimization, in part because they live in places where the concentration of convicted violent, repeat, and violent repeat criminals, adult and juvenile, who live in the community and are released back to the community is dozens of times higher than in most of the rest of America. Thus no group of Americans would stand to benefit more from keeping convicted felons, adult and juvenile, behind bars for all or most of their terms than crime-plagued, black inner-city Americans and their children.

As it presently operates, the justice system is a revolving door for convicted predatory street criminals, the vast majority of whom enter the system by plea-bargaining away some of their crimes, exit it before serving even half of their time in confinement, and make a cruel joke out of the terms of their "community-based supervision." By locking the revolving door—curtailing pretrial releases, reducing plea bargaining, and putting dangerous offenders away for long, fixed terms or life—we can begin to protect the truly disadvantaged from their criminally deviant neighbors.

In the seventy-five most populous counties 65 percent of felony defendants are released before trial, including 63 percent of violent defendants, 37 percent of murder defendants, and 54 percent of rape defendants. Nearly a quarter of all pretrial felony defendants fail to appear in court. About 11 percent of murder arrestees and 12 percent of all violent crime arrestees are on pretrial release (for an earlier case) at the time of the offense. More than 20 percent have ten or more previous arrests, and more than 35 percent have one or more previous convictions.[93]

Case management, the bureaucratic euphemism for plea bargaining, means that more than 90 percent of all criminal cases do not go to trial because the offender pleads guilty to a lesser charge. In high-crime jurisdictions where a premium is placed on processing cases as quickly as possible, even violent crimes are routinely plea bargained so that well under half ever go to trial—44 percent of murder cases, 23 percent of rape cases, 15 percent of aggravated assault cases, 13 percent of robbery cases, and 7 percent of burglary cases.[94]

Relative to the number of serious crimes being committed, America has not been on an imprisonment binge. Rather, it has been gradually recovering from the starvation diet it went on in the late 1960s and adhered to throughout the 1970s. For example, according to a recent analysis by Michael Block and Steven Twist, between 1960 and 1980 the imprisonment rate relative to the number of violent crimes committed fell by 69 percent. In 1960, 738 people were in prison for every 1,000 violent crimes committed. By 1980 the number had dropped to 227. As the prison population increased in the 1980s, the number climbed to 423, higher than it was at any point in the 1970s but still 42 percent lower than it was in 1960.[95]

In 1989 more than 4 million persons were under some form of correctional supervision, either in prison (17 percent), in jail (10 percent), on probation (62 percent), or on parole (11 percent).[96] Thus about three-quarters of all convicted criminals were *not* incarcerated. Instead, they were the responsibility of probation or parole agents who had average caseloads in the hundreds and hence no way of providing effective custodial supervision, let alone helping their charges seek drug treatment, find jobs, or otherwise enhance their noncriminal life prospects.

Nationally, within three years of sentencing, and while still on probation, nearly half of all probationers are placed behind bars for a new crime or abscond. Among probationers with new felony arrests, 54 percent had one new arrest, 24 percent had two, and the remaining 22 percent had three or more. About one-fifth of them were rearrested for a violent crime. About 96 percent of probationers arrested for murder were not on probation for murder. Likewise, within three years of their conditional release from prison, while still on parole, nearly half of all parolees are convicted of a new crime. Nearly one in three released violent offenders and one in five released property offenders are rearrested within three years for a violent crime.[97]

The state-level data tell the same tale in more graphic detail. For example, between 1987 and 1991 about 87 percent of the 147,000 felons released from Florida prisons were released early. Fully one-third of these parolees committed a new crime. At times when they would have been incarcerated had they served their full sentence, these parolees committed nearly 26,000 new crimes, including some 4,654 new crimes of violence—346 murders, 185 sexual assaults, 2,369 robberies, and 1,754 other violent offenses.[98]

Unfortunately, no data are kept on precisely how many probationers and parolees from which neighborhoods are convicted of new crimes each year. But we can get a sense of the magnitude of the problem by looking at fractions of arrestees on probation and parole at the time of the offense. According to the Bureau of Justice Statistics National Pretrial Reporting Program, which is based on data gathered from the nation's seventy-five most populous counties and encompasses most big cities, in 1990, 14 percent of murder arrestees were on probation and 7 percent were on parole. Among all violent crime arrestees, 16 percent were on probation and 7 percent were on parole.[99]

More Community-Based Felons?

One common response to such data is to call for improvements in how probationers and parolees are managed. Today the most popular variant of this response is known as intermediate sanctions.[100]

Unlike routine probation and parole, a felon placed in an intermediate sanction is supposed to be closely supervised via such methods as electronically monitored house arrest, weekly contacts with the agent, drug testing, work requirements, community service, monetary fines, and a swift and certain bout of incarceration for acts of noncompliance or new crimes. Those who in the 1960s made the initial push for the widespread use of alternatives to incarceration stressed that caseloads must be kept within manageable limits. A 1967 presidential commission on crime recommended "an average ratio of 35 offenders per officer."[101] Those who in recent years have attempted to salvage the wreck of probation and parole have claimed that by returning to intensive supervision, convicted criminals can be handled on the streets in ways that protect the public and its purse better than either routine probation and parole or incarceration.

In practice, however, intermediate sanctions have done nothing to remedy the problems of probationer and parolee noncompliance and recidivism. For example, a recent study found that more than 90 percent of all probationers were already part of the very graduated punishment system called for by advocates of intermediate sanctions—substance abuse counseling, house arrest, community service, victim restitution programs, and so on. But about half of all probationers still did not comply with the terms of their probation, and only one-fifth of the violators ever went to jail for their noncompliance. As the study concluded, "intermediate sanctions are not rigorously enforced."[102]

Even the most intensive forms of intermediate sanctions have not proven effective. For example, the most comprehensive experimental study of intensive supervision programs for high-risk probationers concluded that these programs "are not effective for high-risk offenders" and are "more expensive than routine probation and apparently provide no greater guarantees for public safety." Similarly, the best experimental study of intensive supervision programs for high-risk parolees found that the "results were the opposite of what was intended," as the programs were not associated with fewer crimes or lower costs than routine parole.[103]

Despite such findings, most criminologists and many others continue to insist that "prison is not the answer" and that "we cannot build our way out of the problem." But if prison is not the answer, then what, precisely, is the question? If the question is how to solve all of America's worst social and urban problems, then prison alone most certainly is not "the answer." But if the question is how best to protect inner-city citizens from known, convicted, violent, and repeat criminals, then prison is far more of an answer than most experts would allow.

Prisoner Profile

The notion that a majority of prisoners are petty, first-time offenders with few previous arrests, no previous convictions, and no history of violence has been promulgated in many places, but it is completely false.[104] Nationally, more than 90 percent of all prisoners are held by the states. In 1991 fully 94 percent of state prison inmates had been convicted of a violent crime or had a previous sentence to probation or incarceration. In other words, only 6 percent of prisoners were nonviolent offenders with no prior sentence to probation or incarceration. Nearly half were serving time for a violent crime, and one-third had been convicted in the past of one or more violent crimes. Two-thirds of violent inmates had killed, raped, or injured their victims. One-fifth of violent prisoners had victimized a minor. Only 1 percent of all prisoners had been sentenced to probation or incarceration in the past for only minor offenses (drunkenness, vagrancy, disorderly conduct).[105]

The individual state-level data speak in the same voice. For example, in 1992 in New Jersey about 46 percent of prisoners were serving sentences for violent crimes, 80 percent had criminal histories involving violence, and prisoners averaged nine prior arrests and six prior convictions.[106] Relative to New Jersey and most other states, the federal prison system holds more property and drug offenders and fewer violent offenders. But of the thirty-five thousand persons newly committed to federal prison in 1991, only 2 percent, or about seven hundred, were convicted of mere drug possession. And even in the ostensibly white-collar federal prison system, in 1989 more than 55 percent of all federal prisoners had two or more previous felony convictions, and 46 percent of all federal prisoners and 92 percent of all prisoners in federal penitentiaries had a history of violence.[107]

These data show clearly that most prisoners are indeed violent or repeat criminals. But for three reasons even these data understate the actual number and severity of crimes committed by prisoners.

First, the data do not reflect the amount and severity of crimes committed by prisoners before they were of age to be legally tried, convicted, and sentenced as adults. Nationally, juveniles (persons age eighteen and younger) account for about one-fifth of all weapons arrests and in 1991 committed a record 2,476 murders. Nearly 60 percent of juveniles in long-term facilities have a history of violent offenses. A number of longitudinal studies show that among juveniles who become involved with crime, 23 to 34 percent are high-rate offenders who commit a mix of violent and property offenses and are responsible for 61 to 68 percent of all crimes committed by all juveniles.[108] Today's high-rate juvenile criminals are tomorrow's adult prisoners, but today's adult criminal records do not comprehend yesteryear's slew of juvenile crimes.

Second, the data do not account for the deflationary effects of plea bargaining on prisoners' criminal records. To my knowledge, there are no systematic empirical studies that estimate how much actual crime is masked by plea bargaining.

Third, the data do not account for the wholly undetected, unprosecuted, and unpunished crimes committed by prisoners when free. Two recent prisoner self-report surveys suggest that, as bad and long as the official adult records of most prisoners are, their true adult records are longer and much worse. A prisoner self-report survey conducted in Wisconsin in 1990 and representing a random sample of 6 percent of the state's prisoner population found that in the year before imprisonment, prisoners committed a median of 12 property or violent crimes and a mean of 141 such crimes, excluding all drug crimes. A prisoner self-report survey conducted in New Jersey in 1993 and representing a random sample of 4 percent of the state's prisoner population found that in the year before imprisonment, prisoners committed a median of 12 property or violent crimes and a mean of 220 such crimes, excluding drug crimes.[109]

These findings suggest at least two things. First, most prisoners have committed more crimes than those for which they have been arrested, booked, convicted, and incarcerated. Second, the spread between the median and the mean indicates that some fraction of prisoners have committed many times more crimes than those for which they have been arrested, booked, convicted, and incarcerated. In sum, the official data make plain that virtually all prisoners are violent or repeat criminals. And the survey data remind us that the number of career predators behind bars is even larger than the official data document.

How long do most of these violent and repeat criminals serve in confinement before being released? In 1991 thirty-four states released nearly 326,000 prisoners. Almost 90 percent of them were released conditionally (that is, to parole). About half of all parolees had served

TABLE 7-1. *Convicted Violent Felons Not Sentenced to Prison, by Number of Conviction Offenses, 1992[a]*

Percent

Most serious conviction offense	Convicted felons not sentenced to prison for one, two, or three or more felony conviction offenses		
	One	Two	Three or more
All violent offenses	47	31	23
Murder	9	5	3
Rape	39	23	20
Robbery	30	21	14
Aggravated assault	61	45	38
Other violent offenses[b]	65	51	36

Source: Bureau of Justice Statistics, *Felony Sentences in State Courts* (January 1995), p. 6.

a. Table reflects prison nonsentencing rates for felons based on their most serious offenses. For example, if a felon is convicted of murder, larceny, and drug possession, and is not sentenced to prison, he or she would be represented in the table under murder (the most serious offense) with three or more offenses.

b. Includes offenses such as negligent manslaughter, sexual assault, and kidnapping.

fourteen months or less in prison before their release. On average, they served 35 percent of their maximum sentence in prison before release. This average held for most categories of criminal conviction. Thus the median time served for murder was six and a half years on a twenty-year sentence, and the median time served for assault was fifteen months on a sentence of four-plus years.[110] And many violent felons with multiple convictions do not go to prison (table 7-1).

Prisons Pay

The social costs and benefits of imprisonment versus other means of handling violent and repeat criminals are extremely difficult to estimate. However, any sensible estimate of the value of prisons must include the costs to society inflicted by probationers and parolees during periods when they could have remained incarcerated.

Whether or not imprisoning Peter keeps Paul honest, imprisoning Peter for all or most of his term saves society from the human and financial toll he would have inflicted if free. It costs society as much as $25,000 to keep a convicted violent or repeat criminal locked up for a year. Every social expenditure imposes opportunity costs (a tax dollar spent on a prison is a tax dollar not spent on a preschool, and vice versa). But what does it cost crime victims, their families, friends, employers, and the rest of society to let a convicted criminal roam the streets in search of victims?

A recent study of the costs of crimes to victims found that in 1992 a total of 33.6 million criminal victimizations occurred. Economic loss of some kind occurred in 71 percent of all personal crimes (rape, robbery, assault, personal theft) and 23 percent of all violent crimes (rape, robbery, assault). The study estimated that in 1992 crime victims lost $17.6 billion in direct costs (losses from property theft or damage, cash losses, medical expenses, lost pay from lost work). This estimate, however, did not include direct costs to victims that occurred six months or more after the crime (for example, medical costs). Nor did it include decreased work productivity, less tangible costs of pain and suffering, increases to insurance premiums as a result of filing claims, moving costs incurred as a result of victimization, and other indirect costs.[111]

Another recent study took a somewhat more comprehensive view of the direct costs of crime and included some indirect costs of crime as well. The study estimated the costs and monetary value of lost quality of life in 1987 due to death and nonfatal physical and psychological injury resulting from violent crime. Using various measures, the study estimated that each murder costs $2.4 million, each rape $60,000, each arson almost $50,000, each assault $22,000, and each robbery $25,000. It estimated that lifetime costs for all violent crimes totaled $178 billion during 1987 to 1990.[112]

Even these numbers, however, omit the sort of detailed cost accounting that is reflected in site-specific, crime-specific studies. For example, a survey of admissions to Wisconsin hospitals over a forty-one-month period found that 1,035 patients were admitted for gunshot wounds caused by assaults. Gunshot wound victims admitted during this period accumulated more than $16 million in hospital bills, about $6.8 million of it paid by taxes. Long-term costs rise far higher. For example, just one shotgun assault victim in this survey was likely to cost more than $5 million in lost income and medical expenses over the next thirty-five years.[113]

How much of the human and financial toll of crime could be avoided by incarcerating violent and repeat criminals for all or most of their terms? All studies that have attempted to analyze the social costs and benefits of imprisonment have employed much cruder and far lower estimates of the social costs of crime than were employed in the studies summarized above. Even so, all have found that, at the margin, the social benefits of imprisonment exceed the social costs. One such study, commissioned by the National Institute of Justice, found that the "lowest estimate of the benefit of operating an additional prison cell for a year ($172,000) is more than twice as high as the most extreme high estimate of the cost of operating such a cell ($70,000)." Another such study, one based on data from the aforementioned Wisconsin prisoner self-report survey, found that imprisoning one hundred typical felons "costs $2.5 million, but leaving these criminals on the streets costs $4.6 million." A third such study, based on data from the New Jersey prisoner self-report survey, found that it costs society more than twice as much to let the typical prisoner out as it does to keep him in.[114]

Saving Black Lives

We do not know precisely how many black lives were ruined by lax sentencing policies, or, conversely, how many could have been saved by stern ones. Still, the available data leave no doubt that the human and financial benefits of ending revolving door justice would be great for all Americans, most especially poor black Americans.

In the 1980s rates of imprisonment rose and crime rates fell. From 1980 to 1982 the ten states that had the highest increase in their prison populations, relative to total FBI index crime, experienced, on average, a decline in their crime rates of more than 20 percent, while the ten states with the smallest increases in incarceration rates averaged nearly a 9 percent increase in crime rates.[115] A 1986 study by the National Academy of Sciences estimated that doubling the prison population between 1973 and 1982 probably reduced the number of burglaries and robberies in the country by 10 to 20 percent. A 1994 review of the statistical literature on the relationship between imprisonment rates and crime rates concluded that a 10 percent increase in the likelihood of being imprisoned after conviction for a violent crime would reduce violent crime by about 7 percent.[116]

It is one thing to say that a person cannot commit a crime while incarcerated and quite another to say that the overall crime rate will go down by the increased use of imprisonment. One recent study suggests that the simple incapacitation effects of imprisonment (how many crimes are averted by keeping known, convicted offenders behind bars or, conversely, the increase in the level of crime caused by an increase in the use of probation or parole) may be socially significant without even being detected in crime rates (rates that can fluctuate for demographic and other reasons having little or nothing to do with sentencing policies or the justice system more generally).[117]

For example, in 1989 there were an estimated 66,000 fewer rapes, 323,000 fewer robberies, 380,000 fewer assaults, and 3.3 million fewer burglaries attributable to the difference between the crime rates of 1973 versus those of 1989 (that is, applying 1973 crime rates to the 1989 population). If only one-half or one-quarter of the reductions were the result of rising incarceration rates, "that would still leave prisons responsible for sizable reductions in crime." Tripling the prison population from 1975 to 1989 "potentially reduced reported and unreported violent crime by 10 to 15 percent below what it would have been, thereby potentially preventing a conservatively estimated 390,000 murders, rapes, robberies, and aggravated assaults in 1989 alone." Increasing by only four and a half months the time served by violent offenders would avert an estimated 40,000 violent crimes each year; if the number of violent offenders sent to prison increased by just nine thousand each year, an estimated 140,000 violent crimes could be prevented each year.[118]

The more sophisticated and sound the study, the stronger are the findings that incarceration cuts crime. For example, a 1994 study found that "in the 1970s and 1980s [imprisonment of] each additional state prisoner averted at least 17 index crimes on average. . . . For several reasons, the real impact may be much greater, and for recent years a better estimate may be 21 crimes averted per additional prisoner." Strikingly similar findings were reported in a 1995 study produced via the National Bureau of Economic Research and other recent studies.[119]

The 1994 federal crime bill contained truth-in-sentencing provisions. More than anything else, however, these provisions testified to a lack of truth in legislating: the measures would have provided federal money to jurisdictions that increased the fraction of the correctional population on probation or parole whether or not they also increased the actual amount of time served in prison by violent offenders. The Violent Crime and Incarceration Act passed by the House in 1995 corrected the fine print in the 1994 federal crime bill and set aside $5 billion for states that incarcerate more violent felons or keep violent offenders behind bars longer than they do at present. The bill also set aside about $5 billion for states that meet the federal government's own sentencing practices by incarcerating violent felons for 85 percent of their time. Few states, however, would ever qualify for this "second-half" money.

At this point, however, a word of caution is needed. A persistent problem with the truth-in-sentencing approach at the federal level as well as in many states is that it fails to discriminate rationally between violent and chronic offenders on the one side and genuinely low-level drug offenders (persons whose only crimes have been petty drug crimes) on the other. The same logic and evidence on incapacitation and public safety that make truth-in-sentencing laws so entirely sensible for serious offenders makes them silly when applied to low-level drug offenders. As the data presented above make plain, such offenders undoubtedly constitute a small fraction of the prison population. Still, it makes sense to identify them and, when possible, to handle them under less expensive forms of supervision.[120] A system that sorted offenders wisely would undoubtedly keep more offenders in prison for far longer periods than we do at present. But it would not blindly incarcerate all convicted or repeat felons for all or even most of their terms, nor impose blanket no-parole policies that are almost as perverse as blanket anti-incarceration policies.

Beyond Criminal Justice

An even bigger mistake would be to suppose that the inner-city crime problem can be addressed mainly or solely via longer prison terms, more cops, or, for that matter, more social programs and "prevention" efforts. Crime and related problems are mainly a function of demographic and social trends over which no government—certainly no republican government in a free society—can or should exercise much direct control.

Where the inner cities are concerned, the hard social facts are frightening and perplexing. A National Academy of Sciences study of adolescents in high-risk settings concluded that adults "in poor neighborhoods differ in important ways from those in more affluent areas." These neighborhoods lack "good role models for adolescents" and have a "far higher percentage of adults who are involved in illegal markets. The poorest of neighborhoods seem increasingly unable to restrain criminal or deviant behaviors."[121]

That is a polite and politic way of saying that some fraction of children who grow up in inner-city neighborhoods today grow up amidst deviant, delinquent, and crime-prone teenagers and elders, many of them felons, ex-felons, and drug addicts. Indeed, as almost every seasoned prison official knows, virtually all prisoners begin their criminal careers quite early in life, and a large fraction of them come from families where fathers, mothers, or siblings have also been in trouble with the law.

Studies show that more than half of young persons in long-term state juvenile institutions have one or more immediate family members (father, mother, sibling) who have also been incarcerated. A study that compared the family experiences of more violent and less violent incarcerated juveniles found that 75 percent of the former group had suffered serious abuse by a family member, while "only" 33 percent of the latter group had been abused. Likewise, 78 percent of the more violent group had been witnesses to extreme violence, while 20 percent of the less violent group had been witnesses.[122]

Most prisoners come from single-parent families, more than one-quarter have parents who have abused drugs or alcohol, and nearly one-third have a brother with a jail or prison record. Many produce the same sad experience for their own children. In 1991 male and female prisoners were parents to more than 825,000 children under age eighteen.[123] The facts about women in state prisons are particularly revealing and disturbing. Women in state prisons in 1991 were most likely to be black (46 percent) and between the ages of twenty-five and thirty-four (50 percent). Between 1986 and 1991 the number of women in state prisons rose by 75 percent. More than 70 percent of female prisoners had served a previous sentence. About 58 percent of them grew up in a household without both parents present; more than half had used drugs, including crack cocaine, in the month before the current offense; 47 percent had at least one immediate family member who had also been incarcerated; 43 percent had been physically or sexually abused; and 34 percent had parents or guardians who abused alcohol or drugs.[124]

There are countless analyses of how best to help inner-city children resist the blandishments of alcohol and drugs, remain in school, and avoid criminal involvement and victimization. For example, a 1993 report by the Office of Juvenile Justice and Delinquency Prevention concluded that the "behavioral factors that contribute to serious, violent, and chronic juvenile crime" are delinquent peer groups, poor school performance, high-crime neighborhoods, weak family attachments, lack of consistent discipline, and physical or sexual abuse. The first of the OJJDP's "key principles for preventing and reducing juvenile delinquency" is "strengthen families."[125]

The punch line to the old joke about the economist marooned on a desert island with unopened cans of food is, "Assume a can opener!" The punch line of virtually all juvenile delinquency prevention research is, "Assume a good family!" or "Assume a better neighborhood!" The problem is that so many children who go on to become serious juvenile offenders and predatory adult criminals begin life in homes and neighborhoods where the teenagers and adults in their midst are hardly more likely to nurture, teach, and care for them than they are to expose them to neglect, abuse, and violence.

As a study of delinquent and high-risk young people in California concluded, we "know from a number of well-designed studies that chronic delinquency usually has its origins in early childhood experiences."[126] A comprehensive review of the literature on criminal behavior concluded that we must "rivet our attention on the earliest stages of the life cycle," for "after all is said and done, the most serious offenders are boys who begin their careers at a very early age."[127] And these very bad boys do come disproportionately from very bad homes in very bad neighborhoods. As a masterful survey of the literature on the need for intensive interventions into the lives of high-risk youths concluded, most juveniles who "engaged in frequent criminal acts against persons and property . . . come from family settings characterized by high levels of violence, chaos, and dysfunction."[128]

As is commonly believed, a good deal of the violence, chaos, and dysfunction in these crime-infested settings is related to drug and alcohol abuse. Studies show that alcohol abuse is a major public health problem in inner-city black neighborhoods. Nearly one-quarter of state prisoners initially became involved in crime to get money for drugs. Children who are exposed regularly to substance-abusing adults are far more likely to develop substance abuse and related problems of their own later in life than otherwise comparable children who are not so exposed.

The simple truth is that children cannot be socialized by adults who are themselves unsocialized (or worse), families that exist in name only, schools that do not educate, and neighborhoods in which violent and repeat criminals circulate in and out of jail.

According to many big-city police officers, school principals, jail officials, adult and juvenile probation officers, corrections researchers, older prisoners, and others who are in a position to grade the problem in terms of such unobtrusive, field-based, street-level measures as their own sense of frustration and fear when in contact with inner-city youth, things are getting worse and worse. The following reflection of Los Angeles district attorney Gil Garcetti is typical: "It is incredible—the ability of the very young to commit the most horrendous crimes imaginable and not have a second thought about it. This was unthinkable 20 years ago."[129]

In the single most important ethnographic study of contemporary urban street criminals, the vast majority of them black, Mark S. Fleisher offers a compelling analysis of how deviant, delinquent, and criminal adults beget deviant, delinquent, and criminal children. Reducing street crime in these neighborhoods, he argues, "depends on creating and maintaining safe, healthy early-life social environments for pre-teenage children." At-risk juveniles "must be protected from parents" who abuse and neglect them and put them on the road to a life of crime. "We must do more," he concludes, than ask these parents "to stop beating their sons and daughters, we must permanently remove children from brutal parents."[130]

Rescue Mission

More than anything else, at-risk inner-city children need to be protected from abuse and crime at the hands of their relatives and neighbors, and educated and raised by caring and capable adults. Arguably, the deeper the intervention into the lives of at-risk children, the more complete will be the cure. We need to begin to think about, debate fairly, do research into, and develop institutions that remove at-risk children from at-risk settings and succeed in giving them as fine a start in life as possible under the circumstances.

No combination of piecemeal, family-centered, community rede-velopment policies can compete with the negative forces at work in the lives of many of today's at-risk inner-city children. That is the real lesson to be drawn from such programs as Head Start. The long-term effects of Head Start are in grave doubt, as is the basic quality of its personnel administration.[131] In the 1994 congressional debate over the program's reauthorization, no body of empirical evidence was pro-duced to show that it had yielded large, positive, and lasting effects measured in terms of IQ, school performance, or the chances of avoid-ing teen pregnancy, landing a job, or avoiding trouble with the law. The largely successful program that inspired Head Start, the Perry Preschool program in Ypsilanti, Michigan, was "not limited to provid-ing children with preschool experiences for twelve-and-a-half hours a week. It also involved an extensive program of home visits."[132]

There are today many worthwhile programs that, like the old Perry program, send "visitors into families' homes to provide infor-mation, health care, or psychological or other support services."[133] With few exceptions, however, these programs focus not on children but on both children and families, and they operate wholly within the constraints imposed by the dysfunctional or crime-infested environ-ments within which the children continue to live.

The self-evident truth assumed in much of the contemporary social policy literature on at-risk young people is that the only effective and legitimate way to save the children is to save simultaneously all and everyone who surrounds them, including the abusive, neglectful, or criminal adults in the homes from which they come. This "truth" is merely a self-deluded reflection of what Heather Mac Donald has aptly described as the "ideology of family preservation."[134]

As uncertain as the benefits of more child-centered social policies might be, the fallacies and flaws of family-centered policies could not be clearer. The family-centered approach to social policy has been in the ascendant at least since the New Deal. From 1850 to 1930, however, many reformers held to a more child-centered philosophy of remov-ing at-risk children from the disease, crime, and moral squalor of their urban environments. Indeed, during those years the members of a child-removal movement relocated some 200,000 children—a minority of them orphans, a majority of them from the slums of big cities, all of them from impoverished or abusive families—to rural areas in the West, the South, New England, and upstate New York.

The effects of this placing-out policy are hard to know. On balance, the best single study of the policy offers a positive assessment: "Faced with what urban life offered the poor—street life, crime, prostitution, overwhelming deprivations, incarceration, and little hope for escape—the argument must swing to (the placing out advocates') heartfelt appeals."[135]

The time has come to take another look at the development of some species of placing-out institutions for at-risk inner-city children. As Mary-Lou Weisman has noted, at the end of 1990, there were about 406,000 children in out-of-home placements, some 65,000 of them in "group homes and residential treatment centers that are the institutional descendants of the orphanage."[136] As James Q. Wilson has argued, we need to think seriously about developing and improving such institutions—call them boarding schools, orphanages, or residential homes—the primary object of which "would be to provide a safe, consistent, and enjoyable mechanism for the habituation of the child—that is, for the inculcation of the ordinary virtues of politeness, self-control, and social skills. Another goal for these schools would be either to place their students into a college or to qualify them for entry into an occupation by means of an apprenticeship program."[137]

Family-centered policies make the mistake of assuming good or easily repairable families; child-centered policies ought not to make the mistake of assuming successful or easily crafted institutions. At present no one has even begun to research what kinds of institutions for at-risk children might work best under what conditions. There are a tremendous number of questions to be addressed. Should the institutions be public or private or public-private? What is really known about the efficacy of institutions that have attempted similar tasks in the past? At what age is even full-scale intervention "too little, too late"? What would be the optimal size of these institutions? Historically, what administrative problems have turned such institutions into nothing more than wretched orphanages, foster care complexes, or hellish reform schools, and how, if at all, can these difficulties be minimized or eliminated? What political, legal, budgetary, and moral considerations should influence how the institutions are structured, where they are located, and whether they are to be voluntary or mandatory?

If we are going to debate, research, and make incremental experiments with this most radical of radical social program proposals at all, then there is no point in avoiding the gut-wrenching questions of public philosophy and administration that it entails. Youth and family service agencies already have criteria for deciding when, where, and for how long a child is to be placed outside the home (group homes, foster homes, medical or psychiatric hospitals, secure facilities, and juvenile lockups, or training schools as they are called in many states). What types of abusive, neglectful, or criminal acts by parents or guardians might legally mandate placing out? How many such acts of which types should trigger placing out? These are the sorts of tough practical and moral questions that await those whose concerns about social policies for children extend beyond the latest recipes for family preservation and encompass the need to remove some small fraction of at-risk children from parents who have done them severe and certain harm.

Boarding Schools

If I were forced to come up with a blueprint for boarding schools by tomorrow morning, it would have four main elements.

First, the schools would have absolutely nothing to do with existing social service and child-welfare agencies. These institutions do not need to be reformed or "reinvented"; they need to be razed. The boarding schools would be staffed and run exclusively by blacks, including retirees, who live in metropolitan areas. The vast majority of urban blacks are doing well economically and live stable, traditional family lives in which religion plays some role.

Second, the schools would be formally connected to churches and be frankly and unapologetically religious in character. Let perverted civil libertarians and others who have worked to prevent inner-city blacks from target-hardening their communities (erecting concrete barriers, putting metal detectors in high schools, automatically evicting drug dealers from public housing) scream bloody murder about the church-state issues this ostensibly poses. The church choir sings louder and better, and most policymakers and citizens—and maybe a few federal judges who have actually read the Constitution—will support the effort.

Third, the schools could turn any child over to family court authorities at any time for any reason. If this leads to "creaming"—

taking on only the youngest kids or the easiest cases—then so be it. Every life rescued is in the plus column, and the history of juvenile institutions shows that a few irredeemably rotten apples will spoil the whole bunch, demoralize staff, and cause the waste of millions of dollars.

Fourth, the schools would receive public funds on a per pupil basis with no strings attached. They would be held strictly accountable for results: producing children and young adults who are literate, well-behaved, and prepared for the challenges of adult life. They would not be subject to the procedural regulations that define our failed bureaucratic networks of youth agencies and foster care complexes.

Our Children

Being born healthy to loving, caring parents of whatever socioeconomic status is the luckiest accident that can befall a human being. Rescuing America's unluckiest kids via boarding schools is probably not possible politically. Even if it were, boarding schools could never do for these kids what a good family could have done for them. What, then, is to be done?

Proponents of judicial activism have traditionally argued that the courts must correct injustices when the other branches of government refuse to do so. The courts are the last resort for those without the influence to obtain new laws, especially the poor and powerless.

In the case of America's black crime gap, however, we are not talking about activist court orders. Instead, we are talking about strict judicial scrutiny and enforcement of existing, democratically enacted federal, state, and local laws, policies, and procedures governing such things as compliance conditions for probationers, drug-free school zones, conditions of confinement in juvenile detention facilities, the administration of foster care and child-welfare systems, and so on.

The courts' first order of business must be to promote the physical security of inner-city children, most especially to protect them against violent and repeat criminals, adult and juvenile. The children in today's inner-city neighborhoods are being deprived of all manner of specific legal protections and civil rights. It is a contorted conception of civil rights that requires government action against segregated schools but does not require it against violence-ridden ones, virtually all of which are located in poor, minority neighborhoods. It is a morally bankrupt jurisprudence that sees a civil rights interest in enabling children to attend the local public school of their choice, but sees none in enabling children to walk to school without having to dodge stray bullets, run from drug dealers, or wear colors that do not offend street gangsters. It is a mere exercise in legalism to fiddle with "rational basis" doctrines while the inner cities burn.[138]

But the ultimate solution to the black crime gap will come (or not) from within the black urban community itself. About three-quarters of all blacks living in metropolitan areas are not in poverty. As Richard P. Nathan has pointed out, there are a growing number of minority working- and middle-class urban neighborhoods, the flip side of the urban underclass.[139] But whether these neighborhoods will survive and flourish and whether, in turn, their success can somehow be turned to the advantage of those left behind in the crime-torn inner cities are open questions that cry out for more public attention and greater research.

Unfortunately, the best prediction about saving at-risk inner-city children is probably the least hopeful one. We will continue with failed criminal justice policies that do little to empower the law-abiding residents of these places to raise their children in peace. We will continue with piecemeal, family-centered (as opposed to comprehensive, child-centered) social programs that have few if any long-term benefits. We will continue with a public discourse that enables policy intellectuals of all ideological persuasions to retread old arguments, policymakers of both parties to pass new but ineffective laws, judges to look the other way, and average citizens of all races to shrug off any sympathies they may feel toward young, faceless fellow citizens whose personal and economic fates are not closely intertwined with their own.

Notes

1. Hugh Pearson, "Black America' s Silent Majority," *New York Times*, May 26, 1994, p. A23.

2. Randall Kennedy, "Blacks and Crime," *Wall Street Journal*, April 8, 1994, p. A14.

3. President Clinton, as quoted in Douglas Jehl, "Clinton Delivers Emotional Appeal on Stopping Crime," *New York Times*, November 14, 1993, p. A1.

4. Bureau of Justice Statistics, *Highlights from 20 Years of Surveying Crime Victims* (October 1993), p. 22, and author's calculations.

5. National Commission on the Causes and Prevention of Violence, *Violent Crime: The Challenge to Our Cities* (George Braziller, 1969), p. 82.

6. *Uniform Crime Report, Commonwealth of Pennsylvania, Annual Report, 1990* (Harrisburg: Pennsylvania State Police Bureau of Research and Development, 1991), pp. A2–A4.

7. Calculated from George B. Palermo and others, "Crime in a Midwestern City: A Statistical Analysis," *International Journal of Offender Therapy and Comparative Criminology*, vol. 36, no. 4 (1992), p. 296; also calculated from Milwaukee Fire and Police Commission Research Services, *City of Milwaukee 1991 Public Safety Report* (Milwaukee Police Department, 1992), appendix D, pp. 64, 67, 73, 74, 76, 78, comparing predominantly black aldermanic districts 1, 4, and 10 to predominantly white districts 11, 13, and 15.

8. Ronet Bachman, *Crime Victimization in City, Suburban, and Rural Areas* (Bureau of Justice Statistics, 1992), p. 1.

9. Calculated from Bureau of Justice Statistics, *Criminal Victimization in the United States, 1992* (1993), table 19, p. 40, and *Criminal Victimization in the United States, 1989* (1991), p. 34.

10. John M. Dawson and Barbara Boland, "Murder in Large Urban Counties, 1988," *BJS Special Report* (May 1993), p. 2.

11. Office of Criminal Justice Plans and Analysis, *Homicide in the District of Columbia* (Government of the District of Columbia, 1988).

12. Barbara Allen-Hagen and Melissa Sickmund, "Juveniles and Violence: Juvenile Offending and Victimization," *Office of Juvenile Justice and Delinquency Prevention: Fact Sheet No. 3*, pp. 1, 3.

13. Lisa D. Bastian and Bruce M. Taylor, "Young Black Male Victims," *Bureau of Justice Statistics Crime Data Brief* (December 1994), p. 1; and Alfred Blumstein, "Prisons," in James Q. Wilson and Joan Petersilia, eds., *Crime* (San Francisco: ICS Press, 1995), pp. 411–12.

14. Carol J. DeFrances and Steven K. Smith, "Crime and Neighborhoods," *BJS Crime Data Brief* (June 1994), p. 1.

15. Lisa D. Bastian and Bruce M. Taylor, *School Crime: A National Crime Victimization Survey Report* (Bureau of Justice Statistics, September 1991), p. 10.

16. As reported in "Soaring Murder Rate Leaves New Orleans Fearful," *New York Times*, May 31, 1994, p. A14.

17. Bureau of Justice Statistics, *Criminal Victimization in the United States, 1992*, tables 47 and 54.

18. National Research Council, *Losing Generations: Adolescents in High-Risk Settings* (Washington: National Academy Press, 1993), p. 164.

19. Stephen P. Klein and others, *Predicting Criminal Justice Outcomes: What Matters?* (Santa Monica, Calif.: RAND, 1991).

20. Bureau of Justice Statistics, *Correctional Populations in the United States, 1990* (1992), and *National Corrections Reporting Program, 1988* (1992).

21. Bureau of Justice Statistics, *Sentencing in the Federal Courts: Does Race Matter? The Transition to Sentencing Guidelines, 1986–90, Summary* (1993).

22. Patrick A. Langan, "No Racism in the Justice System," *Public Interest*,

no. 117 (Fall 1994), p. 51; and Stanley Rothman and Stephan Powers, "Execution by Quota?" *Public Interest*, no. 116 (Summer 1994), pp. 3–17.

23. Alfred Blumstein, "On the Racial Disproportionality of United States Prison Populations," *Journal of Criminal Law and Criminology*, vol. 73 (1982); Patrick A. Langan, "Racism on Trial: New Evidence to Explain the Racial Composition of Prisons in the United states," *Journal of Criminal Law and Criminology*, vol. 76 (Fall 1985); Bureau of Justice Statistics, *Prison Admissions and Releases, 1983* (1986); *Race and Imprisonment Decisions in California* (Santa Monica, Calif.: RAND, 1990); and James Stephan, "Prison Rule Violators," *BJS Special Report* (December 1989).

24. Carl E. Pope and William Feyerherm, *Minorities and the Juvenile Justice System: Research Summary* (Office of Juvenile Justice and Delinquincy Prevention, December 1993).

25. Jan Hoffman, "Quirks in Juvenile Offender Law Stir Calls for Change," *New York Times*, July 12, 1994, p. B1.

26. Reuters, "Tougher Treatment Urged for Juveniles," *New York Times*, August 2, 1994, p. A16.

27. Data from attitude surveys reported in Bureau of Justice Statistics, *Sourcebook of Criminal Justice Statistics, 1993* (1994), sec. 2, pp. 153–243.

28. Ibid., p. 188.

29. Ibid., p. 171.

30. Glenn C. Loury, "Listen to the Black Community," *Public Interest*, no. 117 (Fall 1994), p. 35.

31. National Research Council, *Losing Generations*, p. 153.

32. Not that such suggestions have not been made. See John J. DiIulio Jr., "The Impact of Inner City Crime," *Public Interest*, no. 96 (Summer 1989), p. 46.

33. Amitai Etzioni, "Do Fence Me In," *Wall Street Journal*, December 1, 1992, p. A16; Rochelle L. Stanfield, "Safe Passage," *National Journal*, September 25, 1993, pp. 2305–08; and Jill Smolowe, "Danger in the Safety Zone," *Time*, August 23, 1993, pp. 29–32.

34. "American Housing Survey for the United States," *Current Housing Reports* (Department of Housing and Urban Development and Bureau of the Census, 1983 and biennial).

35. Bureau of Justice Statistics, *Sourcebook of Criminal Justice Statistics, 1990* (1991), pp. 35, 46.

36. James Q. Wilson and George L. Kelling, "Broken Windows: The Police and Neighborhood Safety," *Atlantic Monthly*, March 1982, p. 38.

37. Lawrence W. Sherman, *Police Crackdowns* (Washington: National Institute of Justice, 1990).

38. Steven D. Levitt, "The Effect of Police on Crime," Massachusetts Institute of Technology, Department of Economics, May 1994; and Helen Tauchen and others, "Criminal Deterrence: Revisiting the Issue with a Birth Cohort," *Review of Economics and Statistics*, vol. 76 (August 1994), pp. 399–412.

39. John J. DiIulio Jr., "Community-Based Policing in Wisconsin: Can It Cut Crime?" *Wisconsin Policy Research Institute Report*, vol. 6 (October 1993), table 4, p. 21.

40. David H. Bayley, "The Cop Fallacy," *New York Times*, August 16, 1993, p. A17.

41. DiIulio, *Community-Based Policing in Wisconsin*, table 5, p. 22.

42. Ibid.

43. Wesley G. Skogan, *Disorder and Decline: Crime and the Spiral of Decay in American Neighborhoods* (University of California Press, 1992).

44. John J. DiIulio Jr., Steven K. Smith, and Aaron J. Saiger, "The Federal Role in Crime Control," in Wilson and Petersilia, *Crime*, pp. 445–62; John J. DiIulio Jr., "America's Crime Problem, What Should Washington Do?", testimony before the Senate Judiciary Committee, February 14, 1995; and John J. DiIulio Jr., "A Crime Bill That Would Work," *Wall Street Journal*, February 15, 1995, p. A19.

45. DiIulio and others, "Federal Role in Crime Control"; John J. DiIulio Jr., "Crime," in Henry J. Aaron and Charles L. Schultze, eds., *Setting Domestic Priorities: What Can Government Do?* (Brookings, 1992); John J. DiIulio Jr., "The Next War on Drugs," *Brookings Review*, vol. 10 (Summer 1993), pp. 28–33; and John J. DiIulio Jr., "A Limited War on Crime That We Can Win: Two Lost Wars Later," *Brookings Review*, vol. 10 (Fall 1992), pp. 6–11.

46. "The New Prohibition," *Public Perspective*, vol. 6 (April–May 1995), pp. 32–37.

47. The remainder of this section is drawn from John J. DiIulio Jr., "Broken Bottles: Liquor, Disorder and Crime in Wisconsin," *Wisconsin Policy Research Institute Report*, vol. 8 (May 1995).

48. Jeffrey Fagan, "Intoxication and Aggression," in Michael Tonry and James Q. Wilson, eds., *Drugs and Crime*, vol. 13: *Crime and Justice: A Review of Research* (University of Chicago Press, 1990), p. 292.

49. Philip J. Cook and Michael J. Moore, "Violence Reduction through Restrictions on Alcohol Availability," *Alcohol Health & Research World*, vol. 17, no. 2 (1993), p. 151.

50. Alan R. Lang and Paulette A. Sibrel, "Psychological Perspectives on Alcohol Consumption and Interpersonal Aggression," *Criminal Justice and Behavior*, vol. 16 (September 1989), pp. 321, 301.

51. Arnold S. Trebach and James A. Inciardi, *Legalize It? Debating American Drug Policy* (American University Press, 1993), p. 160; Steven Jonas, "The U.S. Drug Problem and the U.S. Drug Culture: A Public Health Solution," in James A. Inciardi, ed., *The Drug Legalization Debate*, vol. 7: *Studies in Crime, Law and Justice* (Sage Publications, 1991), p. 164; Hannah Clayson, "Alcohol Policy and New York City: A Harm-Reduction Strategy," WWS402d, Woodrow Wilson School, Princeton University, May 10, 1994, p. 7, citing data from Tom Harford, "The Incidence of Alcohol and Other Drug Use," in Ura Jean Oyemade and Delores Brandon-Moyne, eds., *Ecology of Alcohol and Other Drug Use: Helping Black High-Risk Youth* (Department of Health and Human Services, 1987), pp. 46–47; and *Seventh Special Report to the U.S. Congress on Alcohol and Health* (U.S. Department of Health and Human Services, January 1990).

52. John P. Morgan and Lynn Zimmer, "The Social Pharmacology of

Smokeable Cocaine: Not All It's Cracked Up to Be," City University of New York, 1994.

53. Sam Staley, *Drug Policy and the Decline of American Cities* (New Brunswick, N.J.: Transaction Publishers, 1992), pp. 113–14.

54. Ibid, p. 111, citing data from James Ostrowski, "Thinking about Legalization," *Cato Policy Analysis*, no. 21 (Washington: Cato Institute, 1989), p. 47, table 4.

55. Skogan, *Disorder and Decline*, pp. 4, 22.

56. Cook and Moore, p. 151.

57. Douglas Murdoch and others, "Alcohol and Crimes of Violence," *International Journal of the Addictions*, vol. 25 (September 1990).

58. James J. Collins and Pamela M. Messerschmidt, "Epidemiology of Alcohol-Related Violence," *Alcohol Health & Research World*, vol. 17, no. 2 (1993), p. 94, reporting data calculated from two studies in 1988 and one in 1991 by the Bureau of Justice Statistics.

59. "Prisoners and Alcohol," *Bureau of Justice Statistics Bulletin* (January 1983), p. 2.

60. Bastian and Taylor, "Young Black Male Victims"; and Alfred Blumstein, "Prisons," in Wilson and Petersilia, *Crime*, p. 412.

61. Robert Nash Parker, "Alcohol and Theories of Homicide," in Freda Adler and William S. Laufer, eds., *Advances in Criminological Theory*, vol. 4: *New Directions in Criminal Theory* (New Brunswick, N.J.: Transactions Publishers, 1993) pp. 113–41.

62. Patricia Ladouceur and Mark Temple, "Substance Use among Rapists: A Comparison with Other Serious Felons," *Crime & Delinquency*, vol. 31 (April 1985), p. 272.

63. Helene Raskin White and others, "Alcohol Use and Aggression among Youth," *Alcohol Health & Research World*, vol. 17, no. 2 (1993), pp. 144–50.

64. Department of Health and Human Services, *Seventh Special Report*.

65. James J. Collins, "Alcohol and Interpersonal Violence: Less Than Meets the Eye," in Neil Allen Weiner and Marvin E. Wolfgang, eds., *Pathways to Criminal Violence* (Sage, 1989), p. 50.

66. For example, compare Reginald G. Smart, "The Relationship of Availability of Alcoholic Beverages to Per Capita Consumption and Alcoholism Rates," *Journal of Studies on Alcohol*, vol. 38, no. 5 (1977), pp. 891–96; and Brian R. Rush and others, "Alcohol Availability, Alcohol Consumption and Alcohol-Related Damage: The Distribution of Consumption Model," *Journal of Studies on Alcohol*, vol. 47, no. 1 (1986), pp. 1–18. The former study indicated that the relationships among availability, consumption, and problems weakened if one controlled for such socioeconomic variables as urban conditions and unemployment rates. But the latter and more sophisticated study incorporated these very factors as direct causes of aggregate alcohol consumption and as covariates of retail availability. As common sense would have it, the better model and research showed that availability increased consumption, and consumption increased problems. Likewise, see Philip J. Cook and Michael J. Moore, "Drinking and Schooling," *Journal of*

Health Economics, vol. 12, no. 4 (1993), pp. 411–29, which finds that drinking and schooling do not mix (for example, other things being equal, drinking in high school reduces the average number of years of schooling completed following high school).

67. Cook and Moore, "Violence Reduction."

68. Ibid, p. 154.

69. Frank J. Chaloupka, "Effects of Price on Alcohol-Related Problems," *Alcohol Health & Research World*, vol. 17, no. 1 (1993), pp. 46–53.

70. Mark Temple and Patricia Ladouceur, "The Alcohol-Crime Relationship as an Age-Specific Phenomenon: A Longitudinal Study," *Contemporary Drug Problems*, vol. 13 (Spring 1986), pp. 89–116.

71. Chaloupka, "Effects of Price," p. 49.

72. Ibid., p. 52.

73. Henrick J. Harwood and others, *Social and Economic Costs of Alcohol Abuse and Alcoholism* (Research Triangle Institute, 1985). For reports on estimates of the costs of violent crime, see Anne Morrison Piehl and John J. DiIulio Jr., "Does Prison Pay? Revisited," *Brookings Review*, vol. 13 (Winter 1995).

74. Paul J. Gruenwald and others, "The Relationship of Outlet Densities to Alcohol Consumption: A Time Series Cross-Sectional Analysis," *Alcoholism: Clinical and Experimental Research*, vol. 17, no. 1 (1993), p. 38.

75. Ibid., pp. 38, 45.

76. Paul J. Gruenwald and others, "Alcohol Availability and the Formal Power and Resources of State Alcohol Beverage Control Agencies," *Alcohol: Clinical and Experimental Research*, vol. 16, no. 3 (May–June 1992), p. 592.

77. Jerome Rabow and Ronald K. Watts, "Alcohol Availability, Alcohol Beverage Sales and Alcohol-Related Problems," *Journal of Studies on Alcohol*, vol. 43, no. 7 (1982), pp. 767–801.

78. Gruenwald and others, "Alcohol Availability," pp. 591–97.

79. Jerome Rabow and others, "Alcoholic Beverage Licensing Practices in California: A Study of a Regulatory Agency," *Alcoholism: Clinical and Experimental Research*, vol. 17, no. 2 (1993), p. 245, 244.

80. Robert Nash Parker with L. A. Rebhun, *Alcohol and Homicide: A Deadly Combination of Two American Traditions* (SUNY Press, forthcoming), draft, p. 60.

81. David Whitman with David Bowermaster, "A Potent Brew: Booze and Crime," *U.S. News & World Report*, May 31, 1993, pp. 57–59.

82. Skogan, *Disorder and Decline*, pp. 10-11, summarizing the Wilson-Kelling "broken windows" thesis.

83. Parker and Rebhun, *Alcohol and Homicide*, pp. 60–61.

84. Travis Hirschi, *Causes of Delinquency* (University of California Press, 1969); Marvin D. Krohn and James L. Massey, "Social Control and Delinquent Behavior: An Examination of the Elements of the Social Bond," *Sociological Quarterly*, vol. 20 (Autumn 1980), pp. 529–43; Anne C. Case and Lawrence F. Katz, "The Company You Keep: The Effects of Family and Neighborhood on Disadvantaged Youths," Working Paper 3705 (Cambridge, Mass.: National Bureau of Economic Research, 1991).

85. Stanley I. Orenstein and Dominique M. Hanssens, "Alcohol Control Laws and the Consumption of Distilled Spirits and Beer," *Journal of Consumer Research*, vol. 12 (September 1985), p. 208.

86. Case and Katz, "Company You Keep."

87. Parker and Rebhun, *Alcohol and Homicide*, pp. 55–56.

88. Cook and Moore, "Violence Reduction," p. 155.

89. As quoted in Clayson, "Alcohol Policy and New York City," p. 21.

90. Whitman and Bowermaster, "Potent Brew," p. 59.

91. Clayson, "Alcohol Policy and New York City," p. 22.

92. Philip J. Cook and George Tauchen, "The Effect of Minimum Drinking Age Legislation on Youthful Auto Fatalities, 1970–1977," *Journal of Legal Studies*, vol. 3 (January 1984), pp. 169–90.

93. Pheny Z. Smith, *Felony Defendants in Large Urban Counties, 1990* (Bureau of Justice Statistics, May 1993), pp. 5, 9, 11.

94. Patrick A. Langan and John M. Dawson, "Felony Sentences in State Courts, 1988," *Bureau of Justice Statistics Bulletin* (March 1993).

95. Michael K. Block and Steven J. Twist, "Lessons from the Eighties: Incarceration Works," *Commonsense*, vol. 1 (Spring 1994), p. 77.

96. Bureau of Justice Statistics, *Correctional Populations in the United States, 1989* (1991).

97. Patrick A. Langan and Mark A. Cunniff, "Recidivism of Felons on Probation, 1986-1989," *BJS Special Report*, pp. 1, 6; and Lawrence A. Greenfield, *Prisons and Prisoners in the United States* (Bureau of Justice Statistics, 1992), p. xvi.

98. Florida Statistical Analysis Center, "Study Examines Inmate Recidivism," *SAC Notes* (July 1993), tables 1, 3.

99. *Felony Defendants in Large Urban Counties, 1990*, p. 5.

100. I confess to having made this response myself; see John J. DiIulio Jr., "Punishing Smarter: Penal Reforms for the 1990s," *Brookings Review*, vol. 7 (Summer 1989); and John J. DiIulio Jr., *No Escape: The Future of American Corrections* (Basic Books, 1991).

101. President's Commission on Law Enforcement and Administration of Justice, *The Challenge of Crime in a Free Society* (1967), p. 167.

102. Patrick A. Langan, "Between Prison and Probation: Intermediate Sanctions," *Science*, vol. 264 (May 1994), p. 791.

103. Joan Petersilia and Susan Turner, *Intensive Supervision for High-Risk Probationers: Findings from Three California Experiments* (Santa Monica, Calif.: RAND, 1990), pp. ix, 98; and Turner and Petersilia, "Focusing on High-Risk Parolees: An Experiment to Reduce Commitments to the Texas Department of Corrections," *Journal of Research in Crime and Delinquency*, vol. 29 (February 1992), p. 34.

104. Unfortunately, studies that pick apart this myth are few. For one excellent example, see Charles H. Logan, "Who Really Goes to Prison?" *Federal Prisons Journal* (Summer 1991), pp. 57–59.

105. Bureau of Justice Statistics, *Survey of State Prison Inmates, 1991* (1993), pp. 11, 15, 17.

106. Fred De Vesa, "Attorney General Defends Conference," *Star-Ledger*, October 16, 1993.

107. Craig Perkins, *National Corrections Reporting Program, 1991* (Bureau of Justice Statistics, February 1994), tables 5-2, 5-4, pp. 55, 57; Federal Bureau of Prisons, *1989 State of the Bureau* (1990); and Federal Bureau of Prisons, *Federal Prisoners with a History of Violence* (undated).

108. Susan Estrich, "A Teen Kills, and We Protect Him," *USA Today*, June 2, 1994, p. 11A; and Bureau of Justice Statistics, *Violent Crime in the United States* (March 1991), pp. 14, 16.

109. For the raw data from the Wisconsin study, see John J. DiIulio Jr., "Community-Based Policing in Wisconsin: Can It Cut Crime?", *Wisconsin Policy Research Institute Report*, vol. 6 (October 1993). For an analysis of the Wisconsin data, see John J. DiIulio Jr. and Anne Morrison Piehl, "Does Prison Pay?", *Brookings Review*, vol. 9 (Fall 1991), pp. 28–35. For the raw data from the New Jersey study and a preliminary analysis of it, see John J. DiIulio Jr. and Anne Morrison Piehl, *New Jersey Inmate Survey: Results and Implications* (Trenton: New Jersey Sentencing Policy Study Commission, 1993).

110. Perkins, *National Corrections*, p. 23.

111. Patsy A. Klaus, "The Costs of Crime to Victims," *BSJ Crime Data Brief* (February 1994), pp. 1, 2.

112. Ted R. Miller and others, "Victim Costs of Violent Crime and Resulting Injuries," *Health Affairs*, vol. 12 (Winter 1993), pp. 193–94.

113. Neil D. Rosenberg, "Gunshots Shatter Lives, Cost Millions," *Milwaukee Journal*, March 14, 1993, p. 12.

114. David P. Cavanagh and Mark A. R. Kleiman, *Cost Benefit Analysis of Prison Cell Construction and Alternative Sanctions* (Cambridge, Mass.: BOTEC Analysis Corp., 1990), p. 26; DiIulio and Piehl, "Does Prison Pay?" p. 34; and DiIulio and Piehl, *New Jersey Inmate Survey*.

115. Block and Twist, "Lessons from the Eighties," p. 78.

116. Alfred Blumstein and others, eds., *Criminal Careers and "Career Criminals,"* vol. 1 (Washington: National Academy Press, 1986), p. 123, citing the findings of Michael K. Block, Carey Herbert, and Steven J. Twist, "Deterrence: What We Know and What It Means," working paper, University of Arizona, 1994.

117. Langan, "Between Prison and Probation," p. 792.

118. Patrick A. Langan, "America's Soaring Prison Population," *Science*, vol. 251 (March 1991), p. 1573; Langan, "Between Prison and Probation," pp. 792–93; and Block and Twist, "Lessons from the Eighties," p. 79.

119. Thomas B. Marvell and Carlisle D. Moody Jr., "Prison Population Growth and Crime Reduction," *Journal of Quantitative Criminology*, vol. 10, no. 4 (1994), p. 136; Steven D. Levitt, "The Effect of Prison Population Size on Crime Rates: Evidence from Prison Overcrowding," Litigation Working Paper 5119 (Cambridge, Mass.: National Bureau of Economic Research, February 1995); and George A. Mitchell, "Prison Works," *Wisconsin Policy Research Institute Report*, August 1995.

120. DiIulio and Piehl, "Does Prison Pay? Revisited."

121. National Research Council, *Losing Generations*, p. 5.

122. Bureau of Justice Statistics, *National Update* (1992), p. 7; and Ellen Schall, "Principles for Juvenile Detention," in Francis X. Hartmann, ed., *From Children to Citizens*, vol. 2: *The Role of Juvenile Court* (Springer Verlag, 1987), p. 350.

123. Bureau of Justice Statistics, *Survey of State Prison Inmates*, pp. 9, 10.

124. Tracy L. Snell, "Women in Prison," *BJS Special Report* (March 1994), pp. 1, 2.

125. Office of Juvenile Justice and Delinquency Prevention, *A Comprehensive Strategy for Serious, Violent, and Chronic Juvenile Offenders* (1993), p. 7.

126. Peter W. Greenwood, "Reforming California's Approach to Delinquent and High-Risk Youth," in James B. Steinberg and others, *Urban America: Policy Choices for Los Angeles and the Nation* (Santa Monica, Calif.: RAND, 1992), p. 221.

127. James Q. Wilson and Richard J. Hernstein, *Crime and Human Nature* (Simon and Schuster, 1985), pp. 508–09.

128. David M. Altschuler and Troy L. Armstrong, "Intensive Aftercare for the High-Risk Juvenile Parolee: Issues and Approaches in Reintegration and Community Supervision," in Troy L. Armstrong, ed., *Intensive Interventions with High-Risk Youths: Promising Approaches in Juvenile Probation and Parole* (New York: Criminal Justice Press, 1991), p. 48.

129. Gil Garcetti, as quoted in Isabel Wilkerson, "2 Boys, A Debt, A Gun, A Victim: The Face of Violence," *New York Times*, May 16, 1994, p. A1.

130. Mark S. Fleisher, *Beggars and Thieves: An Ethnography of Urban Street Crime* (forthcoming).

131. Douglas J. Besharov, "Fresh Start," *New Republic*, June 14, 1993, pp. 14–16.

132. James Q. Wilson, "In Loco Parentis: Helping Children When Families Fail Them," *Brookings Review*, vol. 11 (Fall 1993), p. 14.

133. Deanna S. Gomby and others, "Home Visiting: Analysis and Recommendations," *The Future of Children*, vol. 3 (Winter 1993), p. 6.

134. Heather Mac Donald, "The Ideology of 'Family Preservation,'" *Public Interest*, no. 115 (Spring 1994), p. 45.

135. Marilyn Irvin Holt, *The Orphan Trains: Placing Out in America* (University of Nebraska Press, 1992), p. 181.

136. Mary-Lou Weisman, "When Parents Are Not in the Best Interest of the Child," *Atlantic Monthly*, July 1994, pp. 42–63.

137. Wilson, "In Loco Parentis," p. 14.

138. *U.S. v. Lopez*, Docket number 93-1260, decided April 26, 1995.

139. Richard P. Nathan and others, "Minority Working- and Middle-Class Urban Neighborhoods: Case Studies of Other New Yorks," prepared for the 1994 annual meeting of the Association for Public Policy Analysis and Management.

Chapter 8

Child Abuse Reporting: The Need to Shift Priorities from More Reports to Better Reports

Douglas J. Besharov with Lisa A. Laumann

FOR THIRTY YEARS, advocates, program administrators, and politicians have joined cause to encourage even more reports of suspected child abuse and neglect. Their efforts have been spectacularly successful, with about 3 million children having been reported in 1993. Large numbers of endangered children still go unreported, but an equally serious problem has developed: upon investigation, as many as 65 percent of the reports now being made are determined to be "unsubstantiated," raising serious civil liberties concerns and placing a heavy burden on already overwhelmed investigative staffs.

These two problems—nonreporting and inappropriate reporting—are linked and must be addressed together before further progress can be made in combating child abuse and neglect. In this chapter I argue that to lessen both problems, there must be a shift in priorities—away from simply seeking more reports and toward encouraging better reports.

Reporting Laws

Since the early 1960s all states have passed laws that mandate designated professionals to report specified types of child maltreatment. Over the years, both the range of designated professionals and the scope of reportable conditions have been steadily expanded.

Initially, mandatory reporting laws applied only to physicians, who were required to report only "serious physical injuries" and "non-accidental injuries," the operative legislative phrases. In the ensuing years, however, increased public and professional attention, sparked in part by the number of abused children revealed by these initial reporting laws, led many states to expand their reporting requirements. Now almost all states have laws that require the reporting of all forms of suspected child maltreatment, including physical abuse, physical neglect, emotional maltreatment, and, of course, sexual abuse and exploitation.[1]

Under threat of civil and criminal penalties, these laws require most professionals who serve children to report suspected child abuse and neglect. About twenty states require all citizens to report, but in every state any citizen is permitted to report.

These reporting laws, associated public awareness campaigns, and professional education programs have been strikingly successful. In 1993 there were about 3 million reports of children suspected of being abused or neglected.[2] This is a twentyfold increase since 1963, when about 150,000 children were reported to the authorities (table 8-1).[3] (As we will see, however, this figure is bloated by reports that later turned out to be unfounded.)

Many people ask whether this vast increase in reporting signals a rise in the incidence of child maltreatment. Recent increases in social problems such as out-of-wedlock births, inner-city poverty, and drug abuse have probably raised the underlying rates of child maltreatment at least somewhat. Unfortunately, so many maltreated children previously went unreported that earlier reporting statistics do not provide a reliable baseline against which to make comparisons. One thing is clear, however: the great bulk of reports now received by child protective agencies would not be made but for the passage of mandatory reporting laws and the media campaigns that accompanied them.

This increase in reporting was accompanied by a substantial expansion of prevention and treatment programs. Every community, for example, is now served by specialized child protective agencies that receive and investigate reports. Federal and state expenditures for child protective programs and associated foster care services now exceed $6 billion a year.[4]

As a result, many thousands of children have been saved from serious injury and even death. The best estimate is that over the past

TABLE 8-1. *Instances of Child Abuse and Neglect Reported, 1976–93*

Year	Number of children reported	Year	Number of children reported
1976	669,000	1985	1,919,000
1977	838,000	1986	2,086,000
1978	836,000	1987	2,157,000
1979	988,000	1988	2,265,000
1980	1,154,000	1989	2,435,000
1981	1,225,000	1990	2,557,000
1982	1,262,000	1991	2,690,000
1983	1,477,000	1992	2,916,000
1984	1,727,000	1993	2,989,000

Sources: Data for 1976–84 are from American Association for Protecting Children, *Highlights of Official Child Abuse and Neglect Reports: 1985* (Denver, 1987), figure 1, p. 3. Data for 1985–93 are from Karen McCurdy and Deborah Daro, "Current Trends in Child Abuse Reporting and Fatalities: The Results of the 1993 Annual Fifty State Survey," working paper (Chicago: National Committee for Prevention of Child Abuse, April 1994), table 1, p. 5. Data include "unfounded" reports, which are now an estimated 60 to 65 percent of all reports.

twenty years, child abuse and neglect deaths have fallen from more than three thousand a year—and perhaps as many as five thousand—to about eleven hundred a year.[5] In New York State, for example, within five years of the passage of a comprehensive reporting law that also created specialized investigative staffs, there was a 50 percent reduction in child fatalities, from about two hundred a year to less than one hundred.[6] (This is not meant to minimize the remaining problem. Even at this level, maltreatment is the sixth largest cause of death for children under fourteen.)[7]

Unreported Cases

Most experts agree that reports have increased over the past thirty years because professionals and laypersons have become more likely to report apparently abusive and neglectful situations. But the question remains, how many more cases still go unreported?

Two studies performed for the National Center on Child Abuse and Neglect by Westat, Incorporated, provide a partial answer. In

1980 and then again in 1986 Westat conducted national studies of the incidence of child abuse and neglect. (A third Westat incidence study is now under way.) Each study used essentially the same methodology: in a stratified sample of counties, a broadly representative sample of professionals who serve children were asked whether, during the study period, the children they had seen in their professional capacities appeared to have been abused or neglected. (Actually, the professionals were not asked the ultimate question of whether the children appeared to be "abused" or "neglected." Instead they were asked to identify children with certain, specified harms or conditions, which were then decoded into a count of various types of child abuse and neglect.)[8]

Because the information these selected professionals provided could be matched against pending cases in the local child protective agency, Westat was able to estimate rates of nonreporting among the surveyed professionals. It could not, of course, estimate the level of unintentional nonreporting, since there is no way to know of the situations in which professionals did not recognize signs of possible maltreatment. There is also no way to know how many children the professionals recognized as being maltreated but chose not to report to the study. (Obviously, since the study methodology involved asking professionals about children they had seen in their professional capacities, it also did not allow Westat to estimate the number of children seen by nonprofessionals, let alone their nonreporting rate.)

Westat found that professionals failed to report many of the children they saw who had observable signs of child abuse and neglect. Specifically, it found that in 1986, 56 percent of apparently abused or neglected children, or about 500,000 children, were not reported to the authorities. This figure, however, seems more alarming than it is: basically, the more serious the case, the more likely the report. For example, the surveyed professionals reported more than 85 percent of the fatal or serious physical abuse cases they saw, 72 percent of the sexual abuse cases, and 60 percent of the moderate physical abuse cases. In contrast, they reported only 15 percent of the educational neglect cases they saw, 24 percent of the emotional neglect cases, and 25 percent of the moderate physical neglect cases.[9]

Nevertheless, there is no reason for complacency. Translating these raw percentages into actual cases means that in 1986 about 2,000 children with observable physical injuries severe enough to require hospitalization were not reported, more than 100,000 children with moderate physical injuries were also not reported, along with more than 30,000 apparently sexually abused children. And these are the rates of nonreporting among relatively well-trained professionals. One assumes that nonreporting is higher among less well-trained professionals and higher still among laypersons.

Obtaining—and maintaining—a high level of reporting requires a continuation of the public education and professional training begun thirty years ago. But now such efforts must also address a problem as serious as nonreporting—inappropriate reporting.

Unsubstantiated Reports

At the same time that many seriously abused children go unreported, an equally serious problem further undercuts efforts to prevent child maltreatment: the nation's child protective agencies are being inundated by inappropriate reports. Although rules, procedures, and even terminology vary—some states use the phrase "unfounded," others "unsubstantiated" or "not indicated"—an unfounded report, in essence, is one that is dismissed after an investigation finds insufficient evidence on which to proceed.

Nationwide, between 60 and 65 percent of all reports are closed after an initial investigation determines that they are unfounded or unsubstantiated.[10] This is in sharp contrast to 1974, when only about 45 percent of all reports were unfounded.[11]

A few advocates, in a misguided effort to shield child protective programs from criticism, have sought to quarrel with estimates that this author and others have made that the national unfounded rate is between 60 and 65 percent.[12] They have grasped at various inconsistencies in the data collected by different organizations to claim either that the problem is not so bad or that it has always been this bad.

To help settle this dispute, the American Public Welfare Association (APWA) conducted a special survey of child welfare agencies in 1989. The APWA researchers found that between fiscal year 1986 and fiscal year 1988, the weighted average for the substantiation rates in thirty-one states declined 6.7 percent—from 41.8 percent in fiscal year 1986 to 39 percent in fiscal year 1988.[13]

Most recently, the existence of this high unfounded rate was reconfirmed by the annual fifty-state survey of the National Committee to Prevent Child Abuse (NCPCA), which found that in 1993 only about 34 percent of the reports received by child protective agencies were substantiated.[14]

The experience of New York City indicates what these statistics mean in practice. Between 1989 and 1993, as the number of reports received by the city's child welfare agency increased by more than 30 percent (from 40,217 to 52,472), the percentage of substantiated reports fell by about 47 percent (from 45 percent to 24 percent). In fact, the number of substantiated cases—a number of families were reported more than once—actually fell by about 41 percent, from 14,026 to 8,326. Thus 12,255 additional families were investigated, while 5,700 fewer families received child protective help.[15]

The Costs of Unsubstantiated Reports

The determination that a report is unfounded can only be made after an unavoidably traumatic investigation that is inherently a breach of parental and family privacy. To determine whether a particular child is in danger, caseworkers must inquire into the most intimate personal and family matters. Often, it is necessary to question friends, relatives, and neighbors, as well as schoolteachers, day care personnel, doctors, clergy, and others who know the family.

Laws against child abuse are an implicit recognition that family privacy must give way to the need to protect helpless children. But in seeking to protect children, it is all too easy to ignore the legitimate rights of parents. Each year, about 700,000 families are put through investigations of unfounded reports. This is a massive and unjustified violation of parental rights.

Few unfounded reports are made maliciously. Studies of sexual abuse reports, for example, suggest that at most 4 to 10 percent of these reports are knowingly false.[16] Many involve situations in which the person reporting, in a well-intentioned effort to protect a child, overreacts to a vague and often misleading possibility that the child may be maltreated. Others involve situations of poor child care that, though of legitimate concern, simply do not amount to child abuse or neglect. In fact, a substantial proportion of unfounded cases are referred to other agencies for them to provide needed services for the family.

Moreover, an unfounded report does not necessarily mean that the child was not actually abused or neglected. Evidence of child maltreatment is hard to obtain and may not be uncovered when agencies lack the time and resources to complete a thorough investigation or when inaccurate information is given to the investigator. Other cases are labeled unfounded when no services are available to help the family. Some cases must be closed because the child or family cannot be located.

A certain proportion of unfounded reports, therefore, is an inherent—and legitimate—aspect of reporting suspected child maltreatment and is necessary to ensure adequate child protection. Hundreds of thousands of strangers report their suspicions; they cannot all be right. But unfounded rates of the current magnitude go beyond anything reasonably needed. Worse, they endanger children who are really abused.

The current flood of unfounded reports is overwhelming the limited resources of child protective agencies. For fear of missing even one abused child, workers perform extensive investigations of vague and apparently unsupported reports. Even when a home visit based on an anonymous report turns up no evidence of maltreatment, they usually interview neighbors, schoolteachers, and day care personnel to make sure that the child is not abused. And even repeated anonymous and unfounded reports do not prevent a further investigation. But all this takes time.

As a result, children in real danger are getting lost in the press of inappropriate cases. Forced to allocate a substantial portion of their limited resources to unfounded reports, child protective agencies are less able to respond promptly and effectively when children are in serious danger. Some reports are left uninvestigated for a week and even two weeks after they are received. Investigations often miss key facts as workers rush to clear cases, and dangerous home situations receive inadequate supervision, as workers must ignore pending cases as they investigate the new reports that arrive daily on their desks. Decisionmaking also suffers. With so many cases of insubstantial or unproven risk to children, caseworkers are desensitized to the obvious warning signals of immediate and serious danger.

These nationwide conditions help explain why from 25 to 50 percent of child abuse deaths involve children previously known to the authorities. In 1993 the NCPCA reported that of the 1,149 child maltreatment deaths, 42 percent had already been reported to the authorities.[17] Tens of thousands of other children suffer serious injuries short of death while under child protective agency supervision.

In a 1992 New York City case, for example, while under the supervision of New York City's Child Welfare Administration, five-month-old Jeffrey Harden died from burns caused by scalding water and three broken ribs. Jeffrey Harden's family had been known to the administration for more than a year and a half. Over this period, the case had been handled by four separate caseworkers, each conducting only partial investigations before resigning or being reassigned to new cases.

It is unclear whether Jeffrey's death was caused by his mother or her boyfriend, but because of insufficient time and overburdened caseloads, all four workers failed to pay attention to a whole host of obvious warning signals: Jeffrey's mother had broken her parole for an earlier conviction of child sexual abuse, she had a past record of beating Jeffrey's older sister, and she had a history of crack addiction and past involvement with violent boyfriends.[18]

Two of the Hardens' caseworkers explained what happened. Their first caseworker could not find Ms. Harden at the address she had listed in her files. She commented, "It was an easy case. We couldn't find the mother, so we closed it." Their second caseworker stated that he was unable to spend a sufficient amount of time investigating the case, let alone to make the minimum monthly visits, because he was tied down with an overabundance of cases and paperwork. He stated, "It's impossible to visit these people within a month. They're all over New York City." Just before Jeffrey's death every worker who had been on the case had left the department.

Ironically, by weakening the system's ability to respond, unfounded reports actually discourage appropriate ones. The sad fact is that many responsible individuals are not reporting endangered children because they feel that the system's response will be so weak that reporting will do no good or may even make things worse. In 1984 a study of the impediments to reporting conducted by Jose Alfaro, coordinator of the New York City Mayor's Task Force on Child Abuse and Neglect, concluded, "Professionals who emphasize their professional judgment, have experienced problems in dealing with the child protective agency, and are more likely to doubt the efficacy of protective service intervention, are more likely not to report in some situations, especially when they believe they can do a better job helping the family."[19]

Shifting Priorities

The emotionally charged desire to "do something" about child abuse, fanned by repeated and often sensational media coverage, has led to an understandable but counterproductive overreaction on the part of the professionals and citizens who report suspected child abuse. For thirty years, advocates, program administrators, and politicians have all pushed for more reporting of suspected child abuse and neglect.

Potential reporters are frequently told to take no chances and to report any child for whom they have the slightest concern. There is a recent tendency to tell people to report children whose behavior suggests that they may have been abused—even in the absence of any other evidence of maltreatment. These behavioral indicators include, for example, children who are unusually withdrawn or shy as well as children who are unusually friendly to strangers. However, only a small minority of children who exhibit such behaviors have actually been maltreated.

Thirty years ago, even fifteen years ago, when many professionals were construing their reporting obligations narrowly to avoid taking action to protect endangered children, this approach may have been needed. Now, though, all it does is ensure that child abuse hotlines will be flooded with inappropriate and unfounded reports.

Few people fail to report because they do not care about an endangered child. Instead, they may be unaware of the danger the child faces or of the protective procedures that are available. A study of nonreporting among teachers, for example, blamed their "lack of knowledge for detecting symptoms of abuse and neglect."[20] Likewise, few inappropriate or unfounded reports are deliberately false statements. Most involve an honest desire to protect children, coupled with confusion about what conditions are reportable.

Confusion about reporting is largely caused by the vagueness of reporting laws—aggravated by the failure of child protective agencies to provide realistic guidance about deciding to report. In 1987 a national group of thirty-eight child protective professionals from nineteen states met for three days at Airlie House, Virginia, under the auspices of the American Bar Association's National Legal Resource Center for Child Advocacy and Protection in association with the American Public Welfare Association and the American Enterprise Institute. The Airlie House group, as it has come to be called, developed policy guidelines for reporting and investigation decisionmaking. (I was the rapporteur for the effort.) One of the group's major conclusions was that there should be better guidelines for public and professional education about what should be reported (and what should not be). This group urged, "Better public and professional materials are needed to obtain more appropriate reporting." The group specifically recommended that "educational materials and programs should: (1) clarify the legal definitions of child abuse and neglect, (2) give general descriptions of reportable situations (including specific examples), and (3) explain what to expect when a report is made. Brochures and other materials for laypersons, including public service announcements, should give specific information about what to report—and what not to report."[21]

Based on these recommendations, a relatively clear agenda for reform emerges.

—*Clarify child abuse reporting laws:* Existing laws are often vague and overbroad. They should be rewritten to provide real guidance about what conditions should, and should not, be reported. This can be accomplished without making a radical departure from present laws or practices. The key is to describe reportable conditions in terms of specific parental behaviors or conditions that are tied to severe and demonstrable harms (or potential harms) to children.[22] Box 8-1 shows one way to do so.

—*Provide continuing public education and professional training:* Few people fail to report because they want children to suffer abuse and neglect. Likewise, few people make deliberately false reports. Most involve an honest desire to protect children coupled with confusion about what conditions are reportable. Thus educational efforts should emphasize the conditions that do not justify a report, as well as those that do.

—*Screen reports:* No matter how well professionals are trained and no matter how extensive public education efforts are, there will always be a tendency for persons to report cases that should not be investigated. Until recently, most states did not have formal policies and procedures for determining whether to accept a call for investi-

BOX 8-1. *The Basis of Child Abuse Reports*[a]

Direct Evidence

Eyewitness observations of a parent's abusive or neglectful behavior

The child's description of being abused or neglected, unless there is a specific reason for disbelief

The parent's own description of abusive or neglectful behavior, unless it is long past

Accounts of child maltreatment from spouses or other family members

Films, photographs, or other visual material depicting a minor's sexually explicit activity

Newborns denied nutrition, life-sustaining care, or other medically indicated treatment

Children in physically dangerous situations

Young children left alone

Apparently abandoned children

Demonstrated parental disabilities—for example, mental illness, retardation, or alcohol or drug abuse—severe enough to make child abuse or child neglect likely

Demonstrated parental inability to care for a newborn baby

Circumstantial Evidence

"Suspicious" injuries suggesting physical abuse

Physical injuries or medical findings suggesting sexual abuse

For young children, signs of sexual activity

Signs of severe physical deprivation on the child's body suggesting general child neglect

Severe dirt and disorder in the home suggesting general child neglect

Apparently untreated physical injuries, illnesses, or impairments suggesting medical neglect

"Accidental" injuries suggesting gross inattention to the child's need for safety

Apparent parental indifference to a child's severe psychological or developmental problems

Apparent parental condonation of or indifference to a child's misbehavior suggesting improper ethical guidance

Chronic and unexplained absences from school suggesting parental responsibility for the nonattendance

Newborns showing signs of fetal exposure to drugs or alcohol

Source: Douglas J. Besharov, *Recognizing Child Abuse: A Guide for the Concerned* (Free Press, 1990), p. 175.

a. Behavioral indicators, by themselves, are not a sufficient basis for a report.

gation. Such policies should be adopted by all states and they should provide explicit guidance about the kinds of cases that should not be assigned for investigation (box 8-2).

—*Modify liability laws:* Current laws provide immunity for anyone who makes a report in good faith, but give no protection to those who, in a good faith exercise of professional judgment, decide that a child has not been abused or neglected and hence should not be reported. This combination of immunities and penalties encourages the overreporting of questionable situations.

—*Give feedback to persons who report:* If persons who report are not told what happened, they may conclude that the agency's response was ineffective or even harmful to the child, and the next time they suspect that a child is maltreated, they may decide not to report. In addition, finding out whether their suspicions were valid also refines their diagnostic skills and thus improves the quality and accuracy of their future reports. Reporters also need such information to interpret subsequent events and to monitor the child's condition.

—*Adopt an agency policy:* Appropriate reporting of suspected child maltreatment requires a sophisticated knowledge of many legal, administrative, and diagnostic matters. To help ensure that their staffs respond properly, an increasing number of public and private agencies are adopting formal agency policies about reporting. Some state laws mandate them. The primary purpose of these policies, or agency protocols, is to inform staff members of their obligation to report and of the procedures to be followed. Such formal policies serve another important function: they are an implicit commitment by agency administrators to support frontline staff members who decide to report. Moreover, the very process of drafting a written document can clarify previously ambiguous or ill-conceived agency policies.

Prospects for Change

The problem of inappropriate reporting was entirely foreseeable. In fact, as early as 1977 sociologist Saad Nagi predicted that unfounded reports would increase as total reporting rose.[23] As mentioned above, some level of inappropriate reporting is the inescapable result of a system that relies on reports from hundreds of thousands of friends, neighbors, and family members—as well as often poorly trained professionals.

BOX 8-2. *Child Abuse and Neglect Reports That Should Be Rejected*[a]

Allegations clearly fall outside the agency's definitions of child abuse and child neglect, as established by state law. (Prime examples include children beyond the specified age, alleged perpetrators falling outside the legal definition, and family problems not amounting to child maltreatment.)

Caller can give no credible reason for suspecting that the child has been abused or neglected. (Although actual proof of the maltreatment is not required, some evidence is.)

Unfounded or malicious nature of report is established by specific evidence. (Anonymous reports, reports from estranged spouses, and even a history of previous unfounded reports from the same source should not automatically be rejected, but they need to be carefully evaluated.)

Insufficient information is given to identify or locate the child. (This is not technically a rejection; moreover, the information may be kept for later use should a subsequent report be made about the same child.)

Source: Douglas J. Besharov, *Recognizing Child Abuse: A Guide for the Concerned* (Free Press, 1990), p. 179.

a. In questionable circumstances, the agency should recontact the caller before deciding to reject a report. When appropriate, rejected reports should be referred to other agencies that can provide services needed by the family.

What was thoroughly unpredictable was the great resistance to doing something about the problem. As described below, some efforts to reform the system have been made, but many advocates still deny that there is a problem (or at least try to minimize its importance).[24]

Why has it proven so difficult to mount a concerted effort to reduce the number of inappropriate or unfounded reports? First and foremost has been the well-intentioned fear that any attempt to limit inappropriate reporting would inevitably reduce the number of real cases reported. The more careful people are about reporting, and the more aggressive agencies are about screening, the more likely it is that a child in serious danger will escape notice. A formal legal opinion from Iowa's attorney general explained the rationale for this broader approach to reporting: "We will never know if a report of child abuse is valid or not until the appropriate investigation is made."[25]

But this practical wisdom has been taken to unreasonable extremes. Too many advocates have ignored the consequential burden that so many inappropriate cases place on the system's resources. They seem unwilling to make—or even to recognize—the trade-off between gaining large numbers of additional reports and the system's ability to respond.

Second, there has been a certain expediency to well-publicized increases in reports. Ever-rising numbers of reports have helped mobilize public and professional support for expanded funding.[26] News stories about brutal cases of child abuse make our hearts go out to its innocent victims. We all want to do something to alleviate their pain and to prevent other children from suffering a similar fate. Thus advocates and program administrators have had an incentive to remain quiet about the number of cases closed after an initial investigation.

Third, although many of these inappropriate reports did not amount to child abuse or child neglect, they nevertheless involved families who needed social service assistance. Thus accepting and investigating unfounded reports was seen as a means of providing needed services to families in trouble. In effect, the child protective system was being used to fill gaps in what should be community-wide child welfare systems. Even if this strategy had been more likely to succeed, it should have been shunned. The child protective process is coercive—often traumatic—and should be limited to situations in which the child is so endangered that social services must be forced upon unwilling parents.

Fourth, for many years the child protective system was able to absorb the increase in reports by hiring more staff. Although money was never plentiful, the 1970s and much of the 1980s saw expansion in many states. But by the end of the 1980s state budgets became progressively tighter, and programs were being cut rather than expanded.

Change is apparent, however. Most states, as well as most research studies, are now careful to distinguish between total reports and substantiated ones. And as mentioned above, the 1987 recommendations of the Airlie House group gave a legitimacy to those concerned about inappropriate reporting—and provided the outlines for reform. In scattered communities across the nation, various elements of the recommendations listed above (as well as other ideas) are being adopted.

And there is reason to expect still more change. Recently, the flood of unfounded reports has involved more middle-class families than before. Unlike the poor, who have grown used to governmental intrusions, middle-class parents who feel that they have been wrongly accused—and unnecessarily investigated—fight back. Thousands have joined groups like VOCAL (Victims of Child Abuse Laws) to lobby for changes in state and federal laws as well as in agency procedures.

The continuing pressure of state budget cuts has added another group of players to the process. In many states, senior managers have, for the first time, focused their attention on the issue. They are eager, if not desperate, for any ideas that would enable them to do more with existing (or pared down) resources. If they could be convinced that a shift away from simply seeking more reports and toward encouraging better ones would save money without unreasonably endangering children, they would push for the change.

Thus it seems that the coming years will see an acceleration of this shift. And, notwithstanding the opposition of advocates, I believe that reasonable efforts to reduce the number of unfounded reports would strengthen the overall child protective system—as well as public support for it.

Notes

1. See, generally, Douglas J. Besharov, *Recognizing Child Abuse: A Guide For the Concerned* (Free Press, 1990).

2. Karen McCurdy and Deborah Daro, "Current Trends in Child Abuse Reporting and Fatalities: The Results of the 1993 Annual Fifty State Survey," Working Paper 808 (Chicago: National Committee for the Prevention of Child Abuse, April 1994), table 1, p. 5.

3. Children's Bureau, *Juvenile Court Statistics* (Department of Health, Education, and Welfare, 1966), p. 13.

4. Federal expenditures for foster care, child welfare, and related services make up less than 50 percent of total expenditures (state and federal) for these services. In 1992 they amounted to $273.9 million for Title IV-B child welfare services; $1,192.1 million for Title IV-E foster care maintenance; $1,017.7 for Title IV-E foster care administration and training; $70 million for the Title IV-E independent living program; and $219.6 million for Title IV-E adoption assistance. This comes to a total of $2,773.7 million. In addition, states may use a portion of the $2.8 billion federal social services block grant

for such services, though detailed data on these expenditures are not available. Beginning in 1994, additional federal appropriations will fund family preservation and support services (an estimated $60 million in 1994 and $150 million in 1995). "Overview of Entitlement Programs," in *1993 Green Book*, House Committee on Ways and Means, 103 Cong. 1 sess. (Government Printing Office, 1993), table 2, p. 886; and *Budget of the United States Government: Appendix, Fiscal Year 1995*, p. 451.

5. Andrea J. Sedlak, "Supplementary Analyses of Data on the National Incidence of Child Abuse and Neglect," (Rockville, Md.: Westat, 1991), table 2-1, p. 2-2; McCurdy and Daro, "Current Trends in Child Abuse Reporting and Fatalities," table 3, p. 13.

6. New York State Department of Social Services, *Child Protective Services in New York State: 1979 Annual Report* (1980), table 8.

7. Based on comparison data from National Center for Health Statistics, "Advance Report of Final Mortality Statistics, 1980," *Monthly Vital Statistics Report*, vol. 32 (Department of Health and Human Services, August 11, 1983).

8. National Study on Child Abuse and Neglect, *Study Findings: National Study of the Incidence and Severity of Child Abuse and Neglect* (September 1981); and *Study Findings: Study of National Incidence and Prevalence of Child Abuse and Neglect* (1986). The original report for this study contained inaccurate information because of weighting errors by Westat. The revised report is Andrea J. Sedlak, *National Incidence and Prevalence of Child Abuse and Neglect: 1988, Revised Report* (Rockville, Md.: Westat, 1991).

9. Sedlak, "Supplementary Analyses of Data," pp. 3–19.

10. Douglas Besharov, "'Doing Something' about Child Abuse: The Need to Narrow the Grounds for State Intervention," *Harvard Journal of Law and Public Policy*, vol. 8, no. 3 (1985), reporting the author's 65 percent estimate based on a state-by-state analysis by the American Association for Protecting Children, "Highlights of Official Child Neglect and Abuse Reporting: 1985," p. 12, projecting, on incomplete data, a 58 percent unfounded rate.

11. See, for example, New York State Department of Social Services, "Trends in Child Abuse/Maltreatment Reporting, 1974–1976," Albany, 1977, table 5.

12. David Finkelhor, "Is Child Abuse Overreported? The Data Rebut Arguments for Less Intervention," *Public Welfare*, vol. 48 (Winter 1990), pp. 22–29.

13. Toshio Tatara, "Children of Substance Abusing and Alcoholic Parents in Public Child Welfare" (Washington: American Public Welfare Association, December 1990), pp. 17–21, especially p. 18.

14. For 1991 the Fifty State Survey estimated an average substantiation rate of 36 percent. For 1992 it estimated a rate of 35 percent, and for 1993 the average rate was estimated at 34 percent. McCurdy and Daro, "Current Trends in Child Abuse and Fatalities," table 1, p. 5.

15. New York State Department of Social Services, "State Central Register Reporting Highlights, 1974–89," Albany, 1990, table 10; and New York State Department of Social Services, "State Central Register Reporting Highlights, 1974–1993," Albany, 1994, table 13.

16. See Nancy Thoennes and Jessica Pearson, "A Difficult Dilemma: Responding to Sexual Abuse Allegations in Custody and Visitation Disputes," in Douglas J. Besharov, ed., *Protecting Children from Abuse and Neglect, Policy and Practice* (Springfield, Ill.: Charles C Thomas, 1988), pp. 91, 93; Lucy Berliner, "Deciding Whether a Child Has Been Sexually Abused," in E. Bruce Nicholson, ed., *Sexual Abuse Allegations in Custody and Visitation Cases: A Resource Book for Judges and Court Personnel* (Chicago: American Bar Association, 1988); and D. Jones, "Reliable and Fictitious Accounts of Sexual Abuse in Children," *Journal of Inter-Personal Violence*, vol. 3 (1986), table 2, estimating that 8 percent of sexual abuse reports are falsely made (2 percent by children and 6 percent by adults); and Jose D. Alfaro, "What Can We Learn from Child Abuse Fatalities: A Synthesis of Nine Studies," in Besharov, *Protecting Children from Abuse and Neglect*, chap. 9.

17. McCurdy and Daro, "Current Trends in Child Abuse Reporting and Fatalities," table 4, p. 15.

18. Celia W. Dugger, "Litany of Signals Overlooked in Child's Death," *New York Times*, December 29, 1992, p. A1.

19. Jose D. Alfaro, "Impediments to Mandated Reporting of Suspected Child Abuse and Neglect in New York City," report to the Mayor's Task Force on Child Abuse and Neglect, New York, 1984, p. 66.

20. Patricia G. Levin, "Teachers' Perceptions, Attitudes, and Reporting of Child Abuse/Neglect," *Child Welfare*, vol. 62 (January/February 1983), p. 19.

21. Besharov, *Protecting Children from Abuse and Neglect*, p. 346.

22. See Besharov, *Recognizing Child Abuse*, pp. 28–36.

23. In describing the effect of contemporary increases in the number of reports on confirmation rates, he wrote: "As the rates of reporting increased, the rates of confirmed maltreatment increased rapidly up to a certain point, after which the rate of increase tended to lessen considerably. . . . The relations between the rates of reporting and the estimated probability that maltreatment cases will be confirmed, however, exhibited the reverse pattern: the probability of confirming reports of suspected cases dropped sharply as the rates of reporting increased." Saad Zagloul Nagi, *Child Maltreatment in the United States: A Challenge to Social Institutions* (Columbia University Press, 1977), p. 39.

24. See, for example, Finkelhor, "Is Child Abuse Overreported?"

25. Iowa Attorney General, Opinion No. 78-9-12, September 28, 1978, in *Family Law Reporter*, vol. 5 (1978), p. 2015.

26. Barbara J. Nelson, *Making an Issue of Child Abuse: Political Agenda Setting for Social Problems* (University of Chicago Press, 1984).

Conference Participants

Barbara R. Bergmann
The American University

Gary Burtless
The Brookings Institution

Douglas J. Besharov
American Enterprise Institute for Public Policy Research

Timothy J. Besley
Woodrow Wilson School of Public and International Affairs, Princeton University

Andrew J. Cherlin
The Johns Hopkins University

John J. DiIulio Jr.
Woodrow Wilson School of Public and International Affairs, Princeton University

Jameson W. Doig
Woodrow Wilson School of Public and International Affairs, Princeton University

Patrick F. Fagan
Heritage Foundation

Rose E. Firestein
Legal Aid Society

William A. Galston
Domestic Policy Staff, The White House

Irwin Garfinkel
School of Social Work, Columbia University

Amy Gutmann
Princeton University

Stephen F. Hamilton
Cornell University

Marva Hammon
Human Resources Administration, City of New York

Maria J. Hanratty
Woodrow Wilson School of Public and International Affairs, Princeton University

Ronald Haskins
Committee on Ways and Means, U.S. House of Representatives

Hugh Heclo
George Mason University

Jennifer L. Hochschild
Woodrow Wilson School of Public and International Affairs, Princeton University

275

Robert L. Johnson
New Jersey Medical School

Sheila B. Kamerman
School of Social Work, Columbia University

Lorraine V. Klerman
School of Public Health, University of Alabama at Birmingham

Alan B. Krueger
Woodrow Wilson School of Public and International Affairs, Princeton University

Julia Graham Lear
Making the Grade, George Washington University

Robert I. Lerman
The American University and the Urban Institute

Glenn C. Loury
Boston University

Kristin C. Luker
Office of Population Research, Princeton University

Thomas E. Mann
The Brookings Institution

Emily C. Martin
U.S. Department of Justice

Sara S. McLanahan
Woodrow Wilson School of Public and International Affairs, Princeton University

Lawrence M. Mead
John F. Kennedy School of Government, New York University

Ronald B. Mincy
Ford Foundation

Deanna L. Pagnini
Woodrow Wilson School of Public and International Affairs, Princeton University

Deborah A. Phillips
National Research Council

Diane Ravitch
The Brookings Institution and New York University

Peter Reuter
University of Maryland

Cecilia E. Rouse
Woodrow Wilson School of Public and International Affairs, Princeton University

Theda Skocpol
Harvard University

Paul E. Starr
Princeton University

Nomi Maya Stolzenberg
University of Southern California

John F. Witte
University of Wisconsin

Barbara B. Woodhouse
Law School of the University of Pennsylvania

Index